Visual Reference Basics

Microsoft® Publisher 2000

Diana Rain

DDC Publishing

Acknowledgements

Managing Editor
Jennifer Frew

English Editor
Emily Hay

Technical Editor
Robin Drake

Layout and Design
Elsa Johannesson

Cover Design
Amy Capuano

Copyright 1999 by DDC Publishing, Inc.
Published by DDC Publishing, Inc.

All rights reserved, including the right to reproduce this book in any form whatsoever. For information, address:
DDC Publishing, Inc.,
275 Madison Avenue,
New York, NY 10016.
Internet address: http://www.ddcpub.com

10   9   8   7   6   5   4   3   2   1

Printed in the United States of America.

The DDC banner is a registered trademark of DDC Publishing, Inc. Replicating these pages is a violation of copyright law.
Microsoft® and Windows® are registered trademarks of Microsoft Corporation.
IBM is a registered trademark of International Business Machines.
Screen Shots reprinted with permission of Microsoft Corporation.
All registered trademarks, trademarks, and service marks mentioned in this book are the property of their respective companies.

Table of Contents

Introduction .... *v*
Visual index vi

Getting Started *1*
Start Publisher 2
The Publisher Window 3
Hide the Catalog at Startup 4
Customize Toolbars 6
Arrange Toolbars 8
Get Help Using the Office Assistant 10
Get Help Using the Answer Wizard 12
Visit the Office Update Web Site 14

Publications *17*
Create a Publication Using a Wizard 18
Create a Blank Publication 22
Save a Publication 24
Open a Publication 26
Maintain a Personal Information Set 28
Set AutoSave Options 30
Set the Default Publication Folder 32
Disable Publication Wizard Steps 34

Pages *35*
Move Rulers 36
Set the Zero Point 38
Set the Unit of Measure 40
Add Ruler Guides 42
Add Grid Guides 44
Change Page Margins 46
Change the Page Size 48
Snap to Guides and Objects 49
Set Up Facing Pages 50
Change the Page Orientation 51
Add Headers and Footers 52

i

Place Text or Graphics on All Pages 54
Insert a Page 56
View Two Pages 58
Zoom In or Out 60
Set Web Page Properties 62
Run Design Checker 64
Preview Web Pages 66

Add and Edit Text 69

Create a Text Frame 70
Create Connected Text Frames 72
Import Text 76
Flow a Long Story 78
Add Continuation Notices 80
Set Up Columns in a Text Frame 82
Delete Text 84
Type and Edit Text 86
Select Text 90
Edit a Story in Microsoft Word 92
Insert a Symbol 94
Insert the Current Date/Time 96
Find Text 98
Replace Text 100
Check Spelling 102
Hyphenate 106

Format Text 109

Wrap Text Around Pictures 110
Add a Drop Cap 112
Align Paragraphs 114
Align Text Vertically 116
Format Characters 118
Fit Text in a Frame 120
Indent Paragraphs 122
Set Line or Paragraph Spacing 124
Create a Bulleted List 126
Create a Numbered List 128
Set Tabs 130
Create a Style 132
Edit a Style 133
Apply a Style 134
Import Styles from Another Publication 136

Drawing Objects 139

Draw Lines and Arrows 140
Draw Rectangles and Ovals 142
Draw Custom Shapes 144
Draw a Balloon AutoShape 146
Change the Line Style of an AutoShape 148
Change a Line Style of a Drawing Object 150

Pictures 153

Clips: Insert a Picture, Sound, or Video Clip 154
Clips: Organize Clips in the Gallery 156
Clips: Download Clips from the Web 158
Clips: Add Clips to the Gallery 160
Import a Picture 164
Insert a Design Gallery Object 166
WordArt: Create a WordArt Picture 168
WordArt: Change Font and Attributes 170
WordArt: Mold Text into a Shape 172
Crop a Picture 174
Scale a Picture 176

Frames 177

Apply Line Borders to a Frame 178
Apply BorderArt Borders 180
Rotate a Frame 182
Set the Default Formatting for a Frame 184
Select Frames 185
Copy or Move a Frame 186
Resize a Frame 188
Line Up Frames 190
Group Frames and Objects 192
Change Frame Margins 194

Tables 195

Create a Table 196
Apply Table Borders 198
Shade Cell Backgrounds 200
Apply a Preset Table Format 202
Change Column Width or Row Height 204
Insert or Delete Columns or Rows 206
Merge Cells 208
Enter Text in a Table 209
Select in a Table 210

iii

Mail Merge..213
Create an Address List 214
Sort an Address List..216
Merge an Address List with a Publication 218

Print..221
Choose a Printer 222
Change the Paper Size 223
Print Crop Marks 224
Print on a Desktop Printer 226

Introduction

DDC's Visual Reference Basics series is designed to help you make the most of your Microsoft software. Newly updated to reflect changes and enhancements in Microsoft 2000 applications, the Visual Reference Basics are equally useful as instruction manuals or as desktop reference guides for the experienced user. With illustrations and clear explanations of every step involved, they make even complex processes easy to understand and follow.

The most distinctive feature of this series is its extensive use of visuals. Buttons, toolbars, screens, and commands are all illustrated so that there is never any doubt that you are performing the right actions. Most information can be understood at a glance, without a lot of reading through dense and complicated instructions. With Visual Reference Basics, you learn what you need to know quickly and easily.

This book contains one hundred functions—logically sequenced and arranged for ease of use—essential for optimal use of Publisher 2000. Basic skills are covered first; more advanced features then build on these skills. Cross-references in chapters help you find related topics. Notes on each page provide additional information or tips to supplement the directions given. The only thing you need to get the most out of the Visual Reference Basics series is a basic understanding of Windows and the desire to become more familiar with Publisher 2000.

The Visual Reference Basics series is an informative and convenient way to acquaint yourself with the capabilities of your Microsoft application. It is a valuable resource for anyone who wants to become a power user of Microsoft 2000 software.

Visual Index

Layout Grid

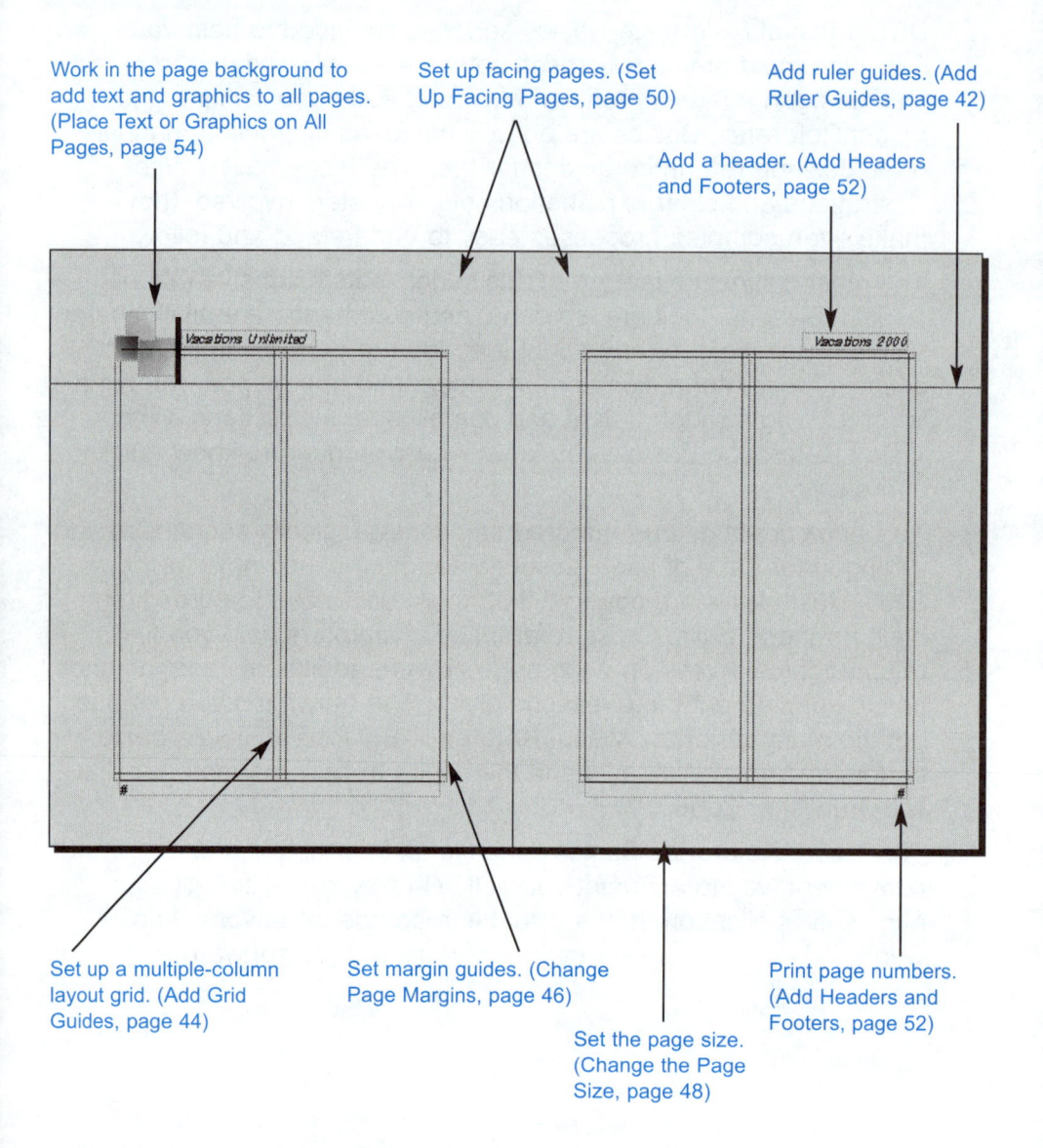

Work in the page background to add text and graphics to all pages. (Place Text or Graphics on All Pages, page 54)

Set up facing pages. (Set Up Facing Pages, page 50)

Add ruler guides. (Add Ruler Guides, page 42)

Add a header. (Add Headers and Footers, page 52)

Set up a multiple-column layout grid. (Add Grid Guides, page 44)

Set margin guides. (Change Page Margins, page 46)

Set the page size. (Change the Page Size, page 48)

Print page numbers. (Add Headers and Footers, page 52)

These sample pages show how to place text and graphics on a page using the layout grid illustrated on the previous page.

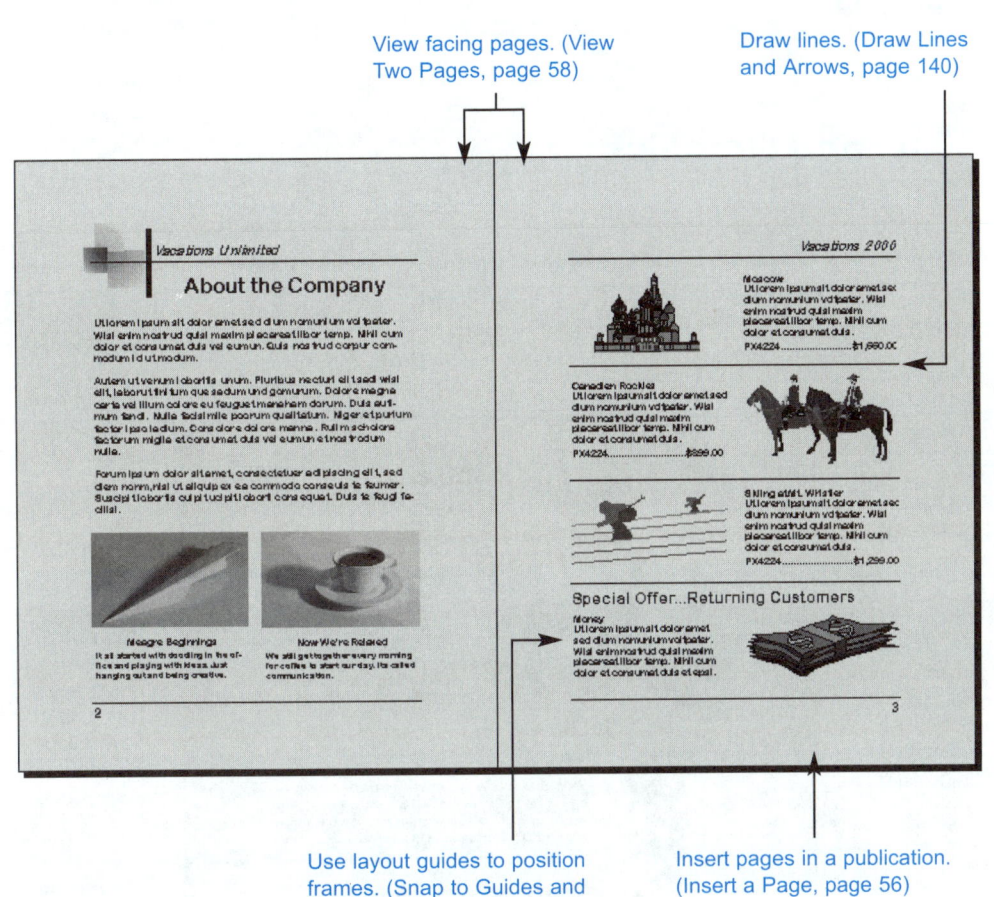

View facing pages. (View Two Pages, page 58)

Draw lines. (Draw Lines and Arrows, page 140)

Use layout guides to position frames. (Snap to Guides and Objects, page 49)

Insert pages in a publication. (Insert a Page, page 56)

vii

Visual Index
(continued)

Text and Graphics

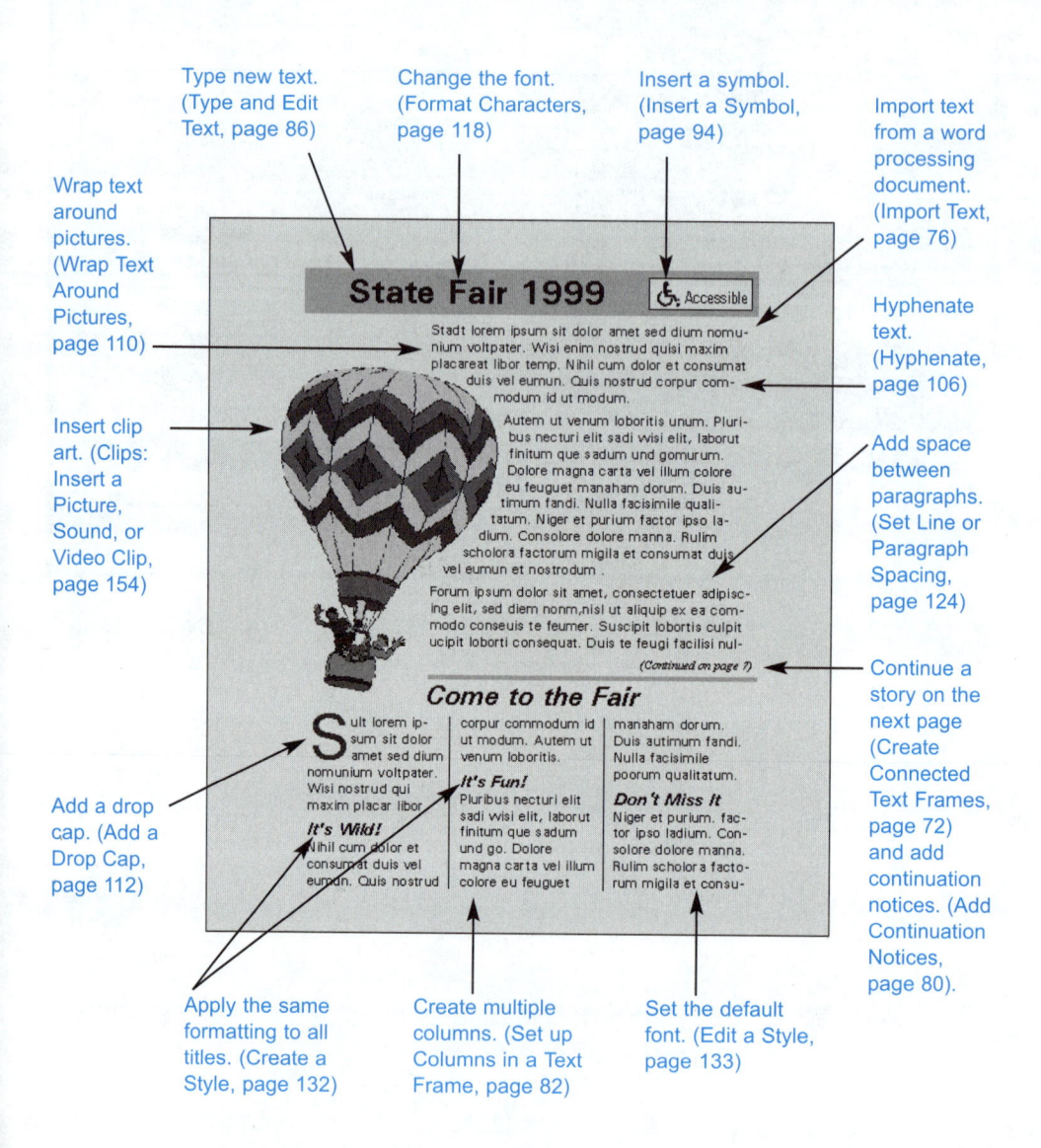

Wrap text around pictures. (Wrap Text Around Pictures, page 110)

Insert clip art. (Clips: Insert a Picture, Sound, or Video Clip, page 154)

Add a drop cap. (Add a Drop Cap, page 112)

Apply the same formatting to all titles. (Create a Style, page 132)

Type new text. (Type and Edit Text, page 86)

Change the font. (Format Characters, page 118)

Insert a symbol. (Insert a Symbol, page 94)

Create multiple columns. (Set up Columns in a Text Frame, page 82)

Set the default font. (Edit a Style, page 133)

Import text from a word processing document. (Import Text, page 76)

Hyphenate text. (Hyphenate, page 106)

Add space between paragraphs. (Set Line or Paragraph Spacing, page 124)

Continue a story on the next page (Create Connected Text Frames, page 72) and add continuation notices. (Add Continuation Notices, page 80).

Frames

Set the amount of space between the contents of the frame and the frame boundaries. (Change Frame Margins, page 194)

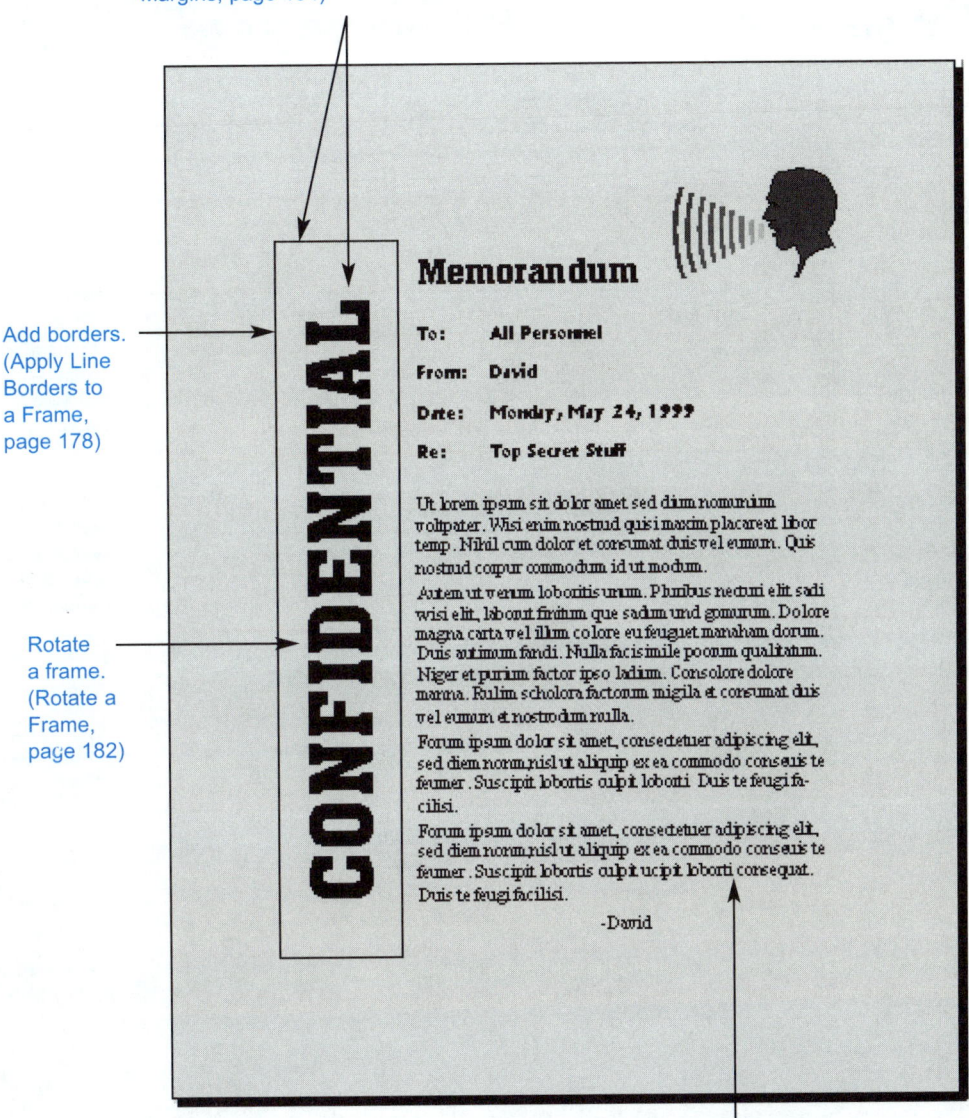

Add borders. (Apply Line Borders to a Frame, page 178)

Rotate a frame. (Rotate a Frame, page 182)

Fit text so that if you resize the frame, text resizes to fill it. (Fit Text in a Frame, page 120)

ix

Visual Index
(continued)

Tables

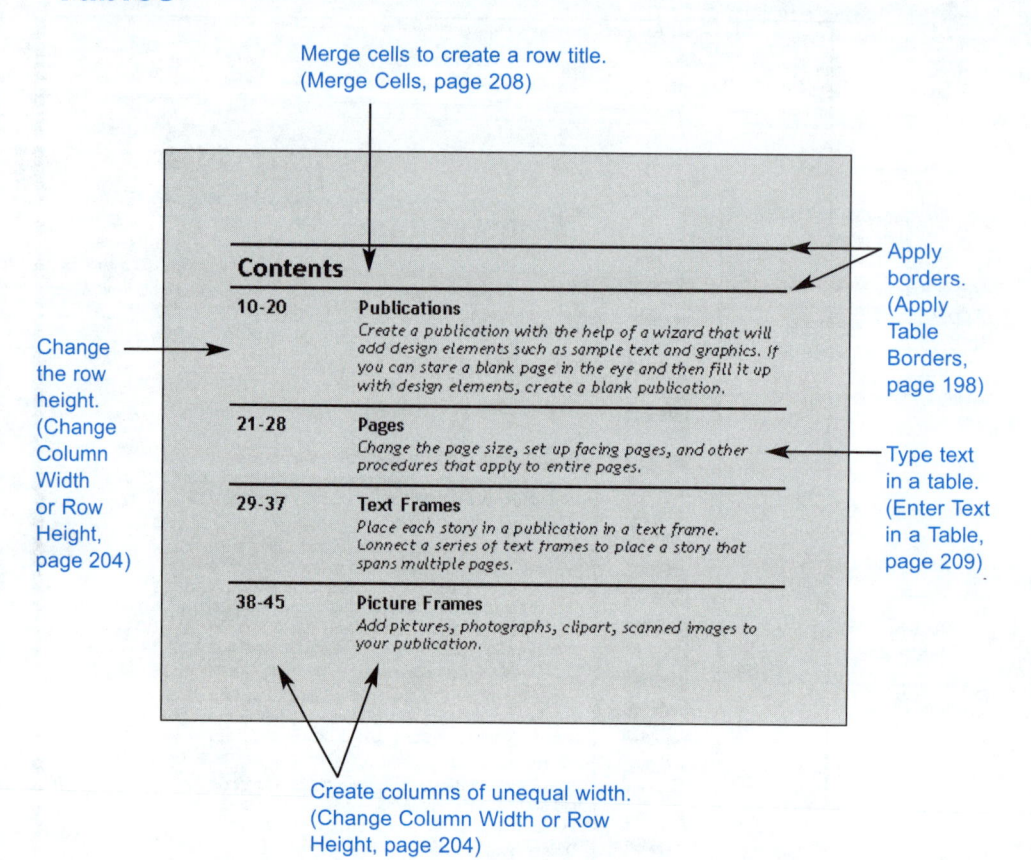

Merge cells to create a row title.
(Merge Cells, page 208)

Change the row height. (Change Column Width or Row Height, page 204)

Apply borders. (Apply Table Borders, page 198)

Type text in a table. (Enter Text in a Table, page 209)

Contents

10-20	**Publications**	Create a publication with the help of a wizard that will add design elements such as sample text and graphics. If you can stare a blank page in the eye and then fill it up with design elements, create a blank publication.
21-28	**Pages**	Change the page size, set up facing pages, and other procedures that apply to entire pages.
29-37	**Text Frames**	Place each story in a publication in a text frame. Connect a series of text frames to place a story that spans multiple pages.
38-45	**Picture Frames**	Add pictures, photographs, clipart, scanned images to your publication.

Create columns of unequal width.
(Change Column Width or Row Height, page 204)

x

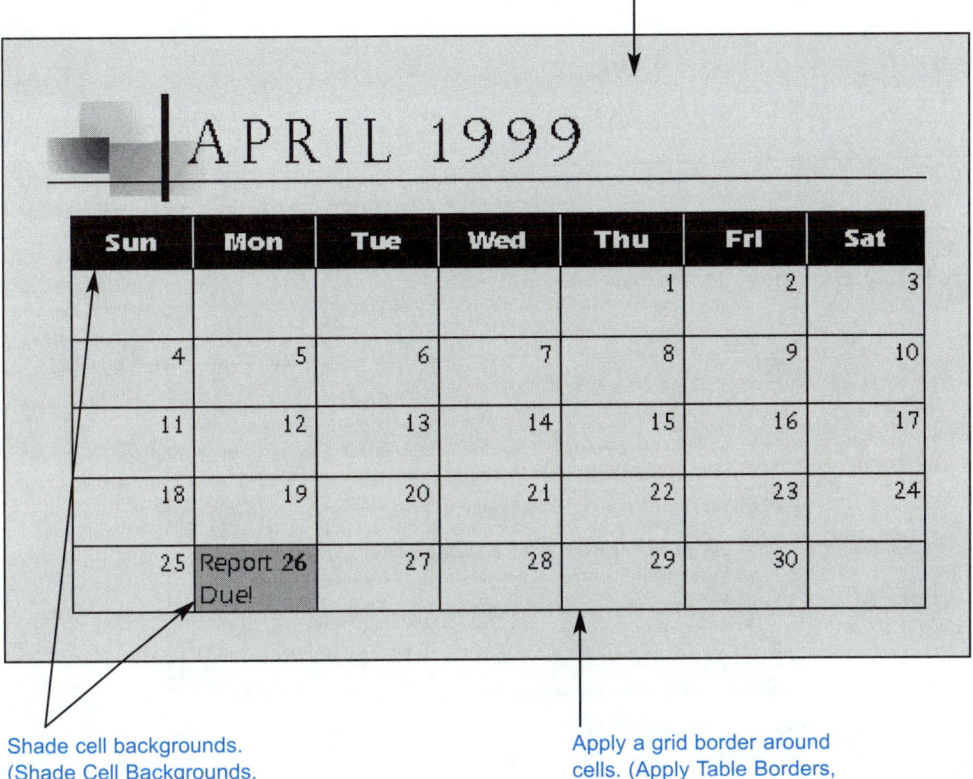

Insert ready-made calendars from the Design Gallery. (Insert a Design Gallery Object, page 166)

APRIL 1999

Sun	Mon	Tue	Wed	Thu	Fri	Sat
				1	2	3
4	5	6	7	8	9	10
11	12	13	14	15	16	17
18	19	20	21	22	23	24
25	Report 26 Due!	27	28	29	30	

Shade cell backgrounds. (Shade Cell Backgrounds, page 200)

Apply a grid border around cells. (Apply Table Borders, page 198)

xi

Visual Index
(continued)

Lists

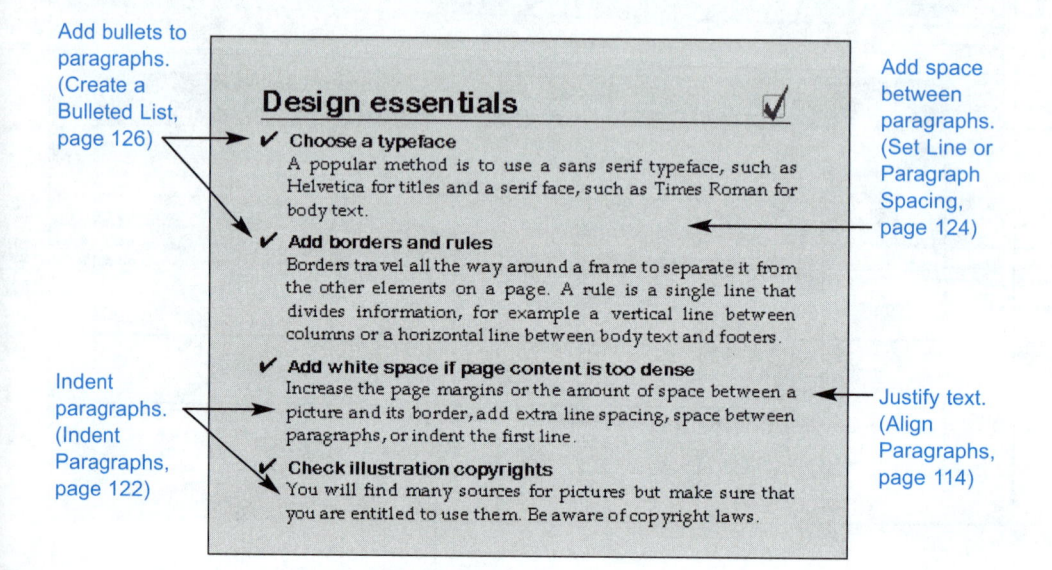

Add bullets to paragraphs. (Create a Bulleted List, page 126)

Indent paragraphs. (Indent Paragraphs, page 122)

Add space between paragraphs. (Set Line or Paragraph Spacing, page 124)

Justify text. (Align Paragraphs, page 114)

Design essentials

✔ **Choose a typeface**
A popular method is to use a sans serif typeface, such as Helvetica for titles and a serif face, such as Times Roman for body text.

✔ **Add borders and rules**
Borders travel all the way around a frame to separate it from the other elements on a page. A rule is a single line that divides information, for example a vertical line between columns or a horizontal line between body text and footers.

✔ **Add white space if page content is too dense**
Increase the page margins or the amount of space between a picture and its border, add extra line spacing, space between paragraphs, or indent the first line.

✔ **Check illustration copyrights**
You will find many sources for pictures but make sure that you are entitled to use them. Be aware of copyright laws.

Number paragraphs. (Create a Numbered List, page 128)

Print a Report
1. Turn on the power
2. Get cup of coffee while waiting for Windows to start up
3. Look at watch—meeting starts in ten minutes
4. Start up software
5. Find report file worked on two weeks ago
6. Open file
7. Read "file damaged, unrecoverable" message
8. Think
9. Break out in sweat
10. Did you make a backup copy last time you worked on it?
11. No? You didn't?

Insert clip art. (Clips: Insert a Picture, Sound, or Video Clip, page 154)

xiii

Visual Index
(continued)

Merge Publications

Place text and graphics on all pages. (Place Text or Graphics on All Pages, page 54)

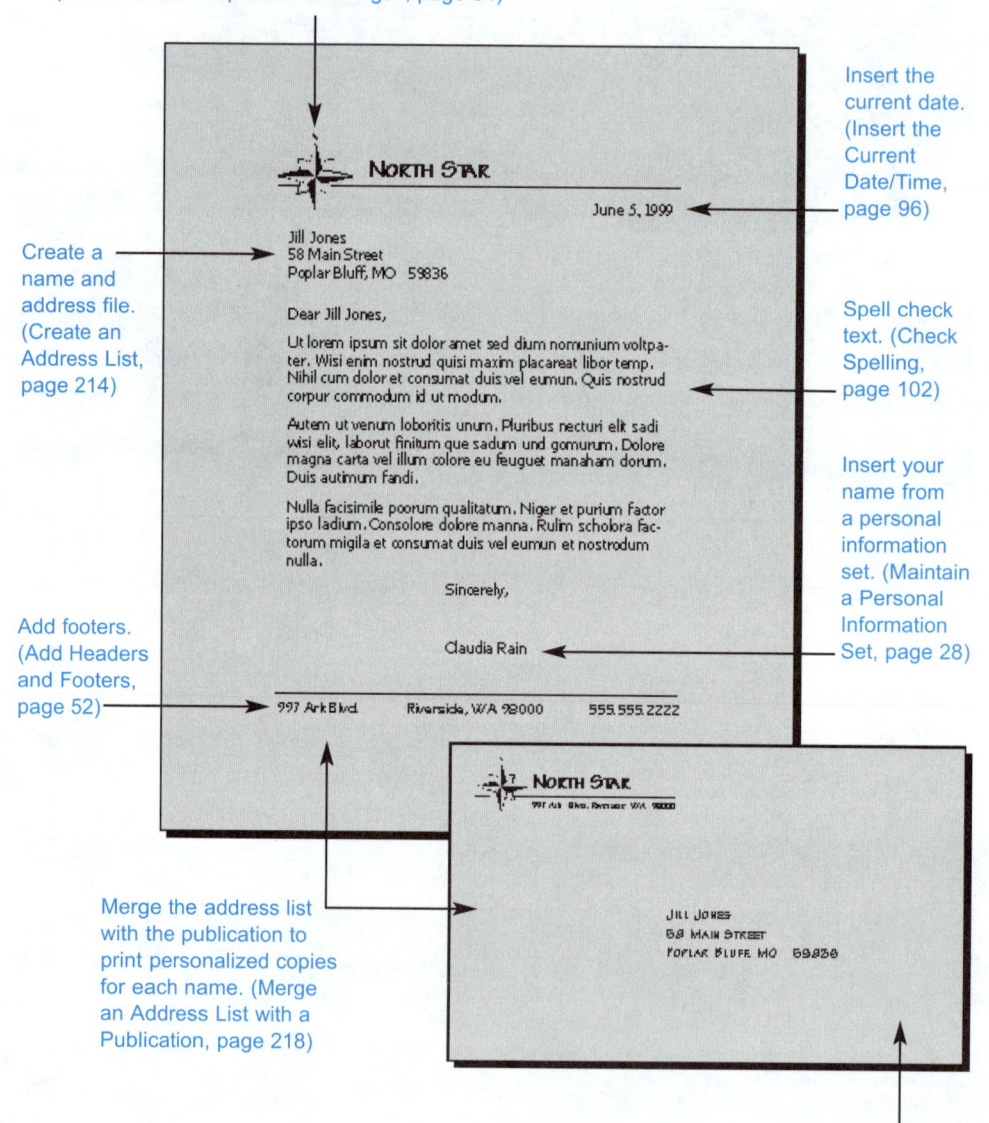

Insert the current date. (Insert the Current Date/Time, page 96)

Create a name and address file. (Create an Address List, page 214)

Spell check text. (Check Spelling, page 102)

Insert your name from a personal information set. (Maintain a Personal Information Set, page 28)

Add footers. (Add Headers and Footers, page 52)

Merge the address list with the publication to print personalized copies for each name. (Merge an Address List with a Publication, page 218)

Create standard envelopes using a wizard. (Create a Publication Using a Wizard, page 18)

xiv

Getting Started

Microsoft Publisher 2000 is a desktop publishing program (DTP). DTPs have replaced old layout methods, where designers had to cut out each design element and paste it onto pages. Now the manual methods have been replaced by computers running DTPs, where you can easily add text and graphics, and then arrange and rearrange these elements on the page for different designs. Because it is so simple to try out various layout combinations, you can have a lot of fun designing pages. Publisher's predesigned layouts provide an expert framework within which you can design creative details.

Use Publisher to create pages with all kinds of design elements such as formatted text, photographs, lines, and pictures. Publisher helps you throughout the entire process of creating a professional publication, starting with wizards that create publications for you in minutes. Wizards come complete with sample text and graphics that you can replace with your own choices. You can check spelling and hyphenate text and even use the Design Checker, which finds potential design problems in your publication.

Use the procedures in this book to create both print publications (such as brochures, newsletters, memos, postcards, and envelopes) and Web publications (pages that you publish on the Internet).

If you are publishing Web pages created in Publisher, work with your Internet service provider to publish the site. Your provider will give you information about where to place your site on their servers, required filenames, and other specifications. Microsoft Publisher is a good program for creating simple Web pages. For larger sites, or to create pages with complex functions, you can use Microsoft FrontPage instead.

Start Publisher

When you install Publisher, the command you use to start it is added to the Windows Start menu on the taskbar.

Start → **Programs**

Notes:

- When you start Publisher, the Catalog displays. Use it to create a new publication. If you close the Catalog, a blank publication is displayed in the Publisher window. At this point, you can create a new publication or open an existing one.

- To bypass the Catalog, see *Hide the Catalog at Startup*. When you start Publisher, a blank publication displays rather than the Catalog.

- See *The Publisher Window* to learn about the different elements in the window.

- You can also start Publisher by double-clicking a publication in Windows Explorer.

1. Click **Start** on the left side of the Windows taskbar.

   OR

   Press **Ctrl+Esc** if the taskbar is hidden.

2. Click **Programs**.

3. Click **Microsoft Publisher**. Publisher starts and displays the Catalog, where you can browse preset publication designs.

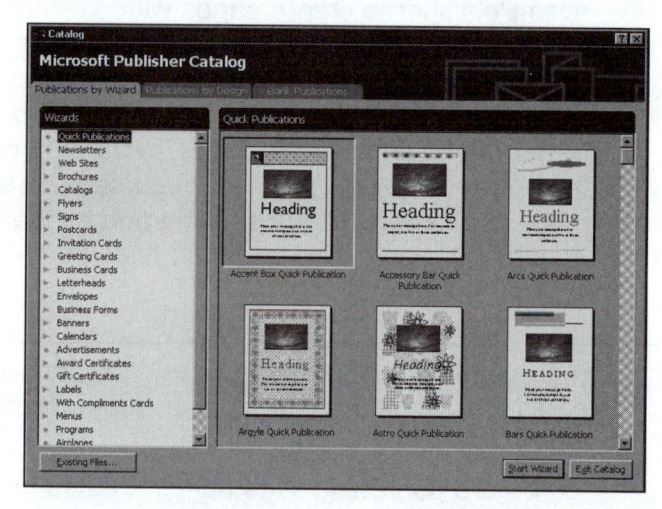

4. To create a new publication, see *Create a Publication Using a Wizard* or *Create a Blank Publication*.

   OR

   To work on an existing publication, see *Open a Publication*.

   OR

   To close the Catalog and display a blank publication, click **Exit Catalog**.

5. To exit Publisher, click **File**, **Exit**.

The Publisher Window

You work with publications in the Publisher window.

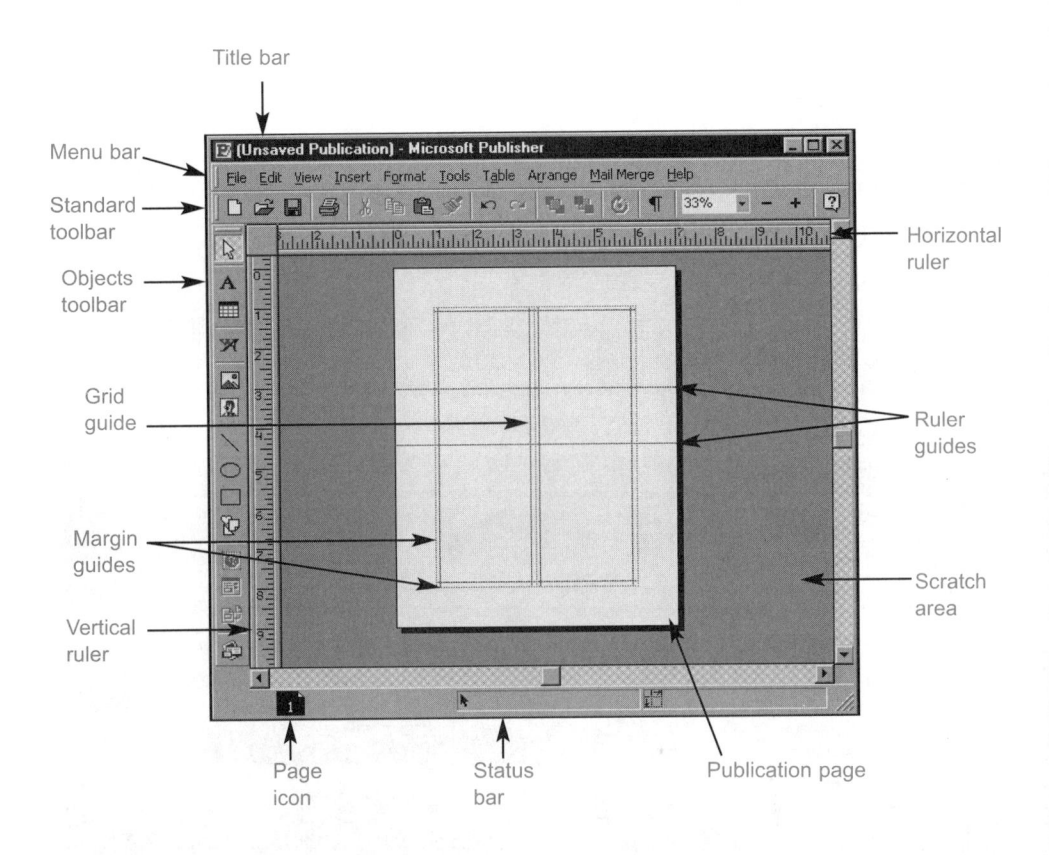

Labels on the window illustration:
- Title bar
- Menu bar
- Standard toolbar
- Objects toolbar
- Grid guide
- Margin guides
- Vertical ruler
- Horizontal ruler
- Ruler guides
- Scratch area
- Page icon
- Status bar
- Publication page

Notes:

- To use rulers, see *Move Rulers, Set the Zero Point,* and *Set the Unit of Measure.* A ruler guide is a nonprinting line useful for lining up frames, as described in *Add Ruler Guides.*

- Grid guides are nonprinting lines that show the page layout, such as the two-column layout in the illustration. See *Add Grid Guides* and *Set Up Facing Pages.*

- Margin guides are nonprinting lines that show page margins. See *Change Page Margins.*

- To work with toolbars and menu bars, see *Customize Toolbars* and *Arrange Toolbars.*

- The status bar shows information about a frame or object that you are creating or that is currently selected.

- The title bar shows the publication name. If it has not yet been saved, it displays **[Unsaved Publication]**.

- The scratch area is a desktop where you can temporarily place pictures and blocks of text that you will use on a page.

3

Hide the Catalog at Startup

The Catalog is a window with a list of preset publication designs that you can select from to create a publication. It appears when you start Publisher. You can also choose to display a new, blank publication when you start Publisher.

Tools → Options...

Notes:

- When you are new to Publisher or if you usually create a new publication when you start the program, it is handy to have the Catalog appear when you start. If you generally open an existing publication when you start Publisher, use the procedure on this page to bypass the Catalog.

- The Catalog displays whenever you choose the **File**, **New** command.

- To return to showing the Catalog each time you start Publisher, repeat this procedure.

1 Click **Tools**, **Options**. The Options dialog box displays.

2 Click the **Use Catalog at startup** check box to clear it. The Catalog will not appear at startup.

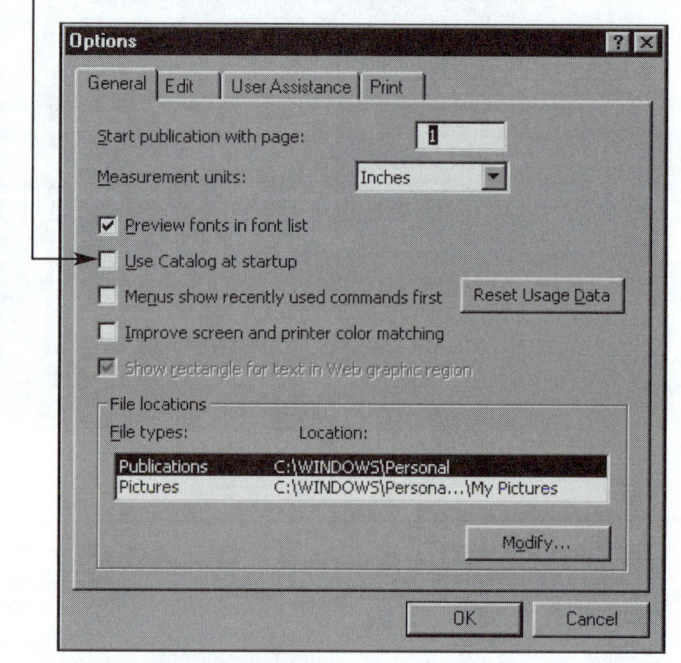

3 Click OK.

4

Continue →

Customize Toolbars

Set the size of toolbar buttons and choose to show or hide ScreenTips (pop-up descriptions of tools and objects on the page). You can also disable personalized menus and select a menu animation effect.

View → Toolbars

Notes:

- These options apply to all toolbars.
- Publisher has two types of ScreenTips that you can customize. Toolbar ScreenTips show the name of a toolbar button when you position the mouse pointer over a toolbar button. Object ScreenTips show the object type when you position the mouse pointer over an object such as a picture frame.
- You can show shortcut keys in toolbar ScreenTips. Shortcut keys show the keyboard alternatives to using a toolbar button or menu command.

1 Click **View**, **Toolbars**, **Options**. The Toolbar Options dialog box displays.

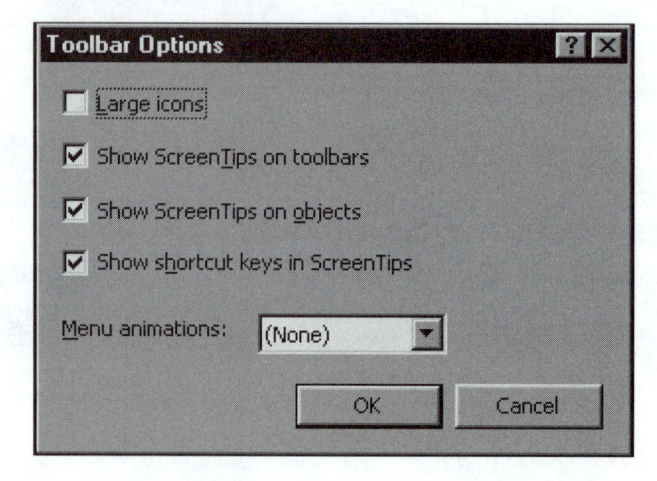

   Toolbar Options dialog:
   - ☐ Large icons
   - ☑ Show ScreenTips on toolbars
   - ☑ Show ScreenTips on objects
   - ☑ Show shortcut keys in ScreenTips
   - Menu animations: (None)
   - OK Cancel

2 Set options as follows:
   - **Large icons**. Set the size of toolbar buttons.
   - **Show ScreenTips on toolbars**. Show or hide ScreenTips when you position the mouse pointer over a toolbar button.
   - **Show ScreenTips on objects.** Show or hide ScreenTips when you position the mouse pointer over an object such as a ruler or a frame.

- **Show shortcut keys in ScreenTips.** Show or hide the keyboard alternatives to toolbar buttons in ScreenTips. The following ScreenTip for the **Cut** toolbar button includes the shortcut keys **Ctrl+X**, which you can press to cut the selected object.

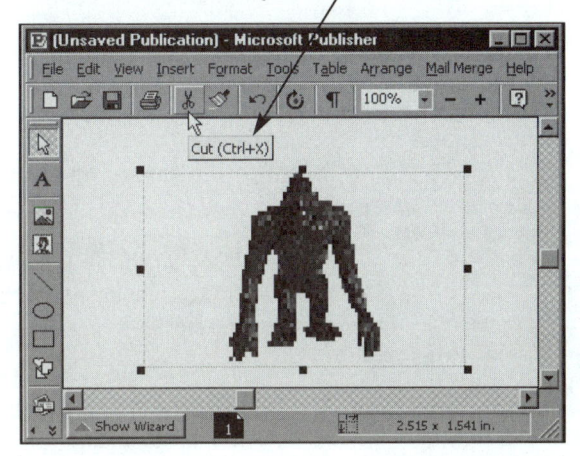

- **Menu animations.** Select a special effect to display when you select a menu command.

3   Click OK .

Notes:

- When personalized menus are enabled, the commands on the menus move so that commands you use most often are at the top of the menu. Commands that you do not use frequently are often hidden.

- By default, personalized menus are enabled.

- If you disable personalized menus, all commands remain in the same place on the menu.

Disable Personalized Menus

1   Click **Tools**, **Options**. The Options dialog box displays.

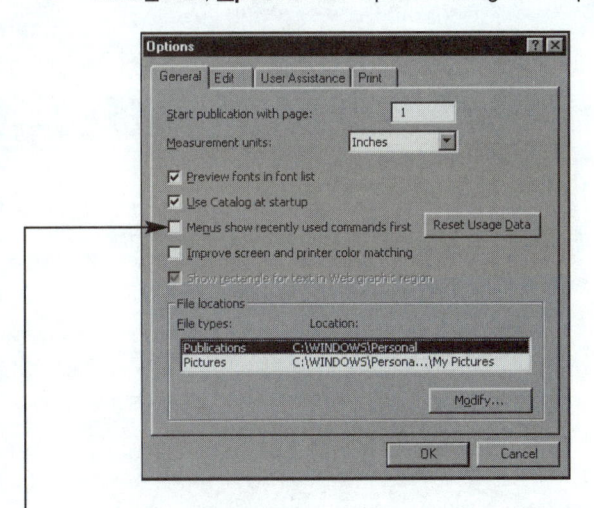

2   Click the **Menus show recently used commands first** check box to clear it.

3   Click OK .

7

Arrange Toolbars

Show and hide toolbars and move them in the Publisher window.

Notes:

- A toolbar is docked when it is located at the top or left side of the window. A floating toolbar can be moved anywhere in the window. Use this procedure to float a docked toolbar and to dock a floating toolbar.

- You can move any toolbar, including the menu bar.

- Floating a toolbar is helpful if you cannot see all of the tools on a toolbar because it does not fit in the window. All buttons on a floating toolbar are visible.

- To float a docked toolbar:

    a. Position the pointer over the move handle at the left side or the top of the toolbar.

    b. Drag the toolbar when the pointer changes to:

    c. Release the mouse button when you have positioned the toolbar.

- To resize a floating toolbar, place the mouse pointer on an edge of the toolbar until it changes to a double-headed arrow and then drag.

- To move a floating toolbar, drag the title bar.

- To dock a floating toolbar, move it to any edge of the window until it snaps into place.

Move handle — *Floating toolbar*

Docked toolbars

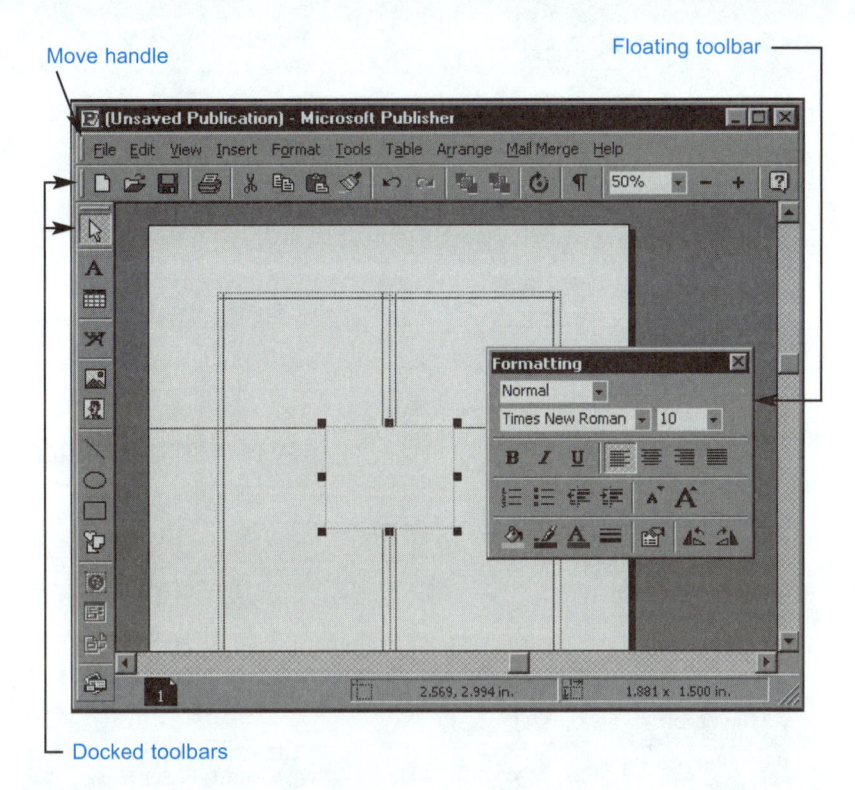

Notes:

- Many toolbars appear automatically when you need to use them. For example, when you select an object, Publisher displays the Formatting toolbar.

- By default, the Standard and the Objects toolbars are always displayed. The Standard toolbar is docked at the top of the window and the Objects toolbar is docked at the left.

Show/Hide a Toolbar

1 Click **View**, **Toolbars**.

2 Click the toolbar to show or hide.

NOTE: A check mark appears on the menu next to each toolbar that is shown.

9

Get Help Using the Office Assistant

The Office Assistant is a cartoon character on the Publisher screen. Use it to locate Help topics or disable it and use the Answer Wizard instead.

Help → Show the Office Assistant

Notes:

- Enter an English-language query such as "prepare a file for a commercial printing service" or "change the font size" to have the Office Assistant search for Help topics related to your question.

- When the Assistant lists Help topics in response to a query, the topics that most closely match your query are at the top of the list.

1. If the Office Assistant balloon is not showing, click the character to display it.

2. Type your query.

3. Click Search. The Assistant shows Help topics that might answer your question.

4. Click **See more** to view more topic titles if the topic you are looking for is not listed.

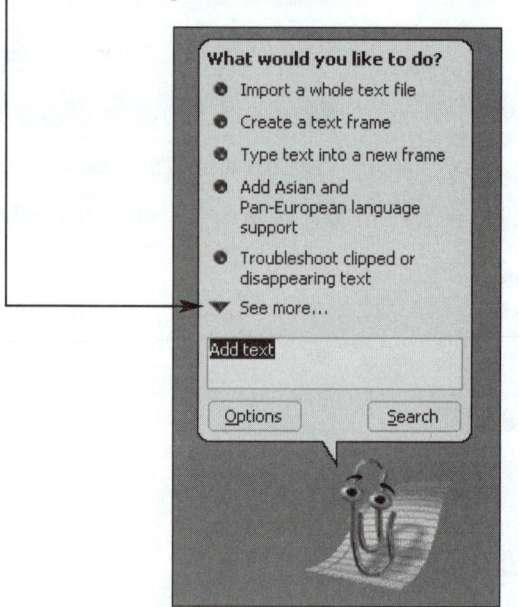

5. Click a topic to display it. The topic opens in the Publisher Help dialog box.

   NOTE: To temporarily hide the Assistant if it is in the way of the Help dialog box, right-click the character and click **Hide**.

10

Notes:

- Disabling the Office Assistant gets it out of your way. You can then use the Answer Wizard to enter queries as described in *Get Help Using the Answer Wizard*.

- If you miss the Office Assistant, repeat this procedure to enable it.

Notes:

- Visit the Office Assistant Gallery and select from different characters.

- Some Assistant characters are more active than others. The least dynamic is the logo. The dot and the puppy are the most active and produce the most sounds.

- If you used a typical installation, only one character is installed. You can install another character from your Publisher CD.

Disable the Office Assistant

1   Click the Office Assistant character.

    NOTE: *If the character is not displayed, click **Help**, Show the **O**ffice Assistant. Even if the Assistant is disabled, this command will display it.*

2   Click **Options**. The Office Assistant dialog box displays.

3   Click the **Use the Office Assistant** check box to clear it.

Use a Different Character

1   Right-click the Office Assistant character.

    NOTE: *If the character is not displayed, click **Help**, Show the **O**ffice Assistant.*

2   Click **Options**. The Office Assistant dialog box displays.

3   Click the **Gallery** tab.

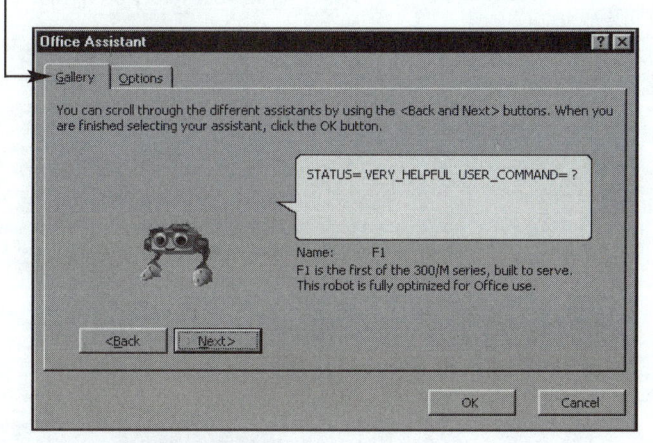

4   Click [**N**ext>] until the character you want to use is displayed.

5   Click [OK].

6   If the character is not installed, the Office Assistant prompts you to install it. Click **Y**es to install it from your Publisher CD.

11

Get Help Using the Answer Wizard

Use this procedure to find Help topics when the Office Assistant is disabled.

Help → ? Microsoft Publisher Help

Notes:

- Use the Answer Wizard tab to enter English-language queries such as "resize a picture frame" or "delete a text frame." The Answer Wizard responds with a list of Help topics related to your question.

- The Answer Wizard is similar to the Office Assistant. You type a question to get a list of topics relating to your question in both the Answer Wizard and the Assistant. However, the Assistant takes up space on the screen since it resides there permanently.

1 Press **F1** or click **Help** [?] to open the Publisher Help window.

> *NOTE: The Office Assistant displays instead of the Publisher Help window if you have not disabled the Assistant. See* Get Help Using the Office Assistant.

2 Click the **Answer Wizard** tab.

3 Type your query and press **Enter**.

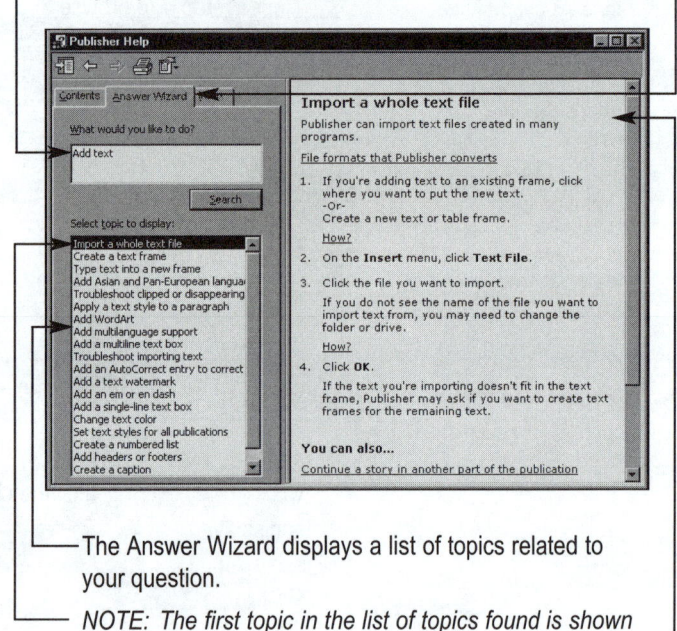

The Answer Wizard displays a list of topics related to your question.

> *NOTE: The first topic in the list of topics found is shown in the right pane.*

12

Notes:

- You can also use the **Contents** tab in the Publisher Help window to see a table of contents of Help topics. However, the table of contents does not include all Help topics.

- When the Answer Wizard lists topics, the topics that most closely match your question are at the top of the list.

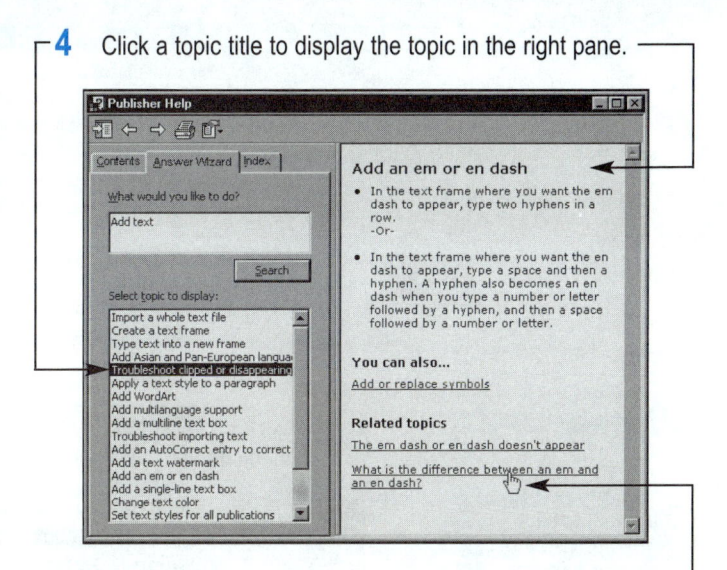

4 Click a topic title to display the topic in the right pane.

5 To browse information mentioned in a topic, click a hyperlink (underlined text).

OR

Repeat step 4 to browse other topics listed in the left pane of the Help window.

OR

Repeat step 3 to rephrase your query if the topic you are looking for is not listed.

6 Click ✖ to close the Publisher Help window.

Publisher Help Toolbar Buttons

- Click **Hide** or **Show** to hide or show the left pane (hiding it leaves more room for topics).

- Click **Back** or **Forward** to move between the topics.

- Click **Print** to print the currently displayed topic.

- Click **Options** to change Internet options (many of these affect Publisher Help).

    NOTE: The Publisher Help window uses an Internet Explorer setting to set the relative text size (from smallest to largest). If set to Smallest, the font will be too small for you to read Help topics. To change the setting, open Internet Explorer. Click View, Text Size, then choose the relative size.

Visit the Office Update Web Site

Visit the Microsoft Publisher Web site to see what's new in Publisher, download Office Assistant characters and Publisher utilities, read articles on using Publisher, and find other items of interest to Publisher users.

Help ➔ Microsoft Publisher Web Site...

Notes:

- You must have a Web browser and Internet service in order to visit the Web site.

- This procedure starts your Web browser (if it is not already started) and connects to the Microsoft Publisher Welcome page in the Microsoft Office Web site.

- Microsoft often updates the Publisher Web pages. Pages might not look like the illustrations you see here.

1 Click **Help**, **Microsoft Publisher Web Site**. Publisher connects to the Publisher Welcome page.

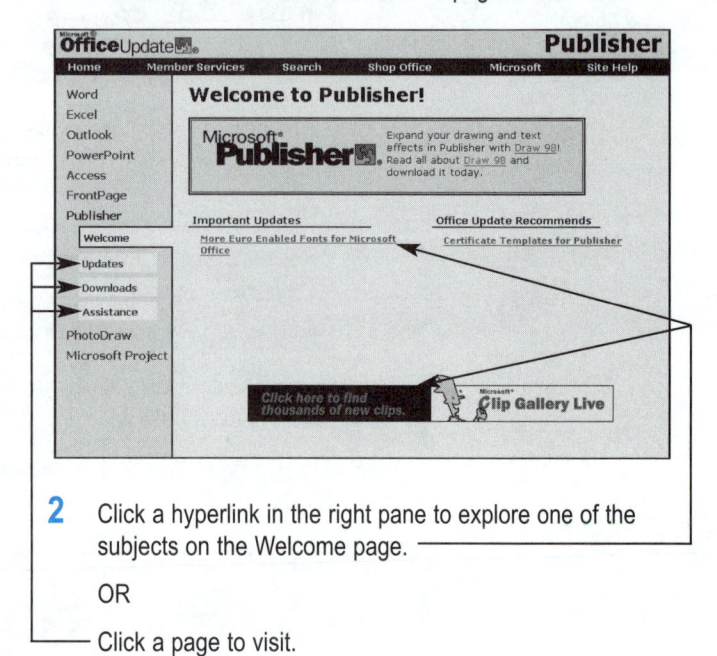

2 Click a hyperlink in the right pane to explore one of the subjects on the Welcome page.

   OR

   Click a page to visit.

The illustration below shows the Download page where you can download utilities, Office Assistant characters, fonts, and other software.

See items selected for downloading, then download.

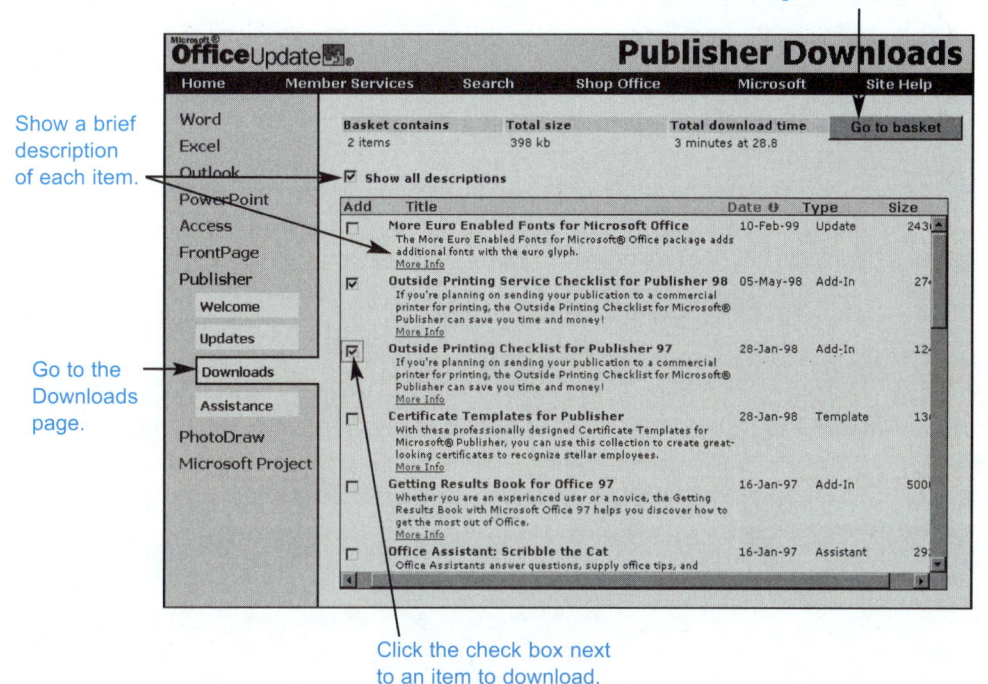

Show a brief description of each item.

Go to the Downloads page.

Click the check box next to an item to download.

3   Exit using your normal Web browser exit procedure.

15

Publications

Documents in Publisher are called publications. Publisher provides wizards to help you quickly create all types of publications, from envelopes to newsletters.

After you create a publication, see the **Pages** section to fine-tune the layout. Then add text and graphics as described in the **Add and Edit Text** and **Pictures** sections.

Create a Publication Using a Wizard

Use a wizard to quickly create a publication that includes a layout, sample text, and graphics. Publisher has wizards that create all types of publications for you.

File ➡ New...

Notes:

- Wizards create publications from preset designs. The design specifies the page layout for the publication. For example, a design for a tri-fold brochure includes fold lines indicating where the page should be folded. A label design sets the label size, how many labels are in each row, and how many rows of labels are on a page.

- Wizards prompt you for information on the publication you are creating. The screens that you see vary depending on the publication type. The illustrations in this example procedure show you the Envelope Wizard screens.

1 If the Catalog is not displayed, click **File**, **New**.

2 Click the publication type in the Wizards list.

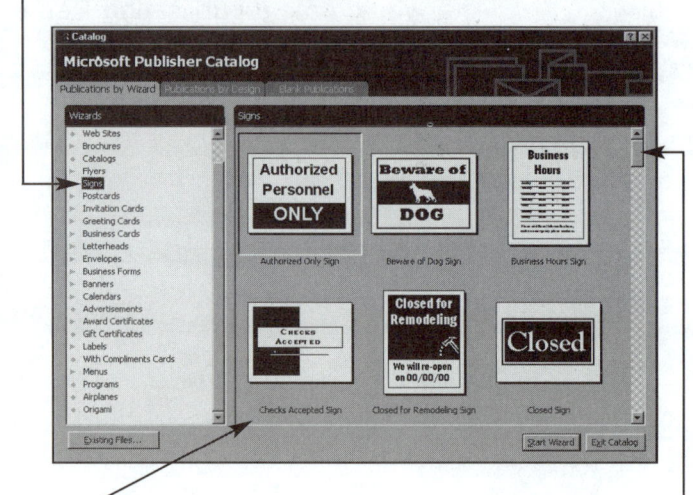

The right pane shows designs for the publication type you selected.

- Use the scroll bar to scroll down to see more designs.
- Publisher includes layouts for Paper Direct papers. These are papers with preprinted graphics. If you choose a Paper Direct layout, the graphics on the page will not print. These are replicas of the graphics that are printed on the actual paper and are used in Publisher as guides so that you can place text around the graphics. Paper Direct layouts are listed in the Special Papers category on the **Publications by Design** tab.
- The designs listed on the **Publications by Design** and the **Publications by Wizard** tab are the same. Layouts are grouped by design (such as all publications you can create using the Checkers or the Waves design) rather than by type (such as all brochures or postcards) on the **Publications by Design** tab.

18

Notes:

- Wizards prompt you for information about the publication that you are creating. For example, the Postcard wizard asks how many postcards to print per page.

- See *Choose a Printer* to select a printer. Publisher displays the publication in the Publisher window as it will print on the selected printer. If you do not have the correct printer selected, your printed output could be very different from what you see in the Publisher window.

- If the publication will be printed at a commercial printing service, use the **Tools**, **Commercial Printing Tools** command to set up the publication for printing. Work with your printing service to set these options properly.

3 If selecting a publication type in the left pane opens a list of subcategories, click a subcategory. For example, the following illustration shows Thank You Postcard designs.

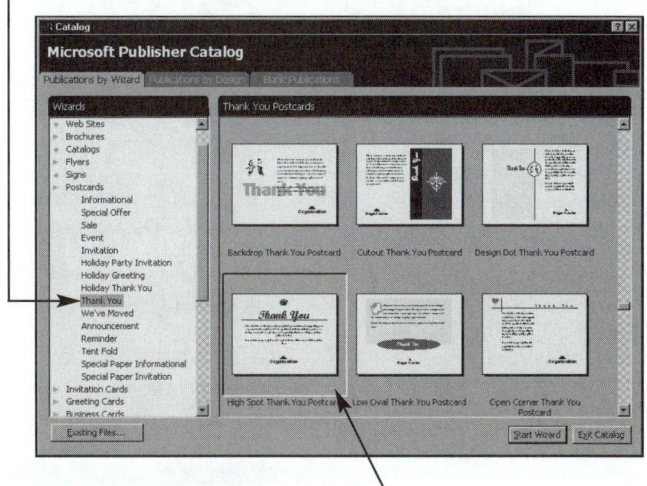

4 Click the publication to create.

5 Click `Start Wizard`.

6 If the wizard prompts you to enter color scheme, layout, or other information:

    a. Enter information as requested. Wizard prompts appear in the left pane. The following screen shows an Envelope Wizard prompt requesting a color scheme.

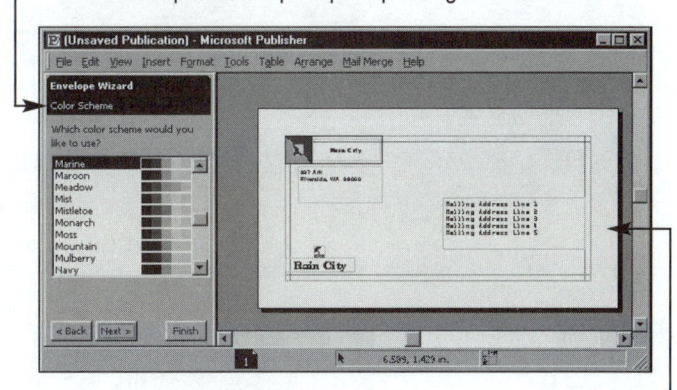

The right pane shows a sample publication with the specifications you entered.

    b. Click `Next >` to continue.

19

Create a Publication Using a Wizard
(continued)

Notes:

- You can disable wizard steps so that when you start a wizard Publisher simply creates the publication without prompting you for information. You can use the Wizard pane to customize the publication layout. See *Disable Publication Wizard Steps*.

- Some wizards use **personal information sets** to add information about you or your company to a publication.

- Many publications include sample text and graphics. After you create the publication, replace placeholder text and graphics with your own. See *Delete Text* to delete sample text.

c. Repeat steps a. and b. as necessary to enter the requested information.

   NOTE: Click [< Back] to return to a previous screen to change the information that you entered.

d. When finished, click [Finish]. The publication is displayed in the Publisher window.

7 Use the Wizard pane to edit the publication. You can change the page size, personal information, color scheme, and other specifications.

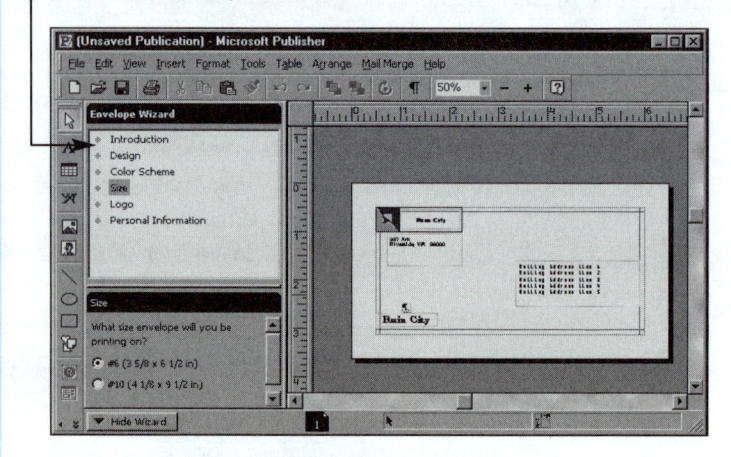

8 Click [▼ Hide Wizard] to close the Wizard pane and use the entire Publisher window to work on your publication, as shown in the next illustration.

20

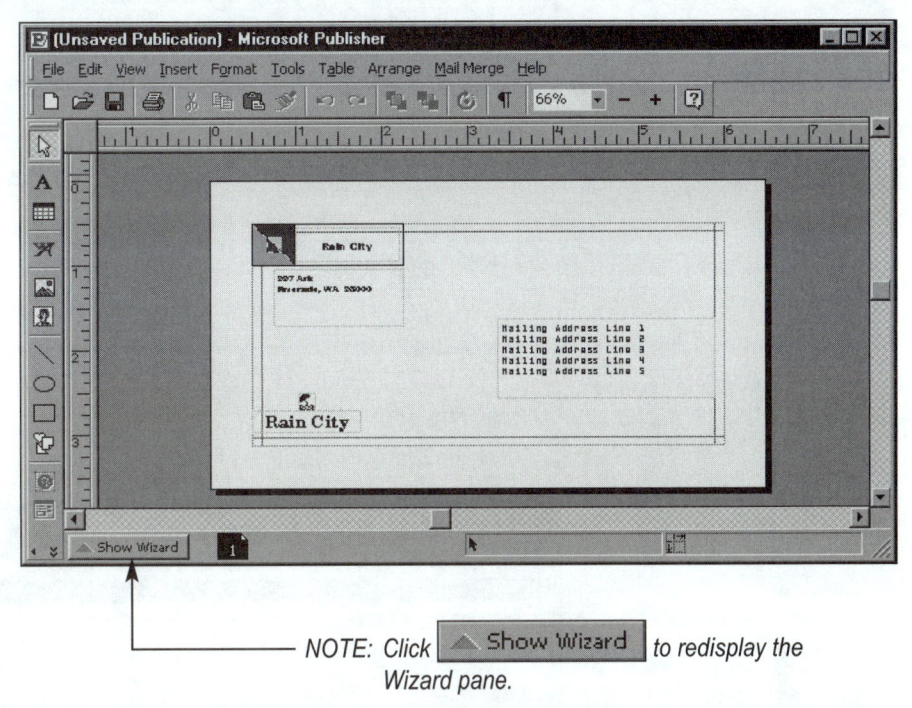

NOTE: Click [Show Wizard] *to redisplay the Wizard pane.*

9 To save the publication, see *Save a Publication*.

Create a Blank Publication

Create a publication that does not include placeholder text and graphics.

File → New...

Notes:

- To create a blank publication, enter page specifications such as the page size, margins, and fold lines.

- Choose a preset standard page size for your publication or define a custom page size by entering the page height and width.

- See *Choose a Printer* to select a printer. Publisher displays the publication in the Publisher window as it will print on the selected printer. If you do not have the correct printer selected, your printed output could be very different from what you see in the Publisher window.

1 Click **File**, **New**. The Catalog dialog box displays.

2 Click the **Blank Publications** tab.

3 Click a publication type in the left pane. Preset layouts for that type appear in the right pane.

4 Click a preset layout in the right pane and click Create.

OR

To specify a custom page size for a print publication, click Custom Page... and enter page specifications (see *Change the Page Size*). Click OK.

OR

To set up a custom size for a Web publication, click Custom Web Page... and enter page specifications. Click OK.

22

Notes:

- If you will send the publication to a commercial printing service, use the **Tools**, **Commercial Printing Tools** command to set up the publication for printing. Work with your printing service to set these options.

5 If you used a preset layout, the Publisher window includes the Quick Publication Wizard pane for modifying the layout.

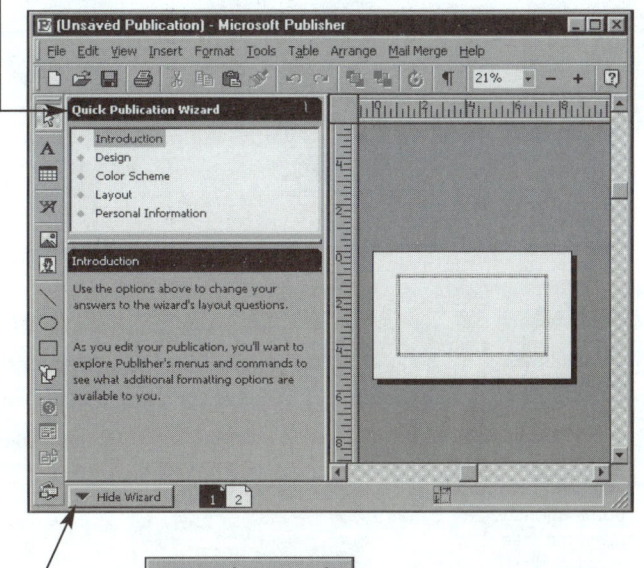

- Click [▼ Hide Wizard] to close the Wizard pane and use the entire Publisher window to work on your publication.
- You can redisplay the Quick Publication Wizard by clicking [▲ Show Wizard] in the status bar.
- If you entered a custom page size, the Quick Publication Wizard pane is not displayed.

6 To save the publication, see *Save a Publication*.

Save a Publication

After you create a publication, save and name it. Save your changes periodically while editing a publication.

File ➡ Save

Notes:

- Organize your publications in folders where you can quickly find them again. For example, you might place all publications for a particular client or project in one folder.

- Create new folders when you save a new publication for the first time. Or, use Windows Explorer to create folders.

- You can automatically save a backup copy each time you save a publication. Then, if the original is damaged, you have a copy. Backup copies use the name of the original file plus **Backup of**. For example, the backup name of a publication called **ClientList.pub** is **Backup of ClientList.pub.**

1 Click **Save** or press **Ctrl+S**.
   - If you are saving a publication for the first time, the Save As dialog box displays.
   - If you are saving an existing publication, the publication is saved after you complete step 1. The Save As dialog box does not display. Continue working on the publication or click **File, Close** to close it.

2 To create a new folder:

   a. Click **Create New Folder** in the toolbar at the top of the Save As dialog box. The New Folder dialog box displays.

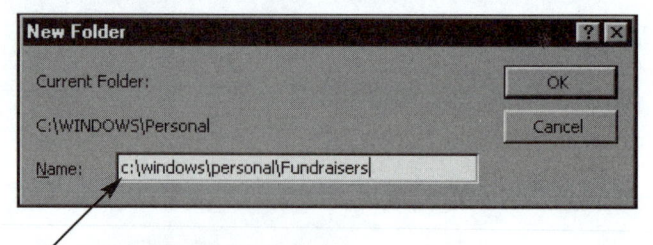

   New Folder
   Current Folder:
   C:\WINDOWS\Personal
   Name: c:\windows\personal\Fundraisers
   OK   Cancel

   b. Type the pathname of the new folder.

   c. Click OK to create the folder and close the dialog box.

24

Notes:

- Save your work often. The AutoSave feature prompts you to save every 15 minutes. See *Set AutoSave Options*.

- When you save a publication for the first time, Publisher displays the default publication folder in the Save As dialog box. See *Set the Default Publication Folder* to specify the default folder.

3   Display the folder in which to save the publication in the **Save in** list.

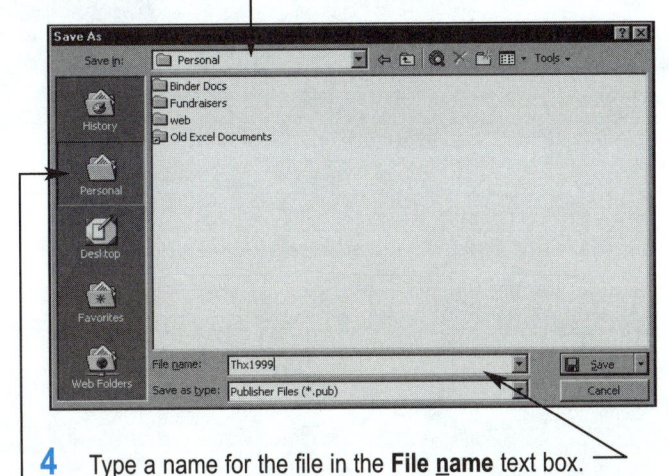

4   Type a name for the file in the **File name** text box.

   NOTE: *The buttons at the side of the Save As dialog box are shortcuts to folders or to the desktop. For example, clicking the **Personal** button opens the Personal folder.*

5   Click the [Save] arrow and click **Save with Backup** to create a backup copy whenever you save this publication.

   OR

   Click the [Save] button.

6   To close the publication, click **File**, **Close**. If you have not saved your latest changes, Publisher prompts you to save before closing.

Open a Publication

Open a publication that you have previously created and saved.

File ➔ Open...

Notes:

- Publisher displays the default publication folder when you open a publication. See *Set the Default Publication Folder* to specify the default folder.

- You can browse folders on your computer to locate a publication.

- You can only have one publication open at a time.

1 Click **File**, **Open**.

OR

If the Catalog is open, click Existing Files...

2 Browse the folders on your computer in the **Look in** list, if necessary, to display the file to open.

NOTE: *Use the **Tools**, **Find** command to search for a publication, if necessary.*

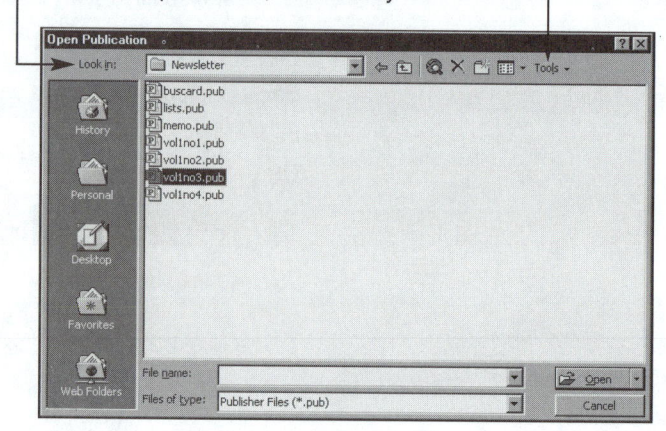

3 Double-click the file to open.

OR

Click the file to select it and click Open.

Notes:

- Publisher lists the last four publications that you opened at the bottom of the **File** menu. Use the menu to quickly open a publication you have used recently.

Open a Recently-Opened Publication

1 Click **File**.

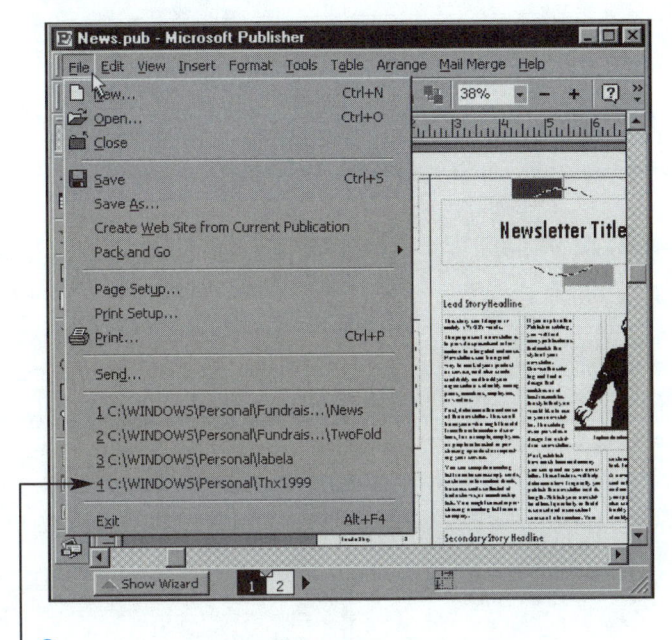

2 Type the underlined number next to the publication.

OR

Click the publication to open.

27

Maintain a Personal Information Set

A personal information set contains information about you or your company. You can quickly insert this information into any publication.

Notes:

- Personal information sets save you time. After you enter the information, you can insert it in any publication.

- Use up to four separate personal information sets for: 1) Primary Business, 2) Secondary Business, 3) Other Organization, and 4) Home/Family. Use these personal information sets to keep the information for your home and business separate.

- In addition to name, phone, and address, each set can store a default color scheme that is applied to publications that use the personal information set. You can specify two different color schemes for each personal information set—one for Web publications and the other for print publications.

- When you create some types of publications, wizards add information from personal information sets to create personalized publications. For example, your name and address can be automatically added to letters.

Edit → **Personal Information...**

1. Click **Edit**, **Personal Information**. The Personal Information dialog box displays.

2. Select the information set to edit. Dialog box options display the information for the selected set.

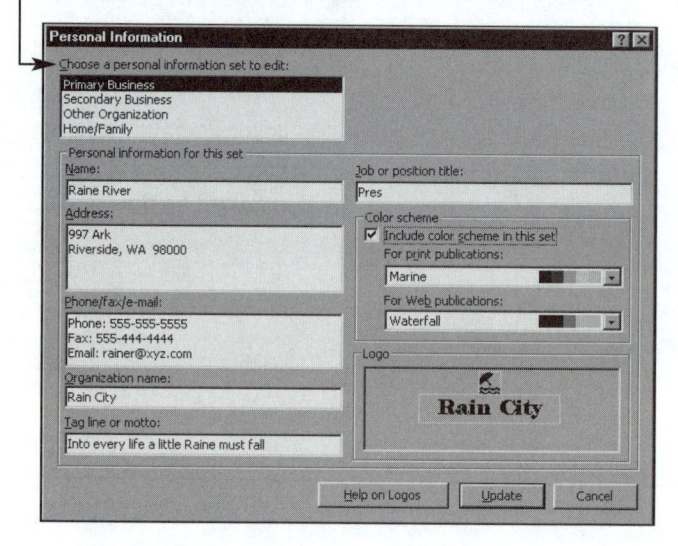

3. Change information such as name, address, and phone numbers as desired.

4. To apply a default color scheme to publications using this personal information set:
   a. Click the **Include color scheme in this set** check box to select it.
   b. Select a color set from the **For print publications** list.
   c. Select a color scheme from the **For Web publications** list.

5. Click **Update**.

Notes:

- Specify which personal information will be used in the current publication.

- All publications use a personal information set even if the information does not appear in the publication. If you do not specify a personal information set for a publication when you create it, Publisher uses the Primary Business set.

Specify the Personal Information Set for a Publication

1. Click **Edit**, **Personal Information**. The Personal Information dialog box displays.

2. In the **Choose a personal information set to edit** list, select the set to apply.

3. Click **Update**.

Set AutoSave Options

Publisher reminds you to save your publication every 15 minutes. This feature is called AutoSave. You must respond to the AutoSave prompt before you can continue working.

Tools → Options...

Notes:

- If you are already in the habit of saving your work often, disable AutoSave so that the reminder does not interrupt your work.

- It is important to save your work often (just press **Ctrl+S**). If you tend to forget to save, leave AutoSave enabled.

- The reminder displays whenever you work in a publication for 15 minutes without saving. When you save, the clock restarts.

- You can specify how often the AutoSave reminder displays. You might, for example, have it display every 10 or 20 minutes rather than every 15.

1 Click **Tools**, **Options**. The Options dialog box opens.

2 Click the **User Assistance** tab.

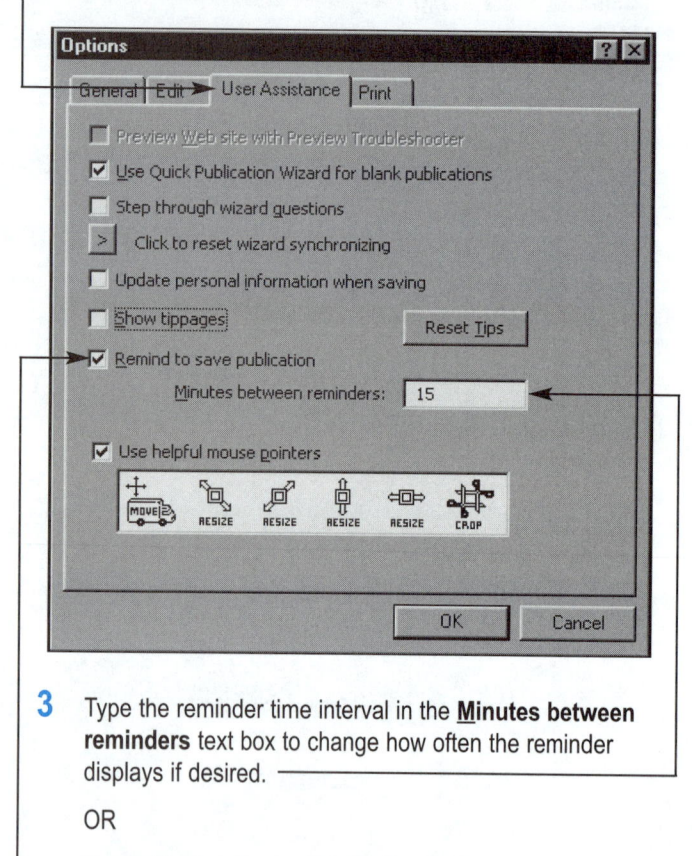

3 Type the reminder time interval in the **Minutes between reminders** text box to change how often the reminder displays if desired.

OR

To disable AutoSave, click the **Remind to save publication** check box to clear it.

4 Click OK.

The following illustration shows the AutoSave reminder.

Click [Yes] to save your work and close the reminder.

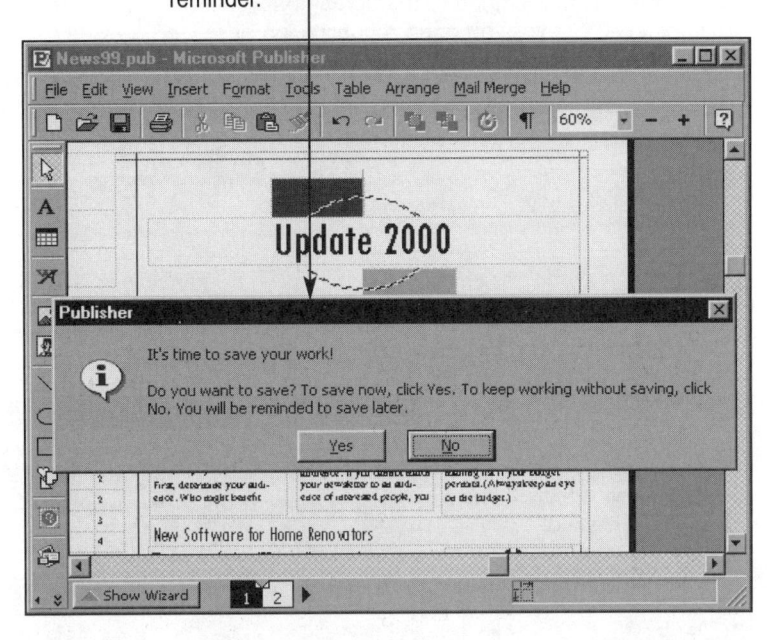

The reminder will pop up again after the specified AutoSave interval.

Set the Default Publication Folder

Publisher assumes that you want to save new publications and open existing publications that are located in the default publication folder. It displays the contents of this folder whenever you open a publication or save a new one.

Tools → Options...

Notes:

- The default publication folder is the folder where you store most of your publications. Save time by setting the default folder so that you do not have to switch folders when you open or save a publication.

- You can create folders when you set the default publications folder.

1. Click **Tools**, **Options**. The Options dialog box opens.

2. Click the **General** tab.

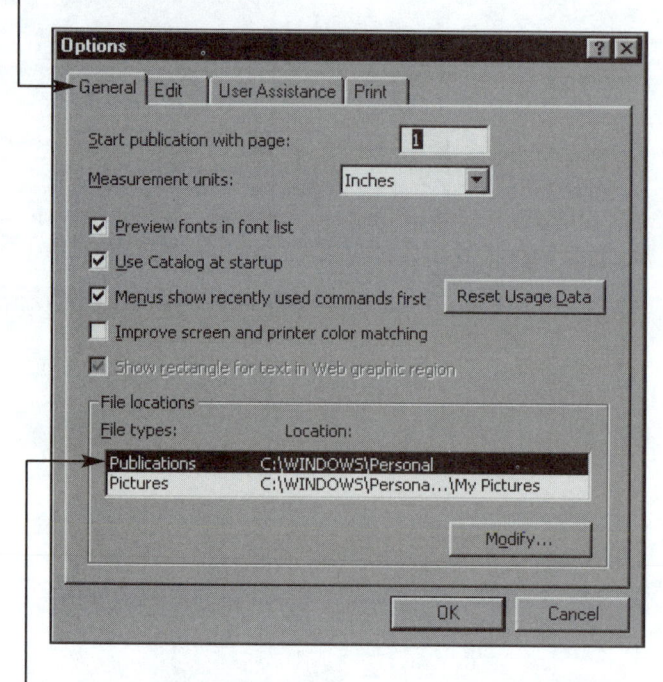

   The current default publications folder is displayed in the **File locations** section.

3. Click Modify... to display the Modify Location dialog box.

32

Notes:

- Create subfolders in the default publication folder to organize publications. For example, in the illustration, the Personal folder is the default publications folder. Subfolders in the Personal folder organize publications by client, publication type, and project.

4   To create a new folder:

a. Click **Create New Folder** in the toolbar at the top of the dialog box. The New Folder dialog box opens.

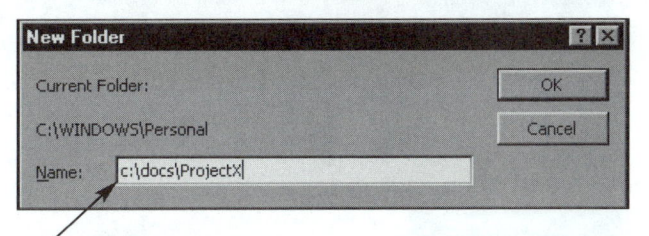

b. Type the pathname of the new folder in the **Name** text box.

c. Click **OK** to create the folder and close the dialog box.

5   In the **Look in** list of folders on your computer, select the folder to be the default.

NOTE: You may not have a Personal folder in the Modify Location dialog box; it may appear as My Documents.

OR

Type the pathname of the default publication folder in the **Folder name** text box.

6   Click **OK**.

33

Disable Publication Wizard Steps

Specify whether or not you are prompted through a series of screens when you create a publication using a wizard.

Tools → Options...

Notes:

- Creating a publication using a wizard displays a series of prompts requesting information about the publication. You can turn off these steps so that wizards create publications without displaying prompts. This is a faster way to create a publication.

- After creating a publication, you can use the Wizard pane to change the color scheme, paper size, and all other specifications set by wizards. See *Create a Publication Using a Wizard,* steps 7 and 8.

- To enable wizard steps, repeat this procedure.

1. Click **Tools**, **Options**. The Options dialog box displays.

2. Click the **User Assistance** tab.

3. Click the **Step through wizard questions** check box to clear it. This disables wizard steps.

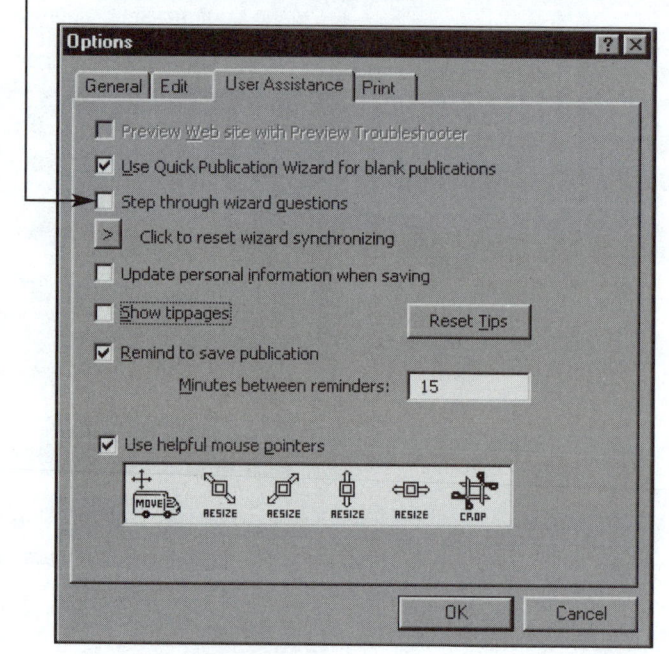

4. Click **OK**.

34

Pages

This section covers working with entire pages in your publication. Place nonprinting guides on the page to define the layout and use them to line up frames and objects on a page. Insert new pages, change the page size, set up a publication that has facing pages, and otherwise work with pages.

All publications have one or two page backgrounds that contain layout guides such as guides that show the page margins. Guides and other objects on the page background appear on all pages in the publication. On the page background, place information that you want to appear on all pages, such as your company's name and phone number or headers and footers.

The design of each page is important. The overall look of a page is a design element in and of itself. Use a consistent design across multiple pages in a publication, particularly those that have facing pages.

Move Rulers

Use the horizontal and vertical rulers to size and position objects on the page.

Notes:

- To move the rulers and the zero point at the same time see *Set the Zero Point*.

- You can have frames "snap" to the nearest ruler mark. This helps you position frames precisely. As you move or size a frame, the frame is pulled to the next ruler mark. The "snap to rulers" feature is enabled by default. Disable it to position or size a frame outside of ruler marks.

- To work closely with a frame, move the rulers to the frame.

- Hide rulers to show more of the page in the window.

- By default, rulers show measurements in inches. To change this to picas, points, or centimeters see *Set the Unit of Measure*.

Move a Ruler

1. Place the mouse pointer over a ruler until the pointer changes to a two-headed arrow.

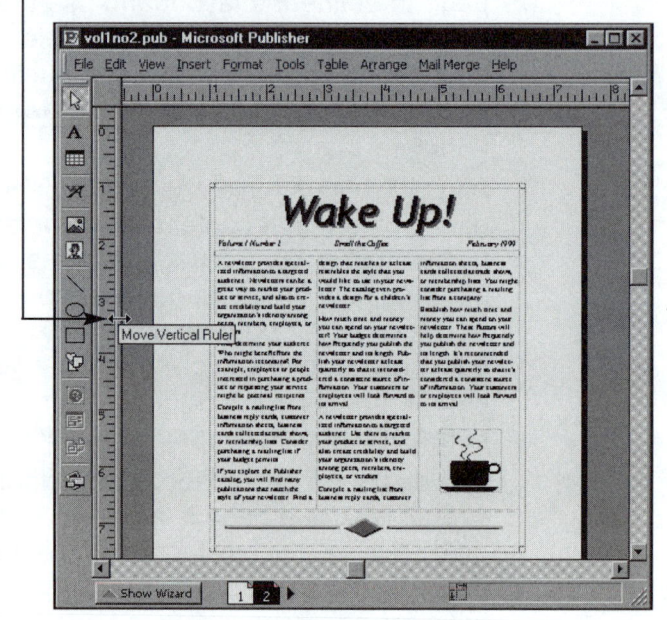

2. Drag the ruler.

Move Both Rulers

1. Place the mouse pointer over the button at the intersection of the rulers until the pointer changes to a two-headed arrow (see the next illustration).

2. Drag to the new position.

   In the following illustration, both rulers are moved to a picture frame in order to work closely with the size and position of the graphic.

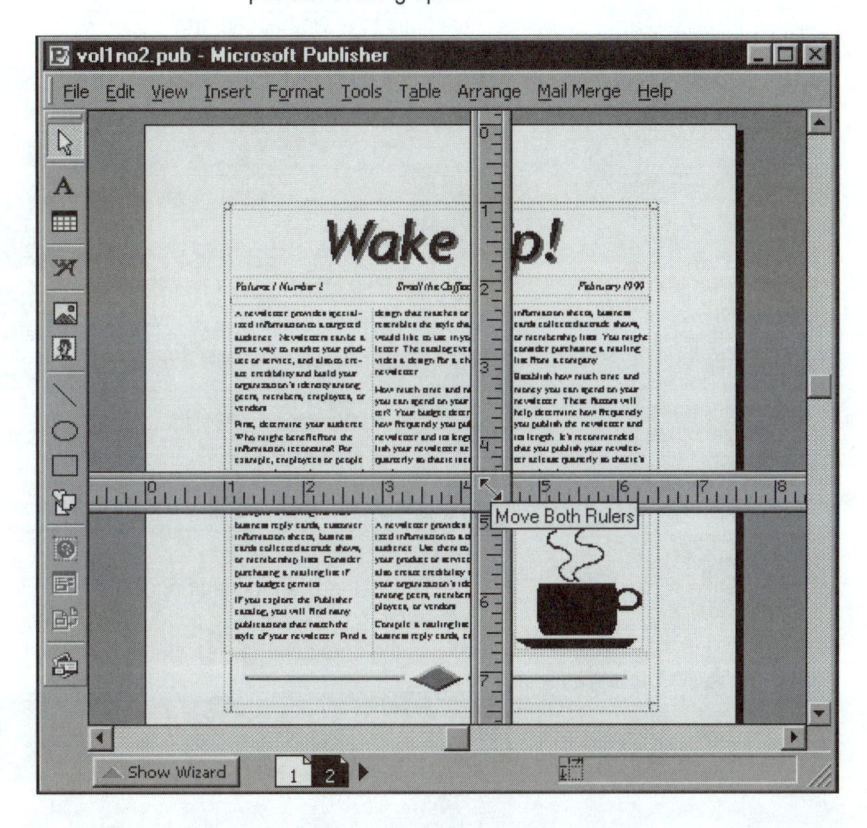

Disable or Enable Snap to Rulers

- Click **Tools**, **Snap to Ruler Marks**.

Show or Hide Rulers

- Click **View**, **Rulers**.

Set the Zero Point

The zero point marks where measurements start from zero on the ruler. Use this procedure to move the zero point on a ruler.

Notes:

- The zero point is the point at which the zero appears on the rulers, normally at the left and top of the page. The ruler measures from this point. The zero on the vertical ruler is at the top of the page. The zero on the horizontal ruler is at the left of the page.

- To work with individual elements on a page, move the zero point. If you move the zero point to the top-left corner of a frame you can work with the measurements of a single frame.

- You can simultaneously move the rulers and reset the zero point. Use this procedure to work with a particular frame.

1 Place the mouse pointer on the ruler until the pointer changes to a two-headed arrow.

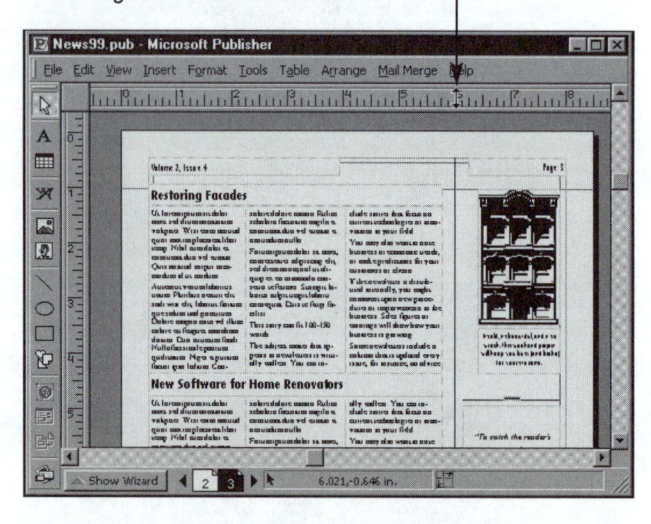

2 Hold down the **Shift** key and right-click the ruler where you want to place the zero point. The following illustration shows the zero point moved on the horizontal ruler.

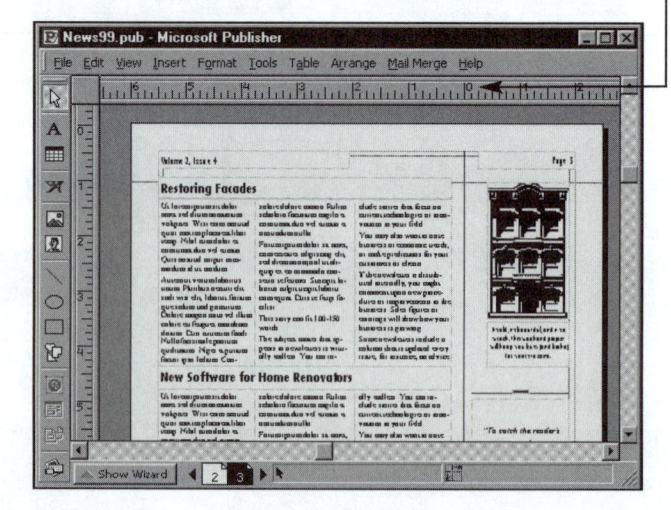

38

Notes:

- When you move the mouse pointer on the page, such as when you are moving a frame with the mouse, the status bar shows the position of the pointer in relation to the zero point. (This information displays only if there is enough room; the window must be large enough to show the entire status bar.)

Move Both Rulers and Set the Zero Point

1. Place the mouse pointer on the intersection of the vertical and horizontal rulers. The pointer changes to a two-headed arrow.

2. Hold down the **Ctrl** key.

3. Drag the rulers to the new position. The following illustration shows the rulers and zero point moved to the upper-left corner of a picture frame.

39

Set the Unit of Measure

By default, Publisher measures pages, frames, and all other sizes in inches. You can switch to picas, points, or centimeters for the unit of measurement.

Notes:

- The unit of measure is the measurement system (inches, picas, points, or centimeters) you use when you enter a measurement in a dialog box. For example, you use the default unit of measure (such as 2.5" or 3.8cm) to enter the size of page margins in the Page Setup dialog box.

- Ruler tick marks and the measurements shown in the status bar appear in the default unit of measure.

- You can type the abbreviation for a different unit of measure (such as cm for centimeters or pt for points) when entering measurements in dialog boxes. The default unit of measure should be the unit that you use most often.

Tools → Options...

1 Click **Tools**, **Options**. The Options dialog box displays with the General tab selected.

2 Select from the **Measurement units** list.

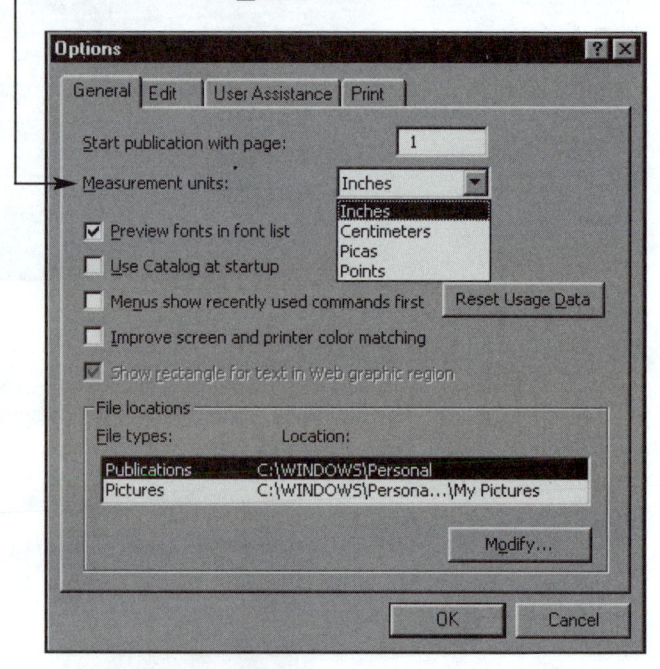

3 Click OK.

Continue →

Add Ruler Guides

Place a ruler guide to line up frames and objects on a page.

Arrange → Ruler Guides

Notes:

- Use ruler guides to quickly add a temporary guide on a page.

- Layout guides are permanent guides that define the layout for all pages in a publication. See *Add Grid Guides* and *Change Page Margins* for information on setting up these types of guides.

- Ruler guides are green. This distinguishes them from layout guides which are pink and blue.

- You can add a horizontal or a vertical guide.

1. Place the mouse pointer on the ruler until the pointer changes to a two-headed arrow.

2. Hold down the **Shift** key. The pointer changes to: (horizontal ruler) or (vertical ruler).

3. Drag from the ruler to the page. The green line that appears is the guide that you are adding.

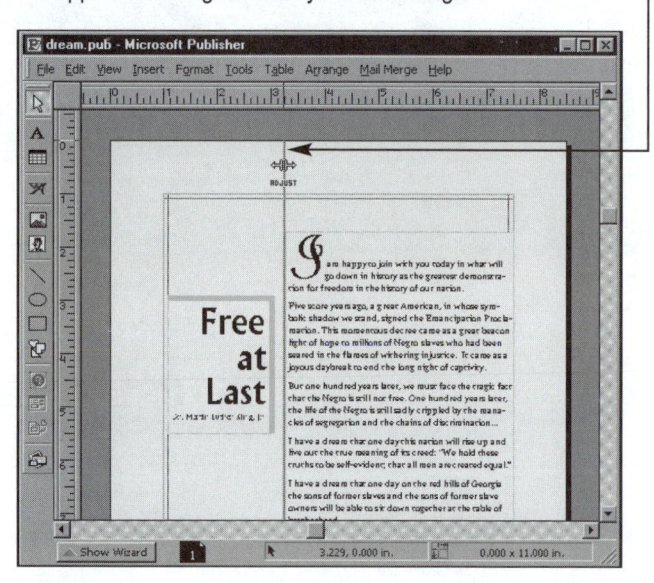

4. Release the mouse button when you have positioned the guide.
   - If the Snap to Ruler Marks feature (on the **Tools** menu) is enabled, the ruler guide will be placed at the nearest ruler mark when you release the mouse button.
   - If guides are hidden, you will not see the guide after you release the mouse button. See *Show or Hide Ruler Guides* on the next page.

5. To move a ruler guide, hold down **Shift** and drag the guide.

42

> *Notes:*
> - Remove a single ruler guide or all ruler guides on the page.

Remove Ruler Guides

- To remove one guide, place the mouse pointer over the guide and hold down the **Shift** key. When the pointer changes shape, drag the guide back to the ruler.

OR

- To remove all ruler guides on the page, click **A**r**range**, **Ruler Gui**d**es**, **C**l**ear All Ruler Guides**.

Show or Hide Ruler Guides

> *Notes:*
> - This procedure shows or hides all guides, including margin guides, grid guides, and frame boundaries.

- Click **V**i**ew**, **Show B**o**undaries and Guides** to see guides.
- Click **V**i**ew**, **Hide B**o**undaries and Guides** to hide them.

  NOTE: *Ruler guides are placed behind the objects on a page. If you cannot see a ruler guide even when guides are displayed, the guide might be hidden behind a frame. To make a frame transparent, click on it and press* ***Ctrl+T****.*

Add Grid Guides

Add guides to every page of your publication. Use these guides to line up frames and objects on each page.

Arrange → Layout Guides...

Notes:

- Grid guides define a layout grid for the pages of your publication. This creates an underlying structure that shows you where to place text and graphics in your publication. A grid helps you to keep a consistent design on each page.

- See *Change Page Margins* to change the margin guides on a page. Page margins should be final before you add grid guides. If you later change the margins you will have to adjust the grid guides.

- Grid guides appear on the screen but do not print.

- Grid guides appear on every page in the publication.

- If the publication has facing pages, guides are mirrored on the left and right pages.

- To have Publisher "snap" frames to the nearest guide when you move or size a frame, see *Snap to Guides and Objects*.

1 Click **Arrange**, **Layout Guides**. The Layout Guides dialog box displays.

2 Type or select the number of vertical guides to add in the **Columns** box.

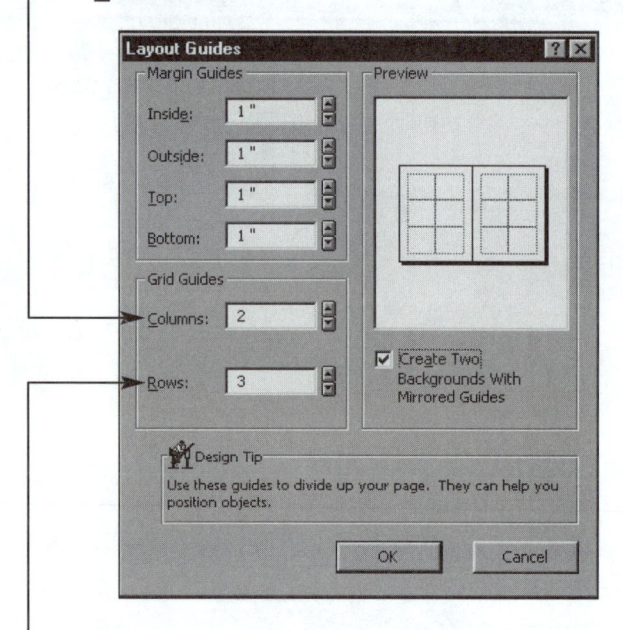

3 Type or select the number of horizontal guides to add in the **Rows** box.

- Guides will be evenly spaced on the page as shown in the Preview pane in the Layout Guides dialog box. To set up a grid with unequal columns and/or rows, see *Move Guides* on the next page.

- If the publication has facing pages, the **Create Two Backgrounds With Mirrored Guides** option is selected and both pages appear in the Preview pane. See *Set Up Facing Pages*.

4 Click OK.

44

Notes:

- Grid guides are added to the page background. In order to move them you must switch to the background.

- Moving a guide in a publication with facing pages moves it on both pages so that the grids on each page are a mirror image of each other. You can see this if you are in Two-Page view when you move the guide.

Notes:

- Grid guides are always visible in the page background. This procedure shows or hides guides in the foreground.

- This procedure shows or hides all guides, including margin guides, ruler guides, and frame boundaries.

Move Guides

1. Click **V̲iew**, **G̲o to Background** to switch to the background.

2. To see both pages in a publication that has facing pages, click **V̲iew**, **Two-Pag̲e Spread**.

3. Hold down the **Shift** key and place the pointer over the guide until it changes shape to: ⇕ADJUST or ⇔ADJUST

4. Drag the guide.

   NOTE: If you have one or more Snap To features enabled, the guide jumps to the nearest guide or object when you position it. See Snap to Guides and Objects.

5. Click **V̲iew**, **G̲o to Foreground** to return to the foreground.

Show or Hide Grid Guides

- Click **V̲iew**, **Show B̲oundaries and Guides** to see guides.
- Click **V̲iew**, **Hide B̲oundaries and Guides** to hide them.

   *NOTE: Guides are placed underneath the frames on a page. If guides are hidden behind a frame, you can make the frame transparent (select the frame and press **Ctrl+T**) so that guides are visible.*

45

Change Page Margins

Define the area of the page in which you will place text and graphics.

[Arrange] → [Layout Guides...]

Notes:

- Pink and blue dotted lines around the outside of the page show you the page margins. These nonprinting lines are called margin guides.

- If a publication has facing pages, set an inside margin to define the gutter margin. The gutter margin is the right margin on left pages and the left margin on right pages (see the illustration). This is where the publication will be bound.

- Headers and footers should be placed outside of the page margins. Set a top and/or bottom margin that is large enough to create space for them if necessary. See *Add Headers and Footers*.

1 Click **Arrange**, **Layout Guides**. The Layout Guides dialog box displays.

   NOTE: *The following dialog box shows options for a publication with facing pages. If your publication does not have facing pages, the dialog box shows left and right margins rather than inside and outside margins.*

2 Type or select margin measurements in the Margin Guides options.

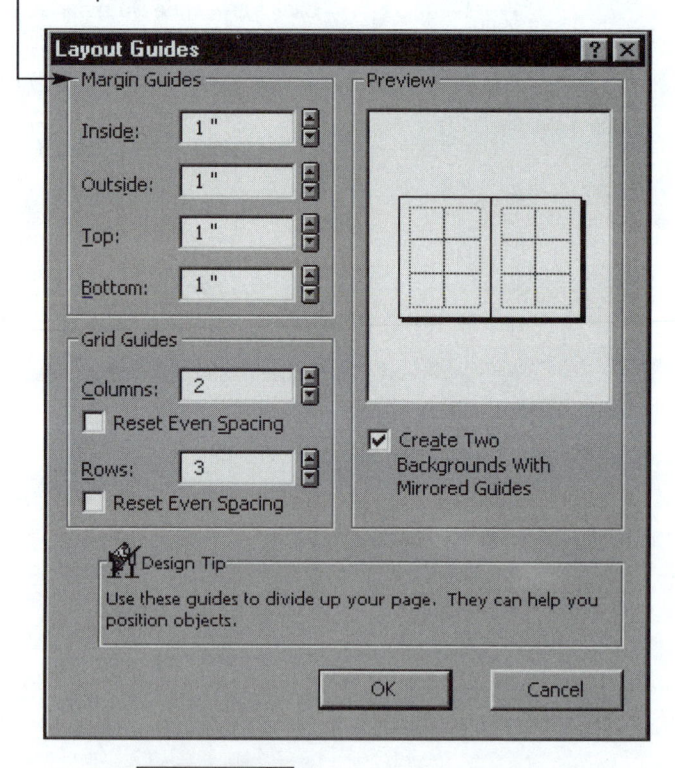

Layout Guides

Margin Guides
- Inside: 1"
- Outside: 1"
- Top: 1"
- Bottom: 1"

Grid Guides
- Columns: 2
- ☐ Reset Even Spacing
- Rows: 3
- ☐ Reset Even Spacing

Preview

☑ Create Two Backgrounds With Mirrored Guides

Design Tip
Use these guides to divide up your page. They can help you position objects.

[OK] [Cancel]

3 Click [OK]. The following illustration shows margins in a publication with facing pages.

Top margin — Inside margins

Bottom margin — Outside margins

Notes:

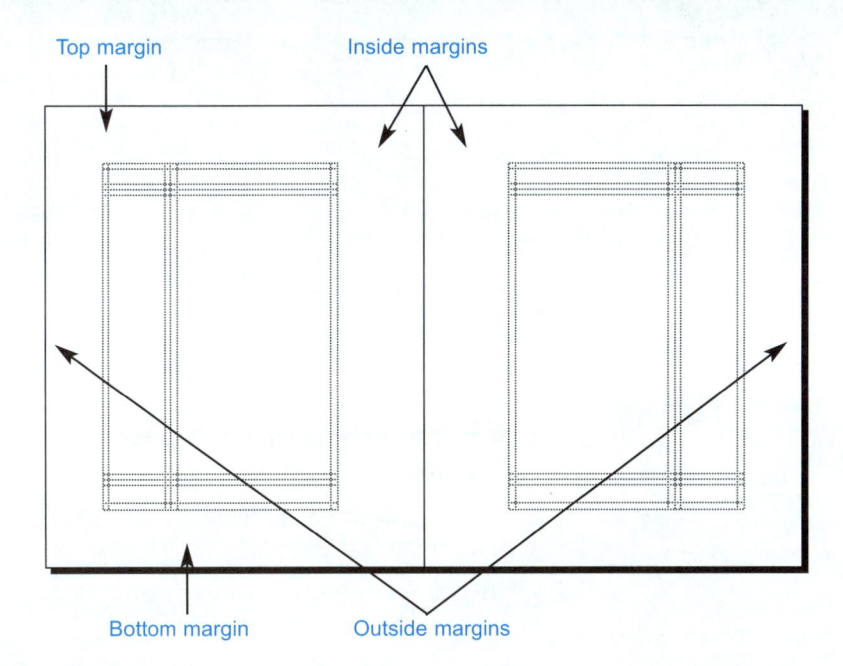

- Switch to the background to move margin guides. Moving a guide changes the margin.
- When you change a margin in a publication that has facing pages, the change is automatically applied to the corresponding margin on the opposite page.

Notes:

- Guides are always visible when you are working in the background. Use this procedure to show or hide guides in the foreground.
- This procedure shows or hides all guides, including ruler guides, grid guides, and frame boundaries.

Change Margins by Dragging Guides

1   Click **View**, **Go to Background**.

2   To see both pages in a publication with facing pages, click **View**, **Two-Page Spread**.

3   Hold down the **Shift** key and place the pointer over a margin until the pointer changes to: ADJUST or ADJUST

4   Drag the margin guide.

5   Click **View**, **Go to Foreground** to exit the background.

Show or Hide Margin Guides

- Click **View**, **Show Boundaries and Guides** to see guides.
- Click **View**, **Hide Boundaries and Guides** to hide them.

Change the Page Size

Change the size of all pages in a print publication.

File ➡ Page Setup...

Notes:

- Choose from a number of preset custom page sizes, such as a 5-foot banner or postcard size. Or, enter any size by entering the paper measurements.

- This procedure sets the publication page size, not the size of the paper that you will print on. For example, if you choose a 10-foot banner page size, you are not setting the paper size to 10 feet. The banner will print on multiple pages which you will need to tape together. To set the paper size, see *Change the Paper Size*.

- You cannot use different sized pages in a single publication. All pages must be the same size.

1 Click **File**, **Page Setup**. The Page Setup dialog box displays.

2 Click a **Choose a Publication Layout** option to specify publication type, if desired.

   NOTE: This allows you to select from standard sizes for different types of publications.

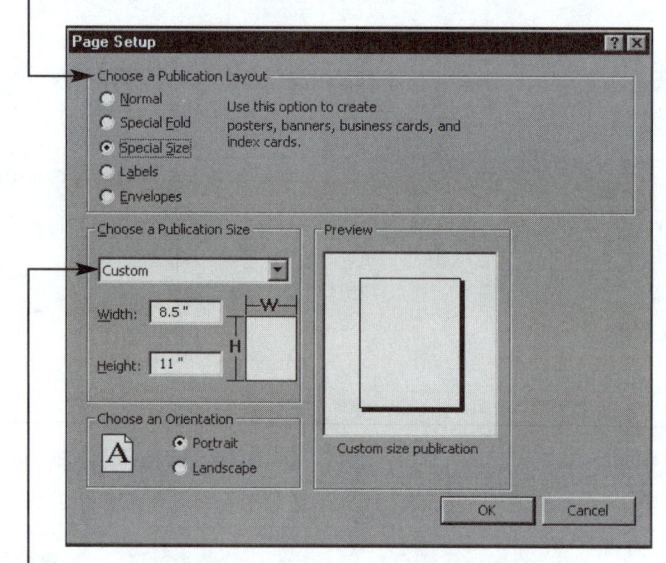

   NOTE: When you select a layout, the dialog box displays options specific to that layout. This illustration shows Special Size layout options.

3 Select a size from the **Choose a Publication Size** list. The **Width** and **Height** of the selected size are shown in the dialog box.

   OR

   If the size that you need is not in the list, type the **Width** and **Height**.

4 Click OK

Snap to Guides and Objects

Use the Snap To feature to have Publisher line up frames with the guides or objects on a page.

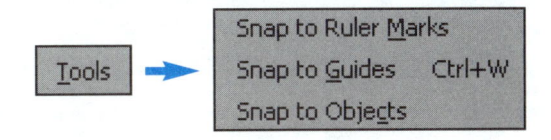

```
Tools  →   Snap to Ruler Marks
           Snap to Guides    Ctrl+W
           Snap to Objects
```

Notes:

- The Snap To feature "snaps" a frame or object to the nearest guide or object on the page when you move or size it. This makes it easy to line up frames precisely in the layout grid.

- You can control what items frames will snap to: guides, ruler marks, or objects on the page.

- If all Snap To commands are enabled, Publisher first snaps to the nearest guide, then to the nearest object, then to the nearest mark on the ruler.

1 Click **Tools**.

2 Click the command for a Snap To feature:

- **Snap to Ruler Marks**. Pulls the frame to the nearest ruler mark. (See *Add Ruler Guides*.)

    NOTE: Rulers must be displayed for this feature to work. Click **View**, **Rulers**.

- **Snap to Guides**. Controls the Snap To feature for grid, margin, and ruler guides. (To set up these guides, see *Add Grid Guides*, *Change Page Margins*, and *Add Ruler Guides*.)

    NOTE: If ruler and grid guides are not visible on the page, click **View**, **Show Boundaries and Guides** to see them. Snap to Guides works even if guides are hidden.

- **Snap to Objects**. Pulls the frame to the nearest object.

3 Repeat the procedure to disable or enable Snap To feature.

NOTE: When a check mark appears next to a Snap To command on the menu, the feature is enabled.

49

Set Up Facing Pages

Create left and right pages for multiple-page print publications such as magazines and books that have pages facing each other.

[Arrange → Layout Guides...]

Notes:

- Publications with facing pages have two background pages: a left page and a right page. For more information on background pages, see *Place Text or Graphics on All Pages*.

- Items on background pages are mirrored (reversed) on facing pages. If you set up a grid on the left page, Publisher mirrors the grid on the right page. See *Add Grid Guides*.

- When you set the page margins, Publisher applies the same margin setting to both the left and right pages. See *Change Page Margins*.

- To view each two-page spread (both the left and the right page) in the publication, see *View Two Pages*.

1 Click **Arrange**, **Layout Guides**. The Layout Guides dialog box displays.

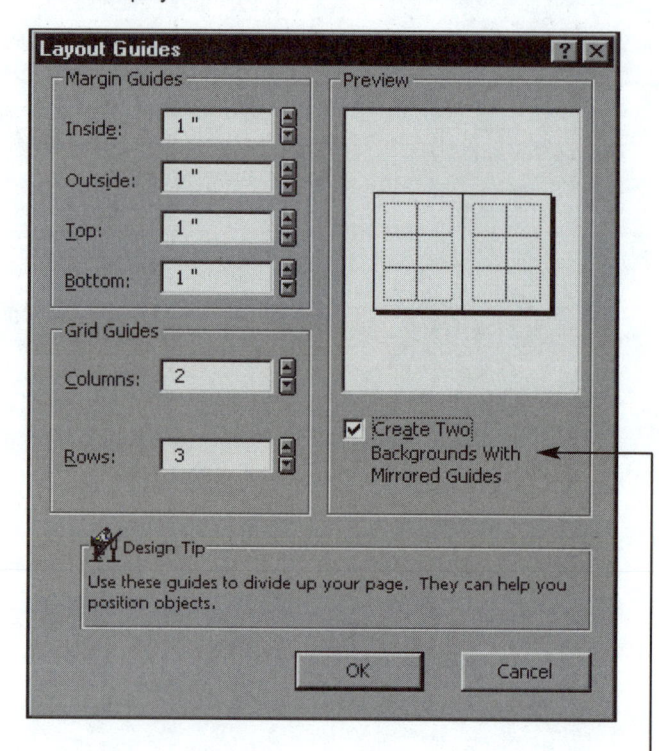

2 Select **Create Two Backgrounds With Mirrored Guides**.

3 Click [OK].

50

Change the Page Orientation

Print pages sideways (landscape orientation) or lengthwise (portrait orientation).

File ➜ Page Setup...

Notes:

- Set the page orientation before you add grid guides, text, and graphics to your publication.

- This procedure changes the orientation for all pages in the publication. You cannot use different orientations in a single publication.

- You can change the page orientation for your printer (**File**, **Print Setup**) to change the default orientation for all new documents created in all Windows programs.

1. Click **File**, **Page Setup**. The Page Setup dialog box displays.

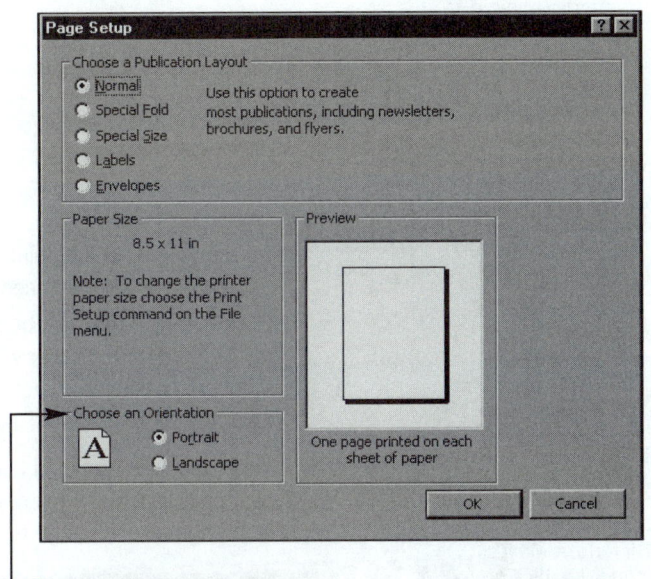

   Page Setup

   Choose a Publication Layout
   - ● Normal — Use this option to create most publications, including newsletters, brochures, and flyers.
   - ○ Special Fold
   - ○ Special Size
   - ○ Labels
   - ○ Envelopes

   Paper Size: 8.5 x 11 in

   Note: To change the printer paper size choose the Print Setup command on the File menu.

   Preview: One page printed on each sheet of paper

   Choose an Orientation
   - ● Portrait
   - ○ Landscape

   OK | Cancel

2. Click **Portrait** or **Landscape**. The Preview pane shows the current orientation.

3. Click OK.

51

Add Headers and Footers

Add a header at the top of every page and/or a footer at the bottom.

View → Go to Background

Notes:

- Headers and footers generally contain information that identifies the publication, such as a title, company name, or logo. They also may contain page numbers for long publications.

- Headers and footers are placed in the page background. Objects on the page background appear on all pages in the publication.

- Place headers and footers outside of the page margins so that they do not interfere with text and graphics on the page. If necessary, see *Change Page Margins* to adjust the top and bottom margins.

1. Click **View**, **Go to Background**.

2. Create a text box for the header or footer. See *Create a Text Frame*.

3. Type the header or footer text in the text frame. See *Type and Edit Text*.

4. To add page numbers:

    a. Type any text that you want to appear with the number. Examples: Page, Page __ of 10

    b. Position the insertion point in the text frame where the page number will be placed.

    d. Click **Insert**, **Page Numbers**. This inserts a pound sign (#) code which Publisher will replace with page numbers (visible when you switch to the page foreground). Examples: Page #, Page # of 10

5. To align separate blocks of text within the frame, see *Set Tabs*. For example, the following footer has a left-aligned title and right-aligned page numbers.

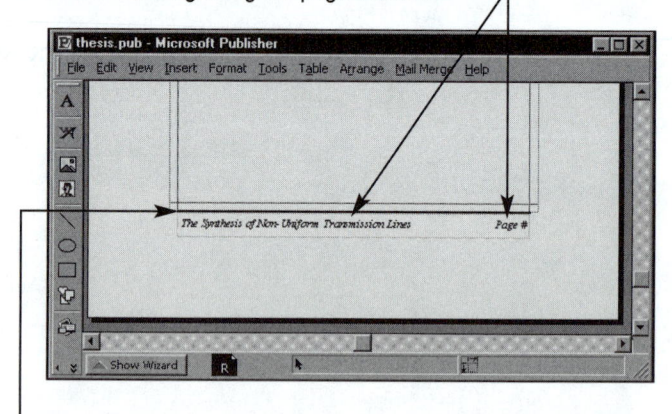

6. Add a rule (line) to separate the header or footer from the body text, as shown in the above illustration. See *Draw Lines and Arrows*.

Notes:

- Leave a blank area of ¼" to ½" around the page, as most printers cannot print to the edge of a page. See your printer documentation to determine the size of the nonprinting area.

- If your publication has facing pages, add headers and footers to both background pages.

7   To format the text font, attributes, and size, see *Format Characters*.

   NOTE: *To see how headers and footers look on a page, click* **View**, **Go to Foreground**. *To edit headers and footers, click* **View**, **Go To Background**.

8   If your publication has facing pages, add headers and footers to the second background page. To see headers and footers on facing pages, click **View**, **Two-Page Spread**.

   The following illustration shows mirrored headers as viewed in the foreground. The position of the page number on the left page is reversed on the right page so that both appear in the outside margin.

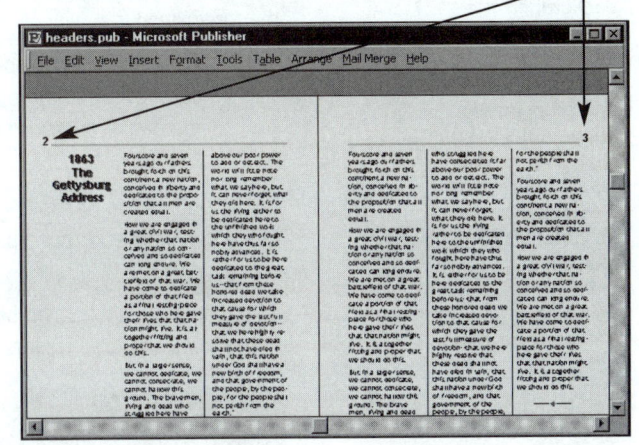

9   When finished working with headers and footers, click **View**, **Go to Foreground**.

Hide Headers and Footers on a Page

1   Go to the page to remove headers and footers.

2   Click **View**, **Ignore Background**.

Notes:

- You may not want to print headers and footers on the first page of a publication.

- This procedure hides all background elements, including guides. You cannot remove just headers and footers.

53

Place Text or Graphics on All Pages

Place an object to appear on all pages in the publication. For example, you could place a watermark or company logo on all pages.

View → Go to Background

Notes:

- The page background is a layer underneath the normal pages where you place text and graphics to appear on all pages. Objects that you place on the page foreground appear only on that page. Objects that you place on the background appear on all pages in the publication.

- Add text and graphics that will appear on all pages before you work in the foreground on individual pages. That way you will not place objects in the foreground on top of background objects.

- Text and objects that are placed in the foreground are not visible when you are working in the background.

1 Click **View**, **Go to Background**.

2 Add text or graphics the same way that you add them in the foreground.

NOTE: If the text or graphic that you want to add appears somewhere in the publication, you can move it to the background using the procedure in this section.

3 If your publication has facing pages, add text and graphics to the second background page, if desired.

The following illustration shows borders that will appear on all pages. This publication has facing pages so the borders are mirrored (reversed) on left and right pages.

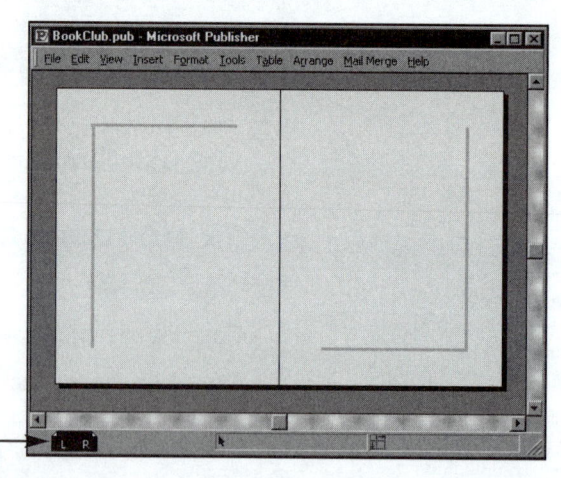

NOTE: In the background, page icons in the status bar show left and right pages rather than page numbers.

4 To view both background pages in a publication with facing pages, click **View**, **Two-Page Spread**.

5 Click **View**, **Go to Foreground** when finished adding background objects.

54

Notes:

- Watermarks should be a pale color so that they do not interfere with text and graphics in the foreground.
- You can remove the background objects from individual pages in your publication. See *Hide Background Objects on a Page* below.

The following illustration shows the same publication as in the previous illustration but in the foreground.

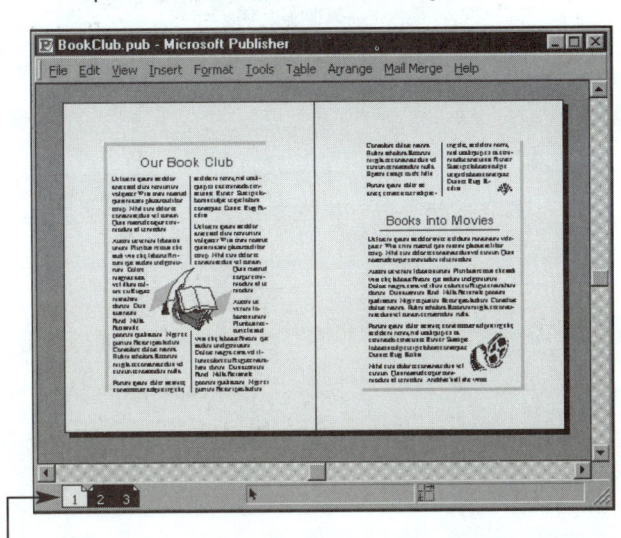

— NOTE: In the foreground, the page icons in the status bar show page numbers.

Notes:

- Move an object from the foreground to the background. Or, move it from the background to the foreground.

Notes:

- In order to move, edit, or otherwise work with text and graphics that appear on all pages, you must go to the background. You cannot access them in the foreground.

Notes:

- This procedure hides all background elements including guides, headers and footers, and any text and graphics that appear on the page background.

Move an Object Between the Foreground and Background

1 Select the object to move.

2 Click **A̲rrange**.

3 Click **Send to Backgro̲und** or **Send to Foregro̲und**.

Change Text or Graphics on the Page Background

1 Click **V̲iew**, **G̲o to Background**.

2 Edit the text or graphic.

3 Click **V̲iew**, **G̲o to Foreground**.

Hide Background Objects on a Page

1 Go to the page to remove background objects.

2 Click **V̲iew**, **I̲gnore Background**.

   TIP: To hide a single background object, create a blank frame and place it over the object in the foreground.

55

Insert a Page

Create new page(s) in your publication.

Insert → Page...

Notes:

- Add a blank page or a page that includes preset design elements. For print publications, you can include a text frame that fills the page. For Web publications, you can select a page type that determines which design elements will be included on the page.

- You can use this procedure to insert a copy of an existing page. The copy includes all frames and their contents and any drawing objects that appear on the original page.

- If adding pages to a print publication, you can add multiple pages.

1. Go to the page where you will insert new page(s).

2. Click **Insert**, **Page**. The Insert Page dialog box displays.

3. If this is a Web publication, the following dialog box displays. If you are creating a print publication, skip to step 5.

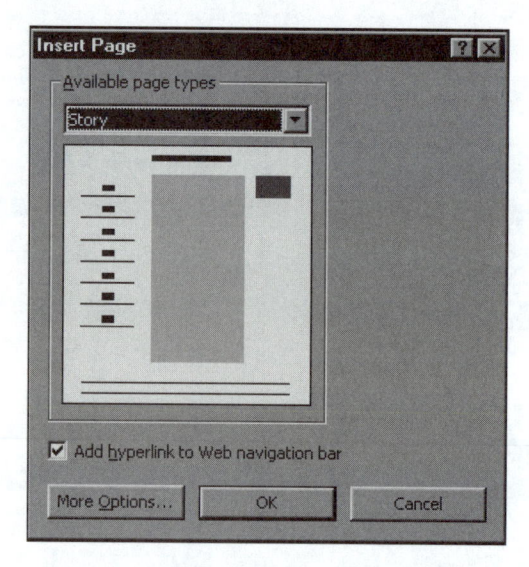

4. To add pages to a Web site:

    a. Select a page type. The sample page in the dialog box shows you a preview of the frames that will appear on the selected page type.

    b. Set the **Add hyperlink to Web navigation bar** option as desired.

    NOTE: Make sure that you include some way to access the page or it will not be accessible in the Web site.

    c. Click More Options... to display the next Insert Page dialog box. This is similar to the one shown on the next page.

5   Type the **Number of new pages** to add.

    NOTE: This option is not available for Web publications.

6   Specify where to add the new page(s).

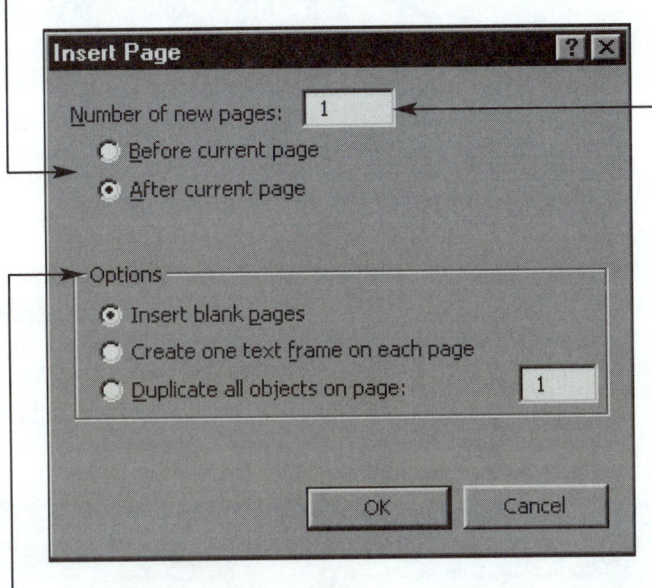

```
Insert Page                                    ? X

Number of new pages:  [ 1 ]

        ○ Before current page
        ⦿ After current page

   ┌─ Options ─────────────────────────────────┐
   │  ⦿ Insert blank pages                     │
   │  ○ Create one text frame on each page     │
   │  ○ Duplicate all objects on page:  [ 1 ]  │
   └───────────────────────────────────────────┘

                          [   OK   ]   [ Cancel ]
```

7   Specify what to include on the new page:

    • **Insert blank pages**. Adds pages without any frames or objects.

    • **Create one text frame on each page**. Adds pages with a text frame that fills the entire page. This saves you a step when creating pages that will be all text.

    • **Duplicate all objects on page**. Use this option to insert a copy of a specified page in the publication.

8   Click [OK].

Notes:

- Find your way around a multiple-page publication. You can go directly to any page if you know the page number.

Notes:

- If the page contains text that is part of a chain of connected text frames, Publisher moves the text to the next frame before deleting the page.

Move Between Pages

• Click a page icon in the status bar: [1 | 2 | 3 | 4 | 5]

OR

• Press **Ctrl+G**. Type the page number and press **Enter**.

Delete a Page

1   If the page contains objects that you want to keep, move them off the page to the scratch area.

2   Display the page to delete.

3   Click **Edit**, **Delete Page**.

57

View Two Pages

View facing pages in a multiple-page publication.

View → **Two-Page Spread**

Notes:

- Facing pages are pages that will face each other when a multiple-page publication is printed. For example, when you open a magazine or a book, you see a left page and a right page at the same time.

- Each set of facing pages in a publication is called a two-page spread.

- Each two-page spread in your publication is a separate design element. Use Two-Page view to make sure that each spread has a consistent design and looks good together.

- Left pages have even page numbers (e.g., 2, 4, 6). Right pages have odd page numbers (e.g., 1, 3, 5).

1 Click **View**, **Two-Page Spread**.

- If you hide boundaries and guides, you can more easily check the appearance of the pages. Press **Ctrl+Shift+O**.

- To fit entire pages in the window, click **View**, **Zoom**, **Whole Page**.

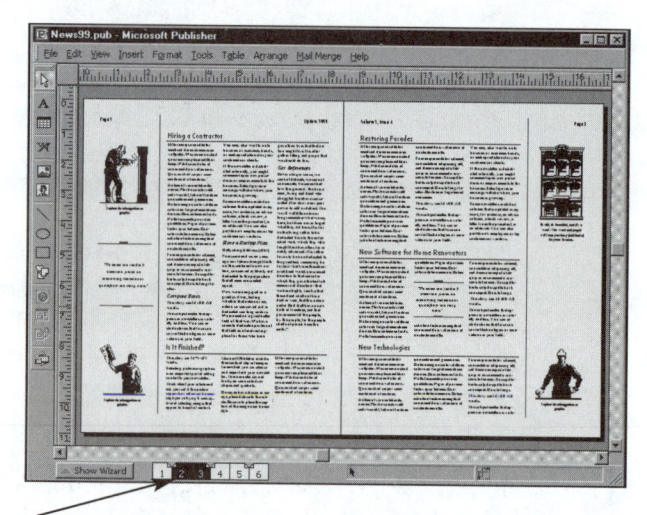

In the illustration, facing pages 2 and 3 are displayed in the window.

When viewing two pages, the icons in the status bar indicate which pages in the publication face each other. The left corner of the icon for the left page is folded over: ⌐4⌐ and the right corner of the right page is folded: ⌐5⌐

2 Click **View**, **Two-Page Spread** to return to viewing one page at a time.

58

Continue →

Zoom In or Out

Zoom in to work closely with items on the page and zoom out to see how all of the elements on a page work together.

View → Zoom

Notes:

- Use the Zoom menu to select from many different preset zoom levels (for example, 50%, 66%). To zoom to a preset level, use the Zoom box on the Standard toolbar.

- When you open a publication or create a new one, it is always displayed at the Whole Page zoom level (the entire page fits in the window).

1 Click **View**, **Zoom**.

2 Click a zoom option:
   - Click a zoom percentage to zoom in or out.
   - Click **Page Width** to fit the entire width of the page in the window.
   - Click **Selected Objects** to zoom in on a selected object on the page.
   - Click **Whole Page** to fit the entire page in the window, as shown in the following illustration. In Two-Page view (**View**, **Two-Page Spread**), both pages fit in the window.

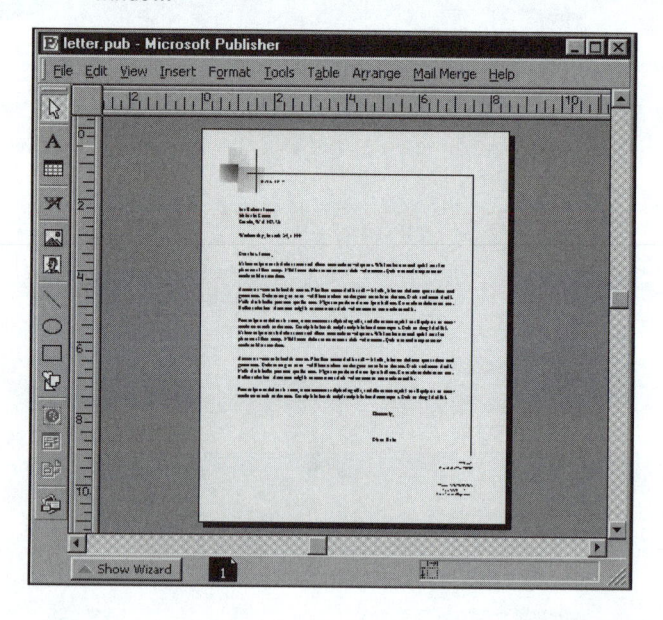

60

Notes:

- In the Zoom box on the Standard toolbar you can zoom to any percentage from 10% to 400%.

- If the Standard toolbar is not displayed, click <u>V</u>iew, <u>T</u>oolbars, Standard.

Zoom Using the Standard Toolbar

- Click **Zoom Out** [−] to view more of the page.

- Click **Zoom In** [+] to zoom in closer to either a selected object or to the center of the page if no objects are selected.

- Click the arrow in the Zoom box to select a preset zoom level from the drop-down menu.

- To zoom to any level:

    a. Click in the Zoom box to activate it. The current zoom level is highlighted.

    b. Type the percentage to zoom.

    c. Press **Enter**.

Switch Between 100% Zoom and the Previous Level

1. Press **F9** to switch to 100% view.
2. Repeat to return to the previous zoom level.

Set Web Page Properties

Enter the page title and file name in the properties. You can also add a sound that will play automatically whenever the page is opened in a Web browser.

File → Web Properties...

Notes:

- You can have a sound file play repeatedly during the entire time that the page is displayed or just once when the page is opened. A sound that plays automatically is called a background sound.

- Add a page title that will be used as the text for hyperlinks to that page. (Changing the title of the home page does not change the text of the Home Page hyperlink on the navigation bar.) The title also appears in the Web browser title bar when the page is displayed. It is also the name used when a user bookmarks the page or adds it to their favorite sites.

1. Display the page whose properties you will set.
2. Click **File**, **Web Properties**.
3. Click the **Page** tab.
4. Type a **File name** for the page.
5. Select a **File extension** for the page file name.
6. Type a page **Title**.
7. To add a sound that will play when the page is opened:

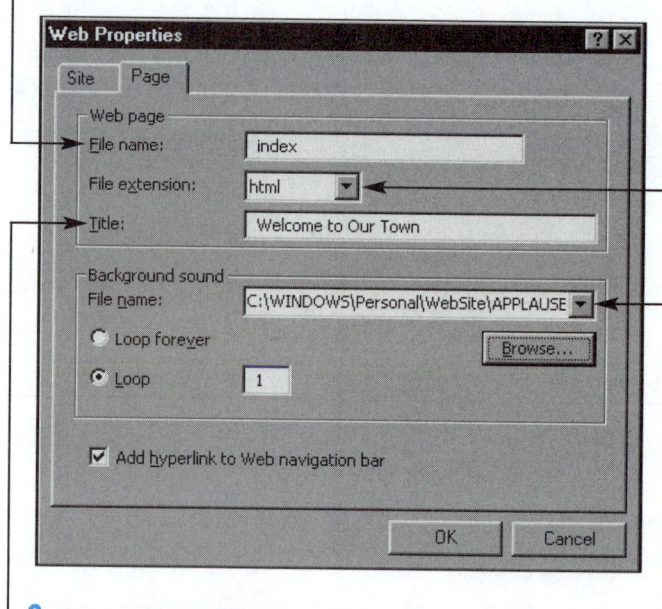

    a. Type the sound file pathname or click **Browse...** to select the file.

    NOTE: Keep the files for a Web publication in a single folder. Place the sound file in the folder containing the publication.

Notes:

- When you publish to the Web, a separate HTML document is created for each page in the Web publication. By default, Web page files use an .html extension (for example, page3.html). Change the extension to .htm if required by the Internet service provider where you will publish the site.

- Most service providers require that the file name for the home page be index.html. Check with your provider.

- Although each page in a Web site is a separate file, the Publisher file for the entire publication has a .pub extension, the same extension that is used for print publications.

b. Click **Loop fore_v_er** to have the sound file play repeatedly for as long as the page is displayed in a Web browser.

OR

Click **Loop** and type the number of times to play the sound when the page is opened.

8 Use **Add _h_yperlink to Web navigation bar** to specify whether or not to include a hyperlink to this page in the navigation bar.

9 Click [OK].

NOTE: The background sound will not play in Publisher. To test it, you must open the publication in a Web browser. See Preview Web Pages.

63

Run Design Checker

Design Checker is a handy feature that analyzes pages and alerts you to possible design mistakes or potential problems such as empty frames.

Tools → Design Checker...

Notes:

- Design Checker can check either individual pages or all pages in the publication.
- You can specify types of errors that Design Checker should ignore when it checks the publication.

1. Click **Tools**, **Design Checker**. The Design Checker dialog box displays.

2. Click **Pages** and type the range of pages to check if you do not want to check all pages in the publication.

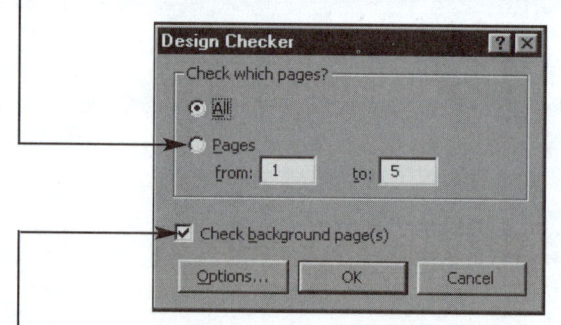

3. Set the **Check background page(s)** option as desired.

   NOTE: *This option is not available for Web publications.*

4. To specify which potential errors to check for:

   a. Click **Options...** to open the Options dialog box.

   b. Click **Check selected features**.

   c. Clear the check box next to each problem that you do not want Design Checker to check.

64

NOTE: Options for print publications and Web publications are different. The illustrated dialog box shows the Design Checker for a print publication.

d. Click **OK** to return to the Design Checker dialog box.

5 Click **OK** to run Design Checker.

6 If Design Checker encounters a potential problem, it displays a dialog box describing the problem.

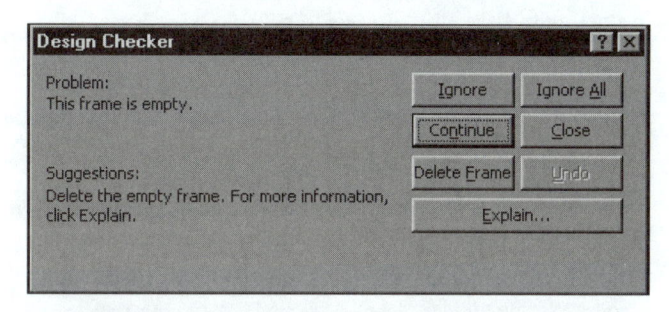

[Design Checker dialog box:
Problem: This frame is empty.
Suggestions: Delete the empty frame. For more information, click Explain.
Buttons: Ignore, Ignore All, Continue, Close, Delete Frame, Undo, Explain...]

The message and buttons on the dialog box vary depending on the problem. In the above illustration, Design Checker has found an empty frame. Click a button:

Ignore — Leaves the object as it is and continues checking.

Ignore All — Leaves the object as it is and continues checking. Stops checking for this type of error during the remainder of the session. In the dialog box illustrated above, clicking this button stops Design Checker from checking for empty frames.

Continue — Continues checking after you have fixed a problem.

Delete Frame — Fixes the problem as suggested on the button. The button text depends on the problem. The example problem is an empty frame so Publisher offers to delete the frame. If the button text is **Change**, the problem frame is activated so that you can edit it without closing Design Checker. This button is not always available.

Undo — Reverses the last change that you made to fix the problem. This button is not always available.

Close — Stops checking and closes the dialog box.

Explain... — Shows a Publisher Help topic explaining this problem.

65

Preview Web Pages

Open a Web publication in your Web browser to work with it in a live environment where hyperlinks, sounds, video, and other objects are active.

File → Web Page Preview...

Notes:

- Although you can see what Web pages look like in Publisher, preview them to see what it is like to navigate the site. You might decide that you have too many pages or notice that important information appears at the bottom of the page where it might be overlooked.

- Preview Web pages to test your publication and make sure that hyperlinks, sounds, and other objects are operating correctly.

- Web pages look different in different Web browsers (and different monitors). At the minimum, test your site in Netscape Navigator and Internet Explorer.

1. Click **File**, **We̲b Page Preview**. The Web Page Preview dialog box displays.

2. Click **Web si̲te** to make all pages of the site available.

   OR

   Click **Current pa̲ge** to preview only the page currently displayed in the Publisher window. Hyperlinks to other pages will not be active.

   The page is displayed in Internet Explorer or your current Web browser.

3. When finished previewing, exit the Web browser.

   If Publisher located any problems with your publication and the Preview Troubleshooter is enabled, it displays a list of Help topic titles that might be relevant.

66

> *Notes:*
>
> - When Preview Troubleshooter is on, Publisher displays a list of Help topics if it locates a problem in your Web publication when you preview it. Problems that the Troubleshooter might detect are animations that do not play, fuzzy text, or hyperlink controls that do not access the target page.
>
> - The Preview Troubleshooter is off by default.

Enable Preview Troubleshooter

1. Click **Tools**, **Options**. The Options dialog box displays.

2. Click the **User Assistance** tab.

3. Click the **Preview Web site with Preview Troubleshooter** check box.

4. Click [OK].

67

Add and Edit Text

Text is one of two basic elements that you will add to a publication (the other is graphics). To add text, first create a text frame and then place text in it. You can type text in the text frame or import text from a file. Each story in your publication goes in a separate text frame. A story is one complete block of text such as a headline or an article. Stories that span multiple pages are placed in connected text frames.

This section tells you how to create text frames and add text. See **Format Text** for procedures on making the text within a frame look good. See also **Frames** for ways to arrange, copy, add borders to, and otherwise work with text frames (and other types of frames) on the page.

Create a Text Frame

Each separate text element in a publication, such as a title or an article, is stored in a text frame. A complete block of text, such as an entire article, is called a story.

Notes:

- Create a new text frame for each story in your publication. Then, you can easily move, format, and otherwise work with each story separately. You might want to place titles in a separate text frame so that you can work with them separately from body text.

- Use the "snap to" feature to create frames that line up with guides. See *Snap to Guides and Objects*.

- The precise size of the frame that you are creating is displayed on the right side of the status bar.

1 Click **Text Frame Tool** [A] on the Objects toolbar.

2 Place the mouse pointer where you would like one corner of the frame to appear. The pointer changes shape to: ┼

3 Click and drag to the opposite corner of the frame to create it.

NOTE: *The boundaries of the frame that you are creating are not visible as you drag. Boundary lines for the frame are displayed in the rulers. These lines mark your location as you drag.*

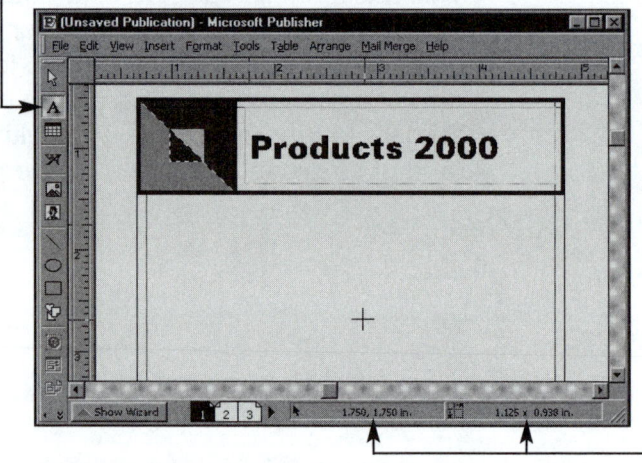

The position and size of the text frame you are creating are displayed in the status bar.

Notes:

- You can resize a frame after you create it.

4 When the frame is the right size, release the mouse button.

NOTE: If "snap to" is on, the frame jumps to the nearest guide or object. See Snap to Guides and Objects.

When you release the mouse button, frame boundaries are visible and the frame is selected. Black squares called handles appear around the border of the frame when it is selected.

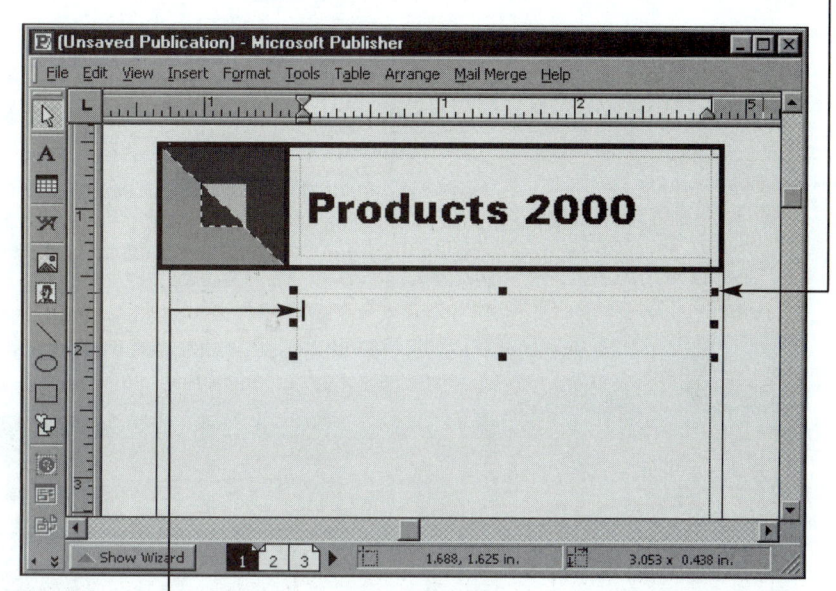

The insertion point is active so that you can type text in the frame.

5 To import text from a file, such as a word processing document, see *Import Text*.

OR

To type text in the frame, see *Type and Edit Text*.

71

Create Connected Text Frames

Create a series of connected text frames to flow a story across multiple frames. Use this procedure when a story does not fit in a single frame.

Tools → Connect Text Frames

Notes:

- All text in a single text frame or in a series of connecting frames is called a story. A story might be short. A title is a very short story. Or, it might be quite lengthy, flowing across any number of text frames and threading its way through multiple pages, as in a newspaper.

- This procedure shows you how to connect text frames before you import a story. To create connected text frames when you import, see *Flow a Long Story*. It is easier to create them before importing if you already know exactly where the text needs to flow to the next frame. For example, you might have a newsletter where the story must begin on the bottom of page 1 and flow to the second column on page 3 above a particular ad.

1. Create each text frame in the series of frames that will contain the story. See *Create a Text Frame*.

   NOTE: Automatic copyfitting for each frame that you will connect must be turned off (**F**ormat, AutoFit Te**x**t, **N**one). Automatic copyfitting is off by default.

2. Go to the page containing the first frame in the series.

3. Click the frame to select it. Small black squares called handles appear around a text frame when it is selected.

   NOTE: The text frame in the illustration has been divided into three columns. (You can divide a text frame into multiple columns either before or after you connect the frames. See Set Up Columns in a Text Frame.)

4. Click **T**ools, **Connect T**ext **F**rames.

Notes:

- A frame can be no larger than the page. If a story does not fit in a single frame, create additional frame(s) to hold it.

- When you add text to connected frames, Publisher automatically flows the text from one frame to the next. When you edit text, it reflows to accommodate added or deleted text. For example, if you delete text, remaining text adjusts to fill the space left empty by the deletion.

- This feature is normally used for long stories that span multiple pages, but you can use it to divide a story into separate frames on the same page. You might use connecting frames to create columns of unequal width. Automatic columns are always of equal width (see *Set Up Columns in a Text Frame*).

- See *Add Continuation Notices* to include a notice that will tell the reader the page number for the next section of the story.

5 Click **Connect Text Frames** on the Connect Frames toolbar. The pointer changes to a pitcher:

6 Go to the next frame in the series and click the Pitcher pointer in the frame. This frame is now connected to the first frame.

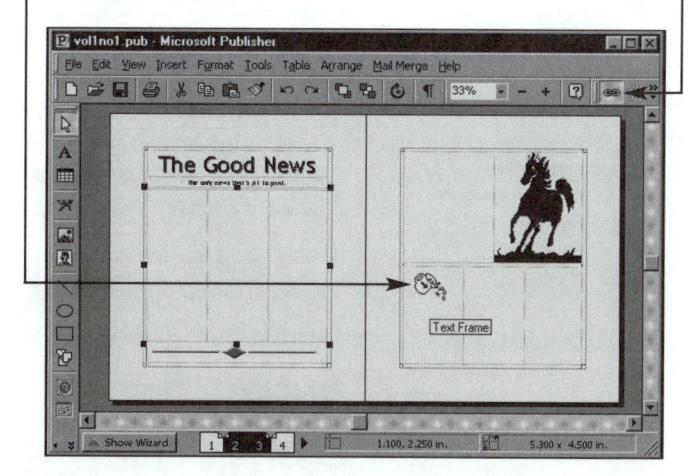

7 If there is another frame, go to the next frame in the series and click the Pitcher pointer in the frame to connect it to the previous frame.

8 Repeat step 7 as necessary to connect all frames in the series.

   NOTE: Text will flow between frames in the order that you connect them.

9 Press **Esc** when you have connected all frames in the series.

10 To import text from a file, such as a word processing document, see *Import Text*.

   OR

   To type text in the frame, see *Type and Edit Text*.

73

Create Connected Text Frames

(continued)

Notes:

- Remove a frame from a series of connected frames.

- When you select a connected frame, the Connect Frames toolbar appears at the top of the window.

Move Between Connected Text Frames

- When you select a connected frame, buttons for moving between the frames in the series appear. The following illustration shows a selected text frame in the middle of a series of connected frames. When selected, the frame shows both the **Go to Previous Frame** and the **Go to Next Frame** buttons. Click a button to move between frames in the series.

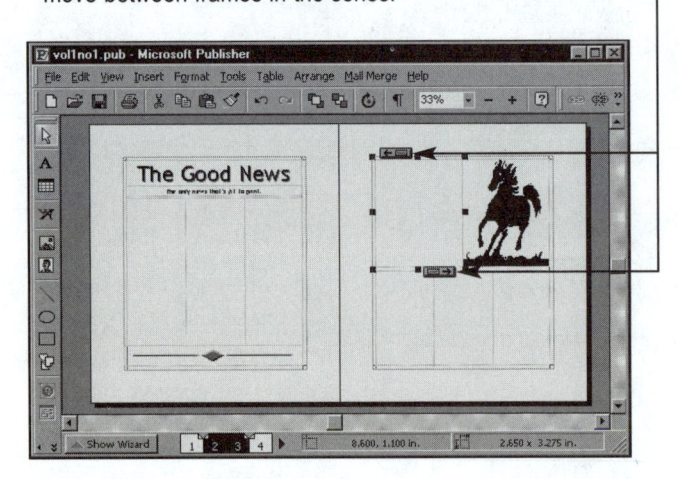

Disconnect a Frame

1 Select the frame to disconnect.

2 Click **Disconnect Text Frames** on the Connect Frames toolbar.

74

Continue →

Import Text

Insert a story from file into a text frame. For example, import text that you entered using a word processing program such as Microsoft Word.

Insert ➡ Text File...

Notes:

- Before you import a story, you must create a text frame to place the story in. Create a text frame (see *Create a Text Frame*) or delete the sample text from a placeholder text frame that was created with a publication wizard (see *Delete Text*).

- If there is more text in the story than will fit in the current text frame, Publisher automatically flows the story to connecting frames, if you have already created them. See *Create Connected Text Frames*.

1 Click the text frame to select it.

2 Click **Insert**, **Text File**. The Insert Text dialog box displays.

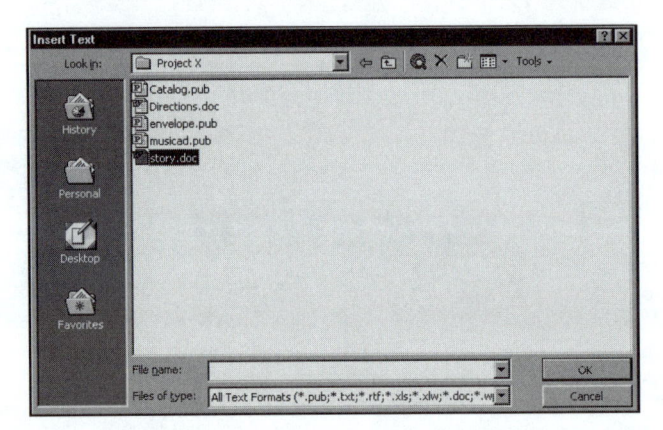

3 Double-click the file to insert. Publisher converts the file into a format it can use and places it in the text frame. If you have created connecting text frames, text automatically flows into the next frame until all of the text is placed.

4 If the text fits in the existing text frame(s), you are finished importing text.

OR

If there is more text than will fit, the following prompt displays:

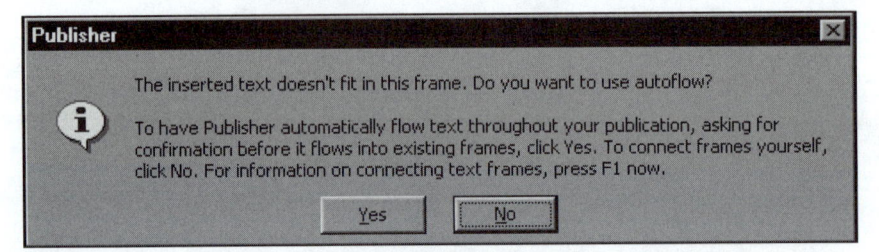

Notes:

- Importing a file into Publisher does not change the contents of the file. It remains on your disk in its original state. Importing simply copies the text from the file into the publication.

5   Choose one of the following procedures:

Have Publisher create connected text frames and flow the story.

OR

Create connecting text frames and flow the story yourself.

Have Publisher create connected text frames and flow the story:

a. Click [Yes] at the prompt. Publisher displays another prompt:

> **Publisher**
> Do you want Publisher to automatically create text frames?
> To have Publisher automatically create text frames and pages for the remaining text, click Yes. To cancel Autoflow now, click No. For information about inserting text files, press F1 now.
> [Yes]   [No]

b. Click [Yes]. Publisher creates a new text frame connected to the current frame in the next available page in the publication. It flows the story into the new frame. It continues creating text frames and flowing the story until the entire story is placed in the publication. If the story will not fit in the publication, Publisher creates as many new pages as are necessary to place the story.

Create connecting text frames and flow the story yourself:

a. Click [No] at the prompt.

Publisher adds the **Text in OverFlow** button [A •••] at the end of the frame. This button represents the part of the story that Publisher is storing in an overflow area.

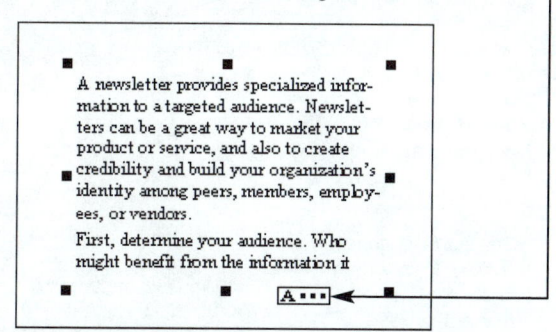

> A newsletter provides specialized information to a targeted audience. Newsletters can be a great way to market your product or service, and also to create credibility and build your organization's identity among peers, members, employees, or vendors.
>
> First, determine your audience. Who might benefit from the information it
>
> [A •••]

b. Go to step 3 of *Flow a Long Story* to create connecting text frames and flow text between them. Publisher will store the text in overflow until you are ready to place it.

77

Flow a Long Story

When you are importing or typing a story with more text than will fit in a text frame, use this procedure to flow the story to additional frames.

Notes:

- Use this procedure if you have not already created connecting text frames for the story before you import or type the text. To create connecting text frames before you import or type a story, see *Create Connected Text Frames*.

- Use connecting text frames to flow a story across multiple pages. For example, a newsletter might have a story that begins in the second column on page one, continues in the third column on page three, and ends on page four.

- Publisher keeps track of the order of connected text frames. When you edit a story that has multiple frames, it reflows the text. For example, if you delete a paragraph, text following the deleted paragraph will reflow to fill the blank space.

- See *Add Continuation Notices* to include a notice that will tell the reader the page number for the next section of the story.

1. Create the first text frame for the story. See *Create a Text Frame*.

2. To import text from a file, such as a word processing document, see *Import Text*.

   OR

   To type text in the frame, see *Type and Edit Text*.

   When you have imported or typed more text than will fit in the frame, the **Text in OverFlow** button [A•••] appears at the bottom of the frame.

3. Create the next text frame:

   a. Go to the page where the story will continue.

   b. Click **Text Frame Tool** [A] in the Objects toolbar.

   c. Drag on the page to create the frame.

4. Return to the page containing the frame with the **Text in OverFlow** button [A•••].

5. Click the frame with the **Text in OverFlow** button [A•••]. The Connect Frames toolbar appears at the top of the window.

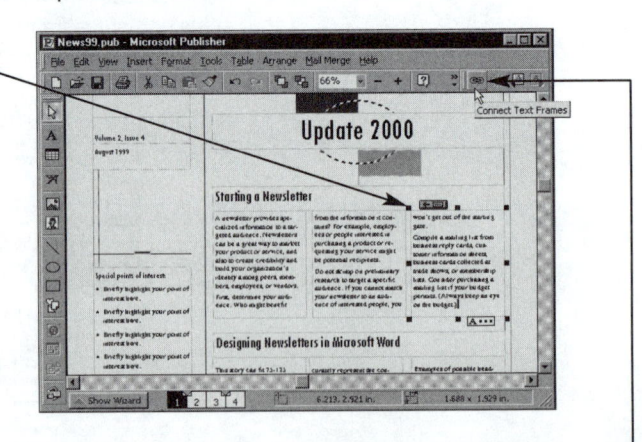

6. Click **Connect Text Frames** [icon] on the Connect Frames toolbar. The pointer changes to:

7 Go to the new text frame created in step 3 and click the Pitcher pointer in that frame.

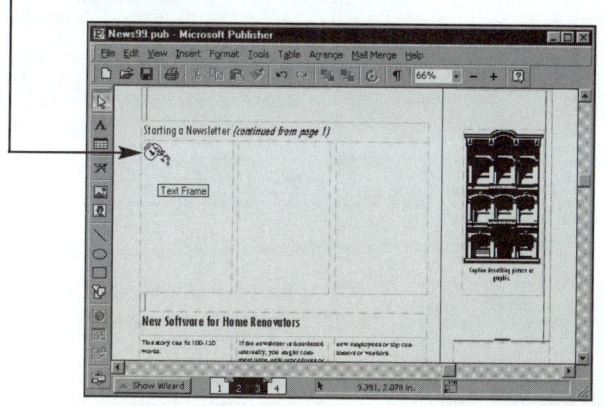

— The story flows into the frame.

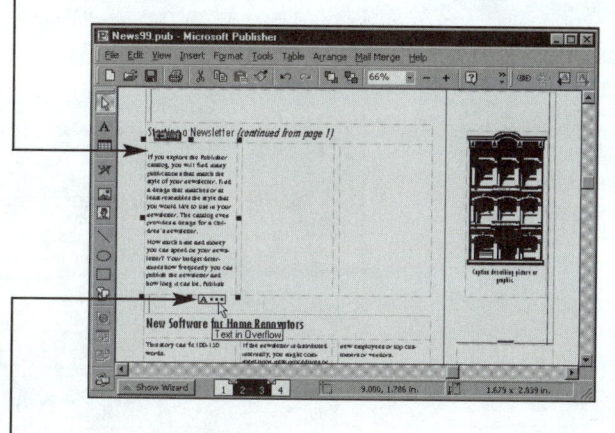

8 If more text remains in overflow, the **Text in OverFlow** button appears at the bottom of the frame. Repeat the procedure starting with step 3 to place overflow text.

Notes:

- Use navigation buttons to go to the next or previous text frame in a series of connected frames.

- Navigation buttons appear when a text frame is selected.

Move Between Connected Frames

- Click **Go to Previous Frame**

- Click **Go to Next Frame**

Add Continuation Notices

When a story spans connected text frames, you can have Publisher automatically add a message that refers the reader to the page on which the story continues.

Format ➔ Text Frame Properties...

Notes:

- When a story continues from the current text frame to connected frame, a continuation notice is placed at the end of the current frame. The message reads, "Continued on page x," with the correct page number filled in. For example, "Continued on page 2."

- When a story is continued from a previous text frame to the current frame, a continuation notice is place at the top of the current frame. The message reads, "Continued from page x" with the correct page number filled in. For example, "Continued from page 1."

- You can have both types of continuation notices in a single frame if the frame is in the middle of a series of connected frames.

1. Select the text frame to contain the continuation notice.

2. Click **Format**, **Text Frame Properties**. The Text Frame Properties dialog box displays.

3. Click the **Include "Continued on page..."** check box to place a continuation notice at the bottom of the frame when the story continues to another frame.

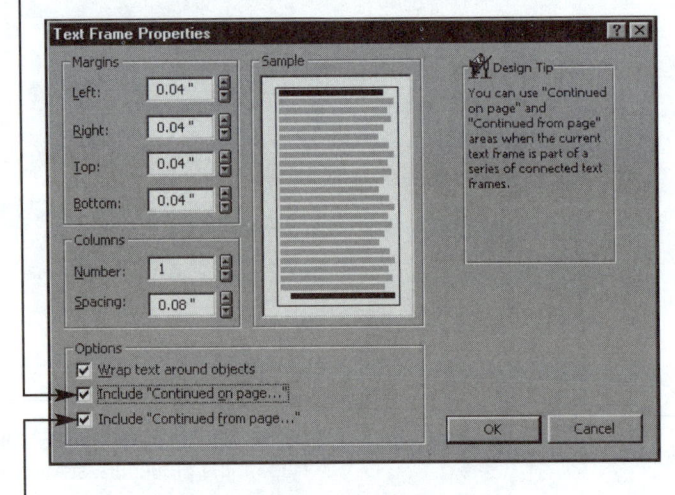

4. Click the **Include "Continued from page..."** check box to place a continuation notice at the top of a frame when the story is continued from a previous frame.

5. Click OK.

Notes:

- Publisher maintains the page numbers in continuation notices so that they are correct even when the page number changes as you edit the publication.

6 Repeat from step 1 to add continuation notices to other connected text frames, as desired.

Publisher adds the specified continuation notices, including automatic page numbers.

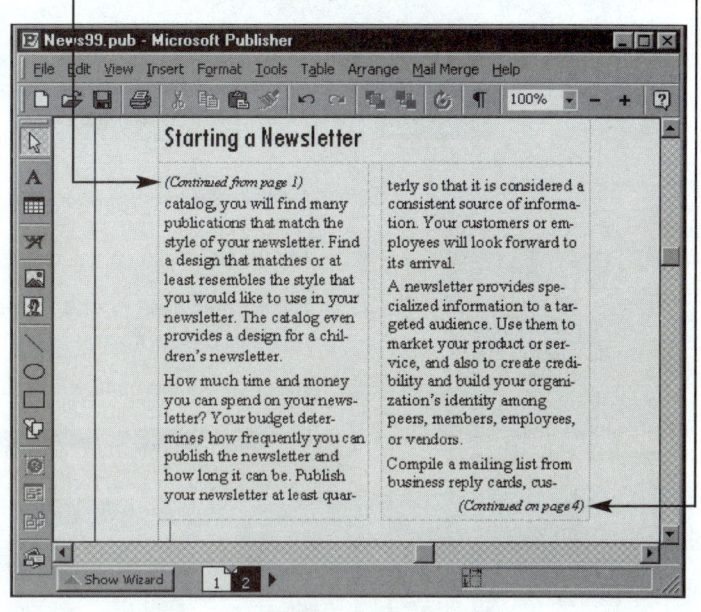

Set Up Columns in a Text Frame

Create multiple newspaper columns in a text frame. Text wraps from the bottom of one column to the top of the next.

Format → Text Frame Properties...

Notes:

- This procedure creates columns of equal width. To create columns of varying widths, create separate text frames for each column and connect them. See *Create Connected Text Frames*.

- You can set up columns in a text frame before or after adding text to the frame.

- Newspaper columns are sometimes called snaking columns.

- To create side-by-side columns, see *Create a Table*. In side-by-side columns, corresponding paragraphs appear next to each other. Text does not wrap between columns.

1. Click the text frame to select it.

2. Click **Format**, **Text Frame Properties**. The Text Frame Properties dialog box displays.

3. Type or select the number of columns.

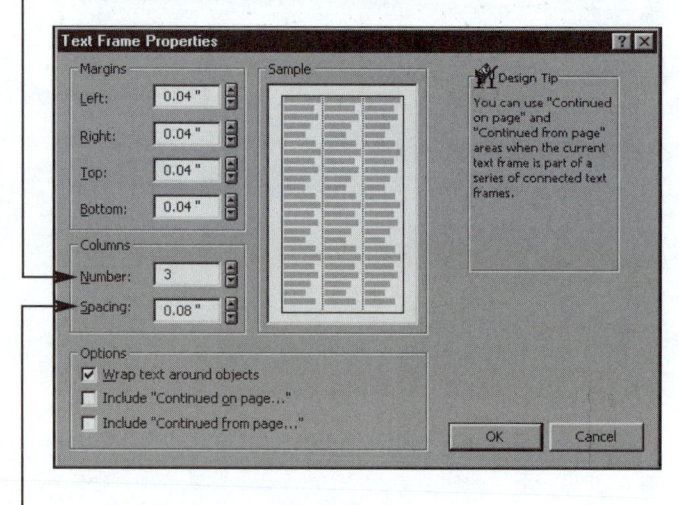

4. Type or select a measurement to set the amount of space between columns.

5. Click OK.

82

Notes:

- To add lines between columns, draw lines using the Line tool. See *Draw Lines and Arrows*.

The text frame shows guides for the columns. When you add text to the frame, it will flow between columns, as shown in the next illustration.

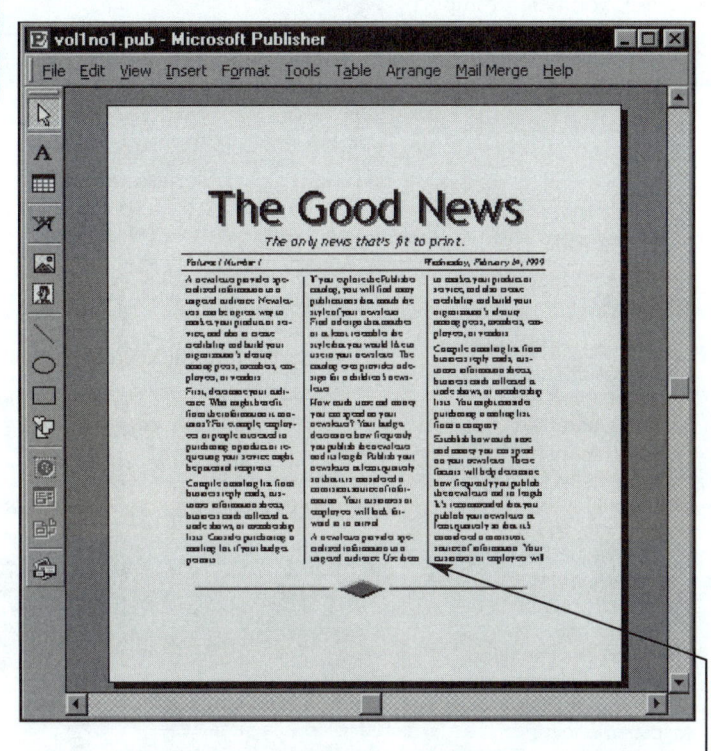

NOTE: Publisher does not add lines between columns. Draw lines over the column guides to create them. See Draw Lines and Arrows.

Delete Text

Deleting placeholder text added by a wizard requires a different procedure from deleting text that you type or import.

Edit → Delete Te*x*t

Notes:

- If you created a publication using a wizard, there will be one or more text frames with placeholder text. Publisher knows which stories are samples placed by a wizard and which are your own stories. Use this procedure to delete placeholder text in a frame so that you can add your own text.

Delete a Sample Story

1 Click the text frame. Publisher selects the story.

 NOTE: *If you start typing text when the sample story is selected, the story is deleted and replaced with the text that you type.*

2 Click **Delete Te*x*t**. The text frame is now empty.

Delete an Imported Story

Use this procedure to delete a story that you typed or imported. The entire story is deleted, even long stories that flow between connected text frames.

1 Click the text frame.

2 Press **Ctrl+A** to select the story.

3 Press **Delete**.

Delete any Text

After you delete, remaining text adjusts to fill the space left empty by the deletion.

1 Select text to delete.

2 Press **Delete**.

Delete a Text Frame

This procedure deletes both the frame and any text in the frame.

1 Right-click the text frame.

2 Click **Delete Object**.

Delete a Character

Use this procedure when you are typing text and make a mistake.

- Press **Backspace** to delete the character to the left of the cursor.

- Press **Delete** to delete the character to the right of the cursor.

Undo the Last Deletion

Use this procedure directly after you delete.

- Click **Undo**. When you place the mouse pointer over the Undo tool, the ScreenTip tells you which action will be undone.

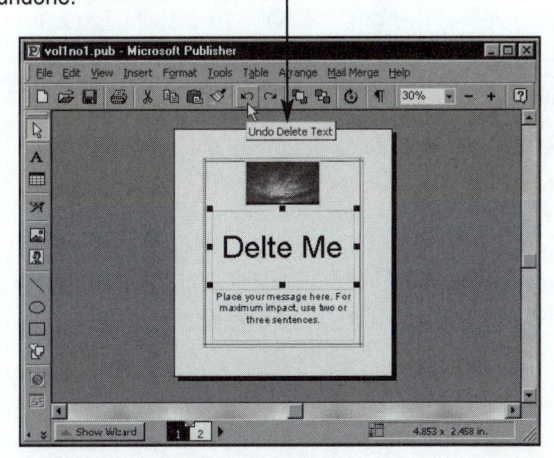

*NOTE: If automatic copyfitting is enabled, the autofit operation will be undone rather than the deletion. Click **Undo** twice: first to undo the autofit operation and then to undo the deletion.*

Type and Edit Text

Add and change text in a text frame.

Notes:

- All text in a publication must be placed in a text frame. See *Create a Text Frame*.

- Publisher does not have an Overtype mode. New text is always inserted.

- When you edit text in a long story that flows across connected text frames, text reflows between the frames to adjust to your changes.

- To select, see *Select Text*.

- To delete, see *Delete Text*.

- If you have extensive editing to do, you can open the story in Microsoft Word to edit it without exiting Publisher. See *Edit a Story in Microsoft Word*.

1. Click the text frame to select it.

   NOTE: If the text frame contains placeholder text placed by a wizard, the text in the frame is selected. Text that you type overwrites the selected text.

2. If the area of the frame is too small to work with, click **View**, **Zoom**, **100%**.

3. Type text.

4. To insert text within existing text, click where you will add the new text. Text is inserted where the insertion point is located.

   OR

   To replace existing text with text that you type, select the text to replace and type new text.

   NOTE: If you add more text than fits in the frame, the **Text in OverFlow** button appears. Increase the size of the frame to accommodate the text. Or, add another frame to continue the story—see *Flow a Long Story*.

5. To undo the last edit, click **Undo** or press **Ctrl+Z**.

> **Notes:**
> - Publisher automatically wraps text to the next line.
> - Text automatically wraps to the next column in a multiple-column text frame. You can, however, insert a column break anywhere.
> - A line break starts a new line without starting a new paragraph.

Insert a Break

Start a new paragraph, line, or column.

- To start a new paragraph, press **Enter**.
- To insert a line break, press **Shift+Enter**.
- To insert a column break in a multiple-column text frame, press **Ctrl+Shift+Enter**.

  *NOTE: Each of these procedures adds a special character that represents the break. For example, a paragraph mark: ¶ shows you where a paragraph ends. Click **View**, **Show Special Characters**.*

> **Notes:**
> - Publisher creates a text frame for the inserted information, if necessary.
> - See *Maintain a Personal Information Set* to add or edit personal information.

Insert Text from a Personal Information Set

1. Click **Insert**, **Personal Information**.
2. Click the information to insert (for example, **Address**).

Copy or Move Text

1. Select the text to copy or move.
2. To copy text, press **Ctrl+C**.

   OR

   To move text, press **Ctrl+X**.
3. To copy or move text to another publication, close the current publication and open the target publication.
4. Click where the text will be inserted and press **Ctrl+V**.

Type and Edit Text
(continued)

Notes:

- When you type quotes, Publisher automatically changes your quotes to smart quotes, or curly quotes (" "). Use this procedure if you want to use straight quotes (") instead.

Use Straight Quotes Instead of Smart Quotes

1 Click **Tools**, **AutoCorrect**. The AutoCorrect dialog box displays.

2 Click **AutoFormat as You Type** tab.

3 Click the **"Straight Quotes" with "Smart Quotes"** check box to clear it.

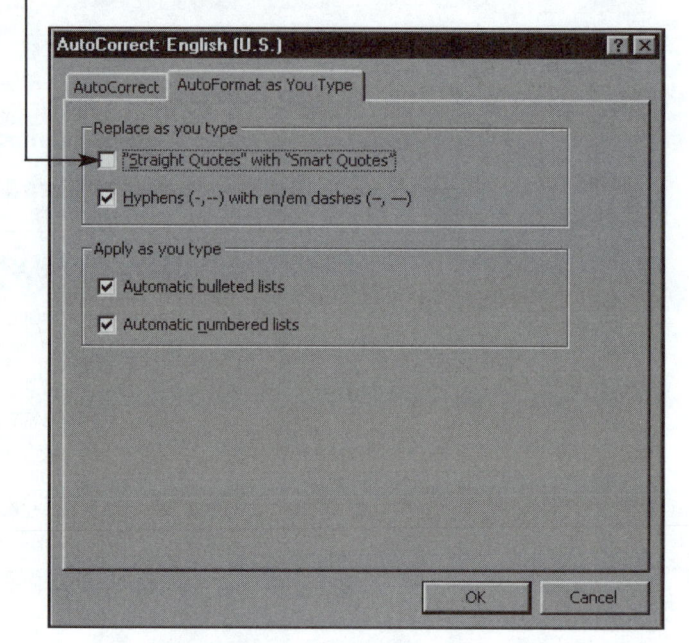

4 Click OK.

88

Continue →

Select Text

Before you copy, move, format, or otherwise edit a block of text, you need to select it.

Notes:

- When you create a publication using a wizard, the wizard adds placeholder text in text frames. You cannot select part of the text in a placeholder story. Clicking anywhere in a frame containing a placeholder story selects the entire story. New text that you type replaces the story. These stories are temporary and meant to be replaced with your own text.

- If you are unable to select characters within a word, disable automatic word selection as described on the next page.

- If you type new text while text is selected, the new text replaces the selected text.

Select by Dragging

1. Click before first character to select.
2. Hold down the mouse button and drag across text.
3. Release the mouse button.

Select by Clicking the First and Last Characters

1. Click before the first character to select.
2. Hold down **Shift** and click the mouse button after the last character to select.

Select Character-by-Character or Line-by-Line

1. Click before the first character to select.
2. Hold down **Shift**.
3. Press arrow keys to select text.

   NOTE: Pressing the left or right arrow keys selects the previous or next character. Pressing the up or down arrow keys selects to the previous or next line.

Selected text appears in reverse video on the screen.

90

More Ways to Select

To select:	Do this:
A word	Double-click word
From the insertion point to the end of the line	**Shift+End**
From the insertion point to the beginning of the line	**Shift+Home**
Entire story (including connected frames)	1. Click in the text frame 2. Press **Ctrl+A**
All objects on the page, including all frames and drawing objects	Click **Edit**, **Select All**

Notes:

- When automatic word selection is enabled, you cannot use the mouse to select text within a word. Publisher assumes that you want to select at least the entire word. In most cases, you will want to disable automatic word selection because there will be times when you want to use the mouse to select characters within a word.

- If automatic word selection is enabled, you can select characters within a word by holding down **Shift** and pressing an arrow key (cursor movement) rather than using the mouse.

Disable Automatic Word Selection

1 Click **Tools**, **Options**. The Options dialog box displays.

2 Clear the **When selecting, automatically select entire word** check box on the **Edit** tab.

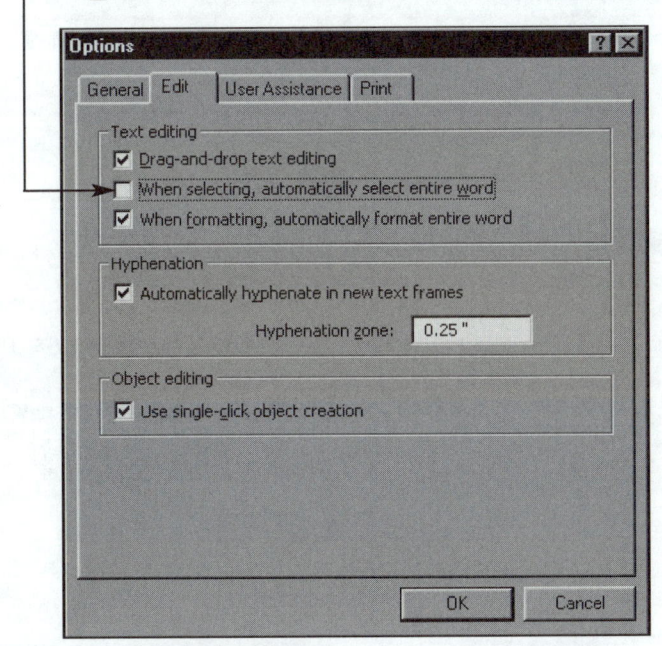

3 Click **OK**.

91

Edit a Story in Microsoft Word

Although Publisher is fine for editing short blocks of text, you might want to use a word processing program to edit long stories. Start Microsoft Word and edit a story without exiting Publisher.

Edit → Edit Story in Microsoft Word

Notes:

- Publisher was not designed for extensive text editing. Unless you have only a few changes to make to a story, use Microsoft Word to edit text rather than Publisher.

- You must have at least Microsoft Word version 6.0 to use this procedure.

1 Right-click the text frame containing the story to edit.

2 Click **Change Text**, **Edit Story in Microsoft Word**. Publisher starts Microsoft Word and displays the story.

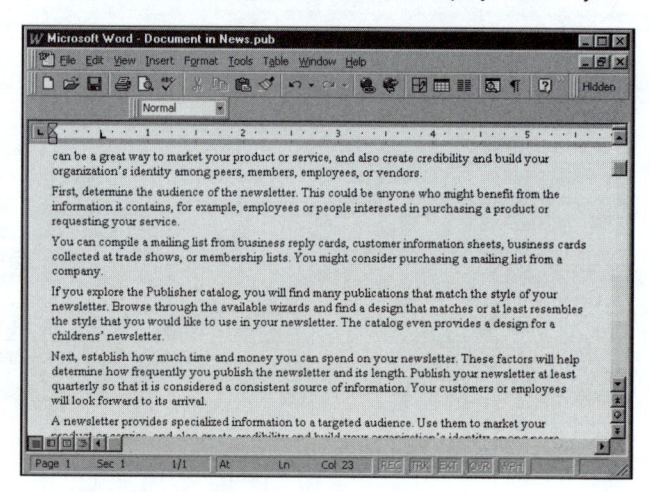

3 Edit the text of the story as desired.

4 To save the story in a Word document:

    a. Click **File**, **Save Copy As**. The Save As dialog box displays.

    b. Type a filename for the new document.

    c. Click **Save**.

Notes:

- Publisher has more text colors than does Microsoft Word. If text loses color, that color is not available in Word. You will need to reapply the color in Publisher.

5 Click **File**, **Exit** to close Microsoft Word and update the story in the publication.

OR

Click **File**, **Close & Return** in Microsoft Word to update the story in the publication and leave Microsoft Word running.

— *NOTE: The name of your publication file is added to the **Close & Return** command. For example, if the Publisher file is named **News.pub**, the command appears as: **Close & Return to News.pub**.*

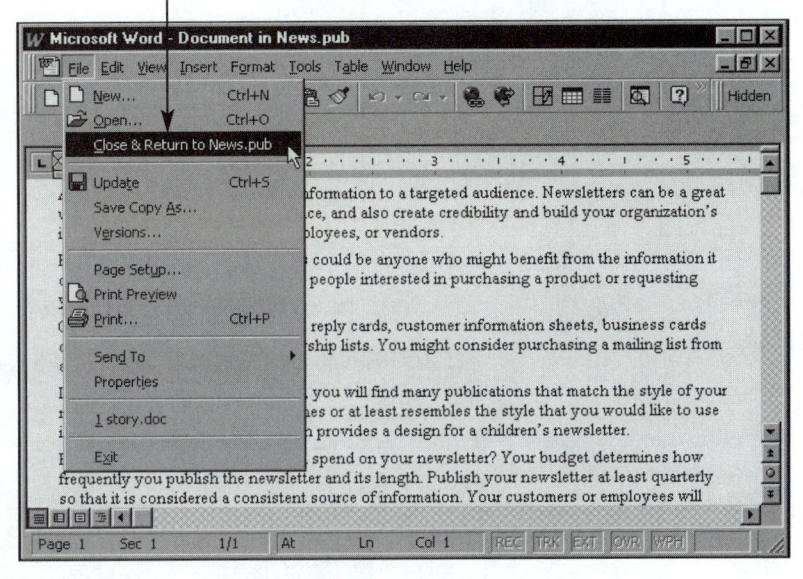

93

Insert a Symbol

Browse symbols (such as em dashes, trademarks, copyrights, yen symbols) available in the fonts installed on your computer and place them in your publication.

Insert ➔ Ω Symbol...

Notes:

- A symbol is a special character that does not appear on the keyboard. For example, the copyright symbol © does not have a corresponding key on your keyboard. You can, however, access it in most typefaces.

- Most typefaces include a number of special symbols that you can access in Publisher.

1 Position the insertion point in a text or table frame where you want to insert the symbol.

2 Click **Insert**, **Symbol**. The Symbol dialog box displays.

3 Select the typeface to view from the **Font** list.

4 If the typeface has a number of character sets, you can select a set in the **Subset** list. (If the Subset list does not appear in the dialog box, the typeface does not have character subsets.)

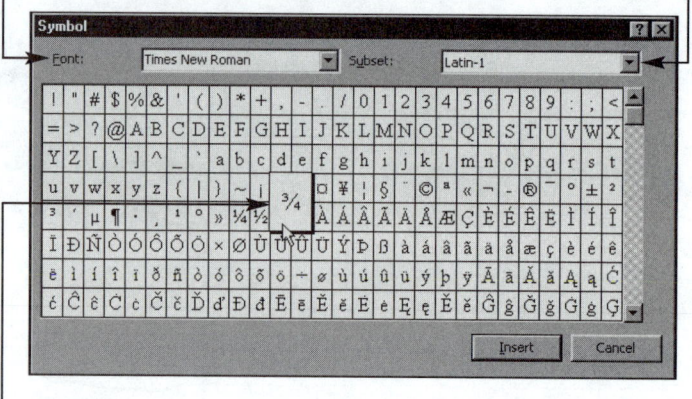

5 To view a larger version of a symbol, point to the symbol and hold down the mouse button. The enlarged symbol displays until you release the button.

6 Click the symbol to insert.

Notes:

- Some typefaces, such as Zapf Dingbats and Wingdings, consist entirely of symbols. Use these to add little graphics to a page. Other typefaces have specialized symbols, such as mathematical symbols, that do not have a key on the keyboard.

7   Click **Insert** to insert the symbol and close the Symbol dialog box.

Use symbols to create flourishes and add graphics to a page. In the following illustration, a heart symbol character makes a headline a little more lively.

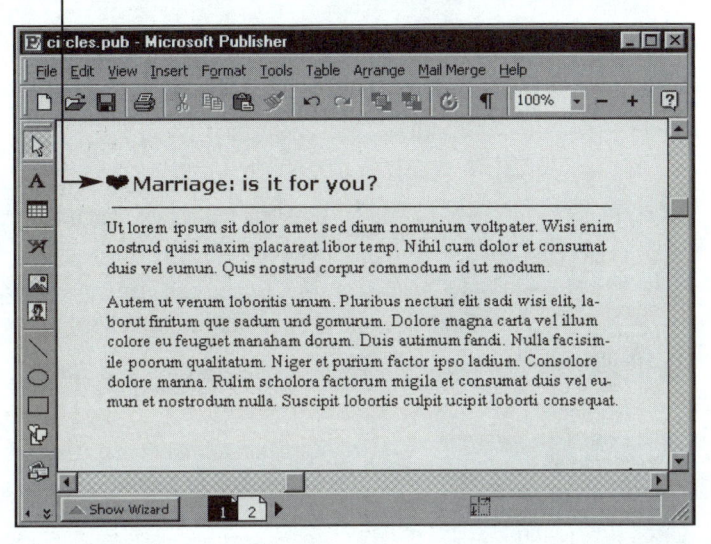

95

Insert the Current Date/Time

Add a date/time stamp to a publication.

Insert → Date and Time...

Notes:

- You can insert a date/time that will automatically update to the current date/time whenever you print or edit the publication. Or, you can insert the current date/time as fixed text, in which case it remains as it appeared when you inserted it.

1. Position the cursor where the date and/or time will be inserted.

   NOTE: You can insert the date/time in either a text frame or a table frame.

2. Click **Insert**, **Date and Time**. The Date and Time dialog box displays.

3. Click the format to use. The format determines the information to be included (such as just the date or just the time) and how it will appear.

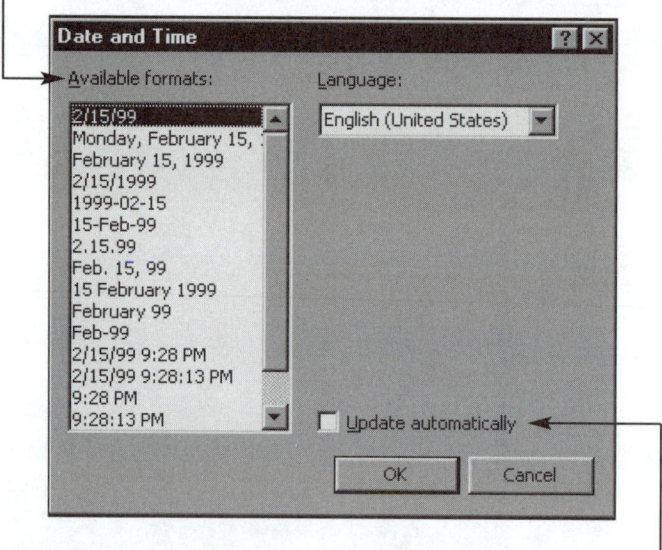

4. If you want the date/time to update so that it is always current, select **Update automatically**.

5. Click **OK**.

Notes:

- The date is sometimes added to the header or footer of a publication. See *Add Headers and Footers*.

The date/time is inserted in the frame, as shown in the following example.

Find Text

Find specific text in a story.

Edit → Find...

Notes:

- Publisher finds occurrences of the text in a single story. If the story spans multiple text frames, all text frames are included. Repeat the operation to find the text in other stories, if necessary.

1 Click the frame to search.

2 Press **Ctrl+F**. The Find dialog box displays.

3 Type the text to find.

   NOTE: *Use the ? character to indicate any character. This is useful if you are unsure of how a word is spelled. For example, if you type ?andy, Publisher will find both Candy and Kandy.*

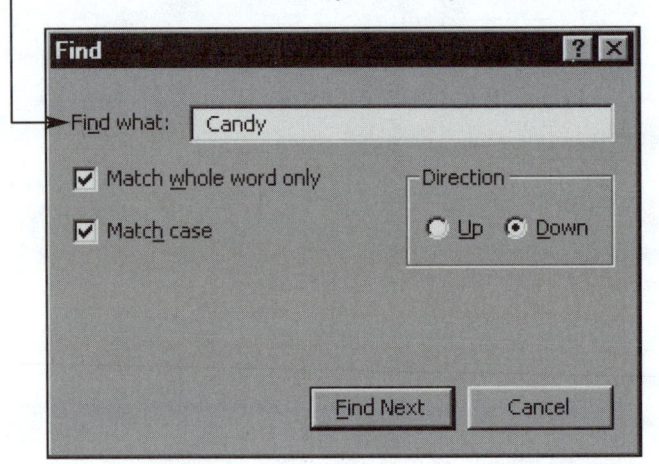

- To find occurrences of the entire word, select **Match whole word only**.
   - If this option is selected, Publisher skips instances of the text buried within other words. For example, if you search for word "in," Publisher will not locate these characters within the words "find" and "cringe."
   - This option is not available if the text that you are searching for is a phrase, such as "Microsoft Publisher."

Notes:
- You can search for text in text frames and table frames.

- To find only instances of the text when the case matches the characters as you typed them, select **Match case**.

    NOTE: For example, if the text to find is "Candy," Publisher will not locate "candy" since the case is different.

- To change the direction in which Publisher will search the story, click **Up**.

    NOTE: By default, Publisher searches from the current frame to the end of the story and then goes to the beginning of the story and continues until it reaches the point at which it started. If the insertion point is active in the frame, it starts searching from the location of the insertion point. If you change the direction, it searches from the insertion point to the beginning of the story.

4 Click [Find Next]. Publisher highlights the next occurrence of the text.

5 Repeat step 4 as desired to find each occurrence.

6 When finished, click [Cancel] to close the Find dialog box.

99

Replace Text

Replace text in a story.

Edit → Replace...

Notes:

- Publisher replaces the specified text in a single story. If the story spans multiple text frames, all text frames are included. Repeat the replace operation for each separate story, if necessary.

1. Click the frame containing text to replace.
2. Press **Ctrl+H**. The Replace dialog box displays.
3. Type the text to replace.

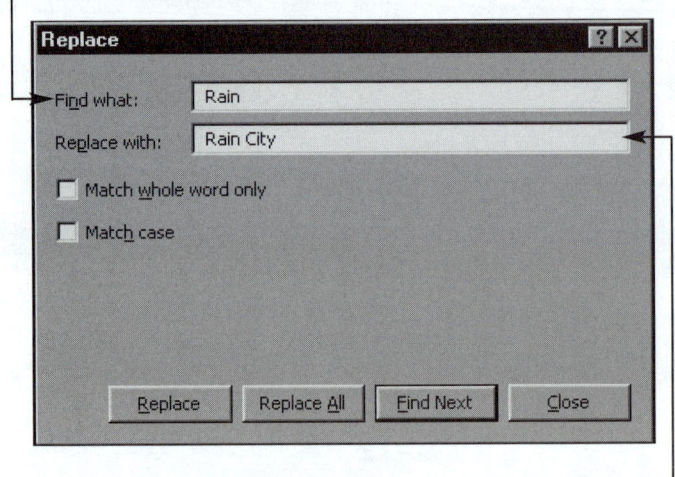

4. Type the replacement text.
   - To find occurrences of the entire word only, select **Match whole word only**.
     - If the option is selected, Publisher skips instances of the text buried within other words. For example, if you replace the word "rain," Publisher will not replace these characters within the word "train."
     - This option is not available if the text that you are searching for is a phrase, such as "Rain City Publications."
   - To find only instances of the text when the case matches the characters in the **Find what** text box, select **Match case**.

     NOTE: For example, if the text to find is "Rain," Publisher will not locate "rain" since the case is different.

Notes:
- You can replace text in text frames and table frames.

5   Click [Find Next]. Publisher highlights the next occurrence of the text.

6   Specify whether or not to replace the text:
   - To replace the highlighted text with the replacement text, click [Replace]. Click [Find Next] to find the next occurrence. Repeat as necessary.
   - To skip this occurrence and go to the next occurrence, click [Find Next].
   - To replace all occurrences in the entire story without a prompt, click [Replace All].

7   When finished, click [Close] to close the Replace dialog box.

101

Check Spelling

The spell check feature checks for misspelled words and repeated words.

Tools → Spelling

Notes:

- You can skip words in all uppercase if a story contains acronyms. Or, you can add the acronyms to the dictionary when you spell check.

- In addition to misspelled words, Publisher brings to your attention words that are typed twice, such as "a a" or "the the."

1 To customize how Publisher checks spelling:

  a. Click **Tools**, **Spelling**, **Spelling Options**. The Spelling Options dialog box displays.

  b. Set the **Flag repeated words** option as desired.

  c. Set the **Ignore words in UPPERCASE** option to determine whether or not Publisher spell checks acronyms such as UNICEF.

  d. Click **OK**.

2 Click the text or table frame to check.

3 Press **F7**. Publisher starts spell checking.

4 If Publisher finds a word that is not in the dictionary, it displays it in the Check Spelling dialog box.

  a. To spell check the entire publication, select the **Check all stories** check box.

  b. Use one of the following options in the Check Spelling dialog box:

  - Type the word as it should appear in the publication in the **Change to** text box. Click **Change** to replace the current occurrence of the word or **Change All** to change all occurrences.

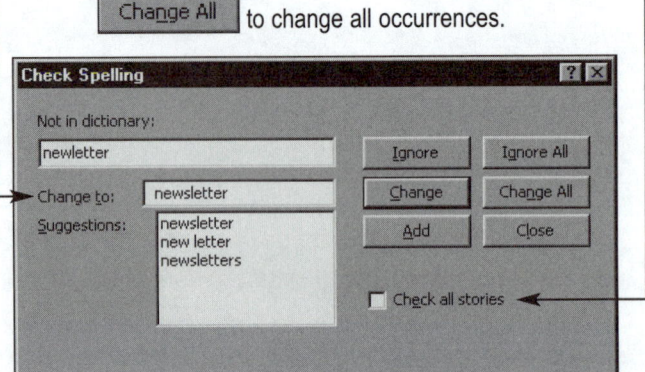

102

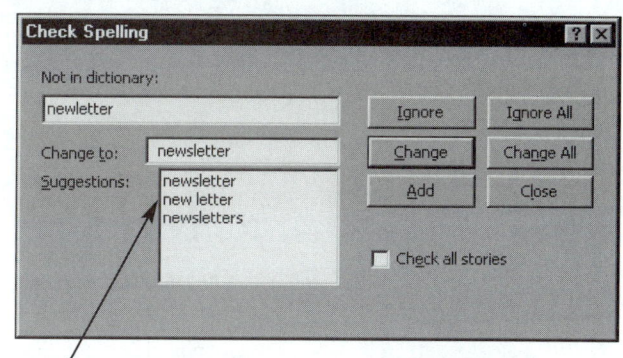

- Click a suggested word. The word is placed in the **Change to** text box. Click [Change] to replace the current occurrence or [Change All] to change all occurrences.

- Click [Ignore] to skip the current occurrence of the word or click [Ignore All] to skip all occurrences.

- Click [Add] to add the word to the dictionary.

5 If Publisher finds a repeated word (such as "the the"), it displays the word in the Check Spelling dialog box.

Click [Delete] to delete one occurrence of the word.

OR

Click [Ignore] to leave the text as is.

6 Repeat steps 4 and 5 as necessary.

NOTE: To cancel spell checking, click [Close].

Check Spelling

(continued)

Notes:

- When automatic spell checking is on, Publisher spell checks as you type. It is turned on by default. When you type a word that is not in the dictionary, Publisher underlines the word with a red wavy line.

- You can leave automatic spell checking on but hide the red wavy lines if they are distracting. When you are ready to look at spelling errors, show the lines.

Automatic Spell Checking

1. To turn automatic spell checking on or off:

   a. Click **Tools**, **Spelling**, **Spelling Options**. The Spelling Options dialog box displays.

   b. Set the **Check spelling as you type** option as desired. Marking the check box enables automatic spell checking and clearing the check box disables it.

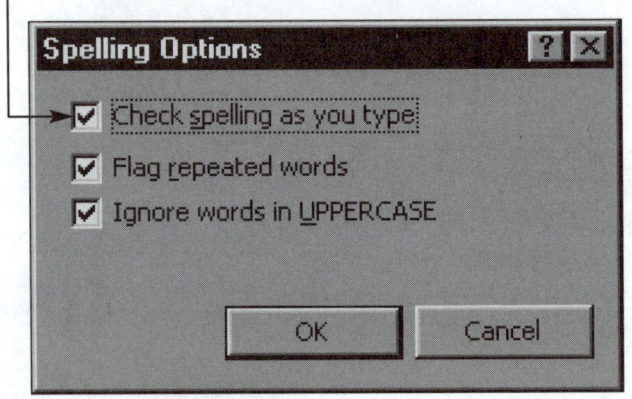

   [Spelling Options dialog box showing:
   ☑ Check spelling as you type
   ☑ Flag repeated words
   ☑ Ignore words in UPPERCASE
   OK / Cancel buttons]

   c. Click [OK].

2. To hide or show red wavy lines when automatic spell checking is on:

   a. Click **Tools**, **Spelling**.

   b. Click **Hide Spelling Errors** or **Show Spelling Errors**.

Continue ➡

Hyphenate

Have Publisher help you hyphenate words in a story. Hyphenated text has a less ragged right edge.

Tools → Language

Notes:

- Usually you will use this procedure when automatic hyphenation is off. You can, however, use it to change where Publisher has placed automatic hyphens. You can check the location of each hyphen in the story and move hyphens.

- Publisher will suggest words that you might want to hyphenate according to the size of the hyphenation zone. See *Change the Hyphenation Zone* on the next page.

- Wait until your story is completely finished before you hyphenate. Adding or deleting even a small amount of text can change the hyphenation for the entire story.

- If you do not want hyphens to appear in your story at all, disable automatic hyphenation using the **Turn Automatic Hyphenation On/Off** procedure.

1. Click **Tools**, **Language**, **Hyphenation**. The Hyphenation dialog box displays.

2. Click Manual... . Publisher hyphenates and highlights the next word that you might want to hyphenate. It displays the word in the Hyphenate dialog box as shown in the illustration. If the word can be hyphenated in multiple places, the suggested location is highlighted.

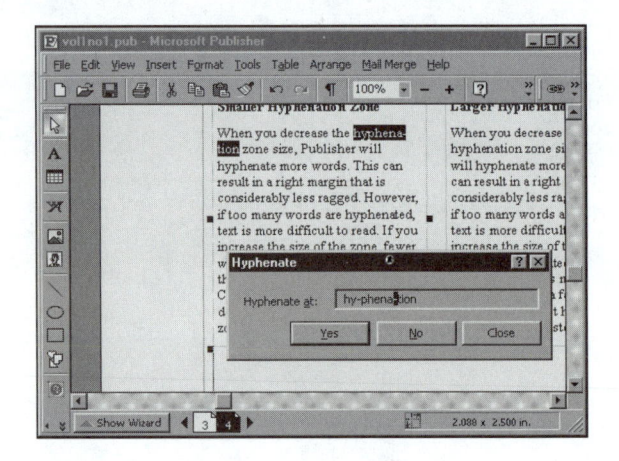

3. Move the highlight to a different place in the word, if desired.

4. To hyphenate the word, click Yes . Publisher places the hyphen and finds the next word that you might want to hyphenate.

   OR

   To skip the word without adding a hyphen, click No . Publisher removes the hyphen and finds the next word that you might want to hyphenate.

5. Repeat from step 3.

6. When finished, click Close .

Notes:

- By default, Publisher automatically hyphenates words. If automatic hyphenation is turned off, words that do not fit on a line are placed on the next line rather than hyphenated.

- You turn automatic hyphenation on or off for individual stories.

- Disabling automatic hyphenation for a story that has already been hyphenated removes hyphens from the story.

- The hyphenation zone is an area at the right edge of text. Publisher hyphenates words located in this zone. For example, if the zone is set to .25", Publisher hyphenates long words located within a quarter of an inch of the right margin of a text or table frame.

Turn Automatic Hyphenation On/Off

1 Click the text or table frame.

2 Click **Tools**, **Language**, **Hyphenation**. The Hyphenation dialog box displays.

3 Click the **Automatically hyphenate this story** check box to select or clear it.

   NOTE: When the option is checked, automatic hyphenation is turned on.

4 Click **OK**.

Change the Hyphenation Zone

1 Click **Tools**, **Language**, **Hyphenation**. The Hyphenation dialog box displays.

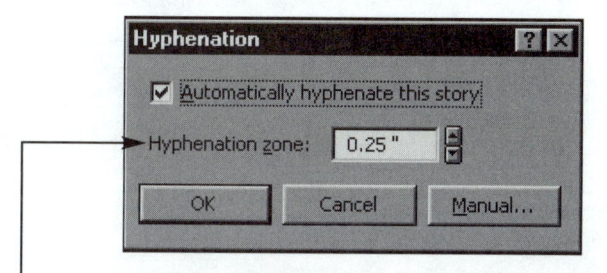

2 Type or select the **Hyphenation zone** measurement.

   NOTE: Decreasing the size of the zone causes more words to be hyphenated. Increasing the size causes fewer words to be hyphenated, although the right edge of the text will be more ragged, as shown in the following illustration.

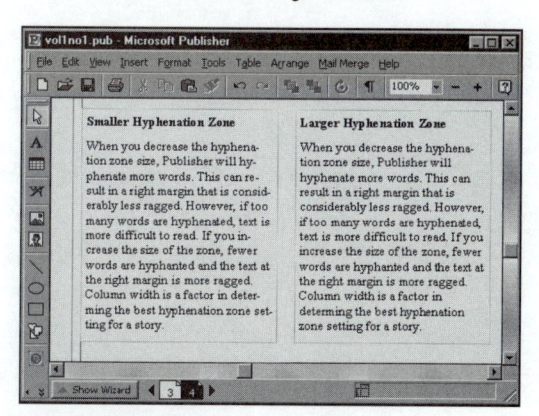

3 Click **OK**.

107

Format Text

These procedures show you how to format the text in a text or table frame. Text is a design element that, when formatted effectively (and with restraint), can give your publication a lively and inviting appearance. Apply fancy fonts, boldfacing, or underlining, wrap text around pictures, create numbered and bulleted lists, and otherwise format text. Experiment with different formatting to create the effect you want to present to the reader, whether it be formal or playful.

Wrap Text Around Pictures

Conform the text in a story to the shape of a picture.

Format ➔ Text Frame Properties...

Notes:

- When you place a picture frame over a text frame, Publisher automatically wraps the text around the picture frame. This wraps text in straight lines since the frame is rectangular. Use the procedure on this page to create an irregular wrap, where wrapped text takes the shape of the picture rather than that of the frame.

- If you don't want text to wrap around a picture, see *Prevent Text from Wrapping* on the next page.

1. Right-click the picture frame. The following illustration shows default text wrapping, where text wraps around the picture frame.

2. Click **Change F**r**ame**, **Frame Prop**e**rties**. The Frame Properties dialog box displays.

3. Click **P**i**cture only** to select it.

4. To set the amount of white space between the picture and text, type or select a measurement in the **O**u**tside** box.

5. Click OK. In the following illustration, text wraps around the picture rather than the frame.

110

Notes:

- If you do not like the way that Publisher has wrapped the text around a picture, use this procedure to fine-tune text wrapping. Bring text closer to the picture or push it further away.

- You can use this procedure only if the text is wrapped around the picture, not the entire frame.

Adjust the Text Wrap

1. Click the picture to select it.

2. Click **Edit Irregular Wrap** on the Formatting toolbar.

   NOTE: If the Formatting toolbar is not displayed, click **View**, **Toolbars**, **Formatting**.

3. Place the mouse pointer over a handle until it changes to:

4. Drag the handle. As you drag, the text moves with the handle.

5. To add another wrap handle, hold down **Ctrl** and click the boundary where Publisher will add the handle.

6. Repeat from step 3 as necessary.

7. Click **Edit Irregular Wrap** when finished.

Notes:

- By default, Publisher wraps text around frames that are placed over the text frame.

- Use this procedure to prevent the text in a particular text frame from wrapping so that you can place a picture beneath a text frame.

Prevent Text from Wrapping

1. Right-click the text frame.

2. Click **Change Frame**, **Text Frame Properties**.

3. Click the **Wrap text around objects** check box to clear it.

4. Click [OK].

   NOTE: Frames have a white background by default. To make a text frame transparent so that a picture beneath it is visible, select the frame and press ***Ctrl+T***.

Add a Drop Cap

Format the first letter of a story with a large capital letter.

Format → Drop Cap...

Notes:

- A drop cap transforms a letter into a graphic element. Use a drop cap to add interest to a plain page (one without a lot of other graphics).

- Sometimes drop caps are formatted in a font other than the text of the story. Preset drop cap styles include letters in various fonts. You can apply a different font to the letter.

1. Change the font of the letter that will be drop cap, if desired. See *Format Characters*.

2. Position the cursor in the paragraph to begin with a drop cap.

3. Click **Format**, **Drop Cap**. The Drop Cap dialog box displays.

4. Drag the scroll bar under the **Available drop caps** list to view drop cap styles.

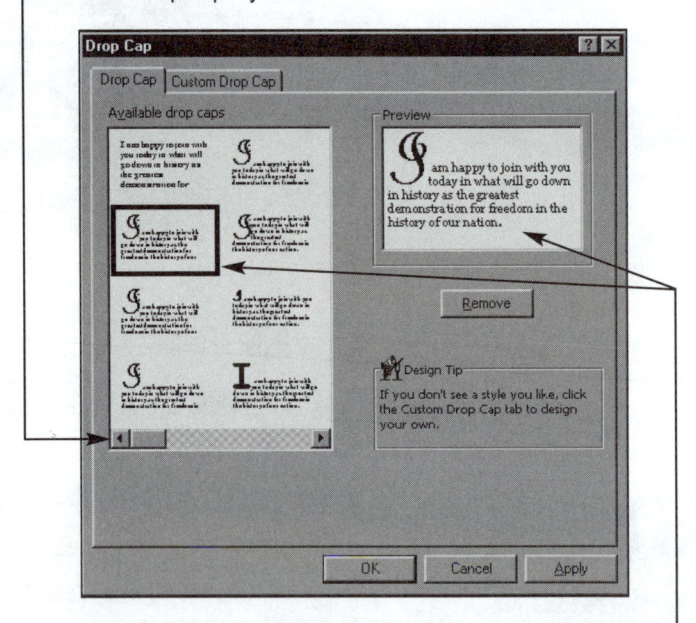

5. Click a style to see your paragraph with the drop cap in the Preview pane.

6. Click **Apply** to apply the selected drop cap style to the text without closing the dialog box.

   NOTE: To move the dialog box so you can see the drop cap in your publication, drag the window title.

112

7 Click [OK] to apply the selected drop cap style and close the Drop Cap dialog box. The following illustration shows a sample drop cap.

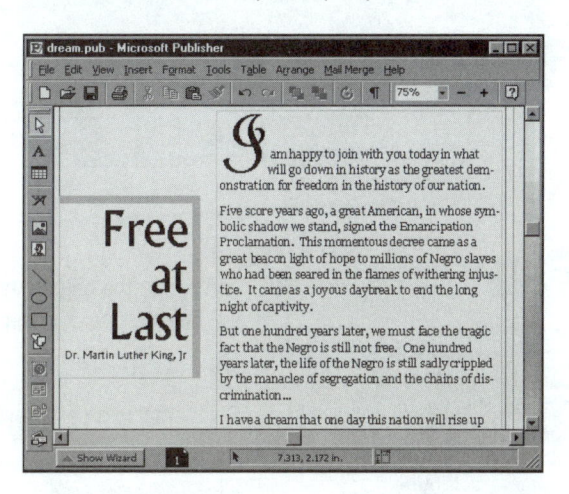

Publisher treats the drop cap as a separate paragraph. If there is space added after the paragraph containing the drop cap, the space will be applied to the drop cap as shown below.

SPACE AFTER PARAGRAPH APPLIED

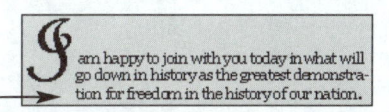

SPACE AFTER PARAGRAPH REMOVED

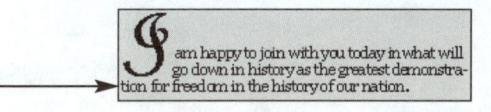

To fix this, remove the paragraph spacing from the paragraph containing the cap. Then add space before the paragraph that follows in order to add the space between the paragraphs. You might also want to adjust line spacing to add more or less white space around the drop cap. See *Set Line or Paragraph Spacing*.

Remove a Drop Cap

1 Position the cursor in the paragraph containing the drop cap.

2 Click **Format**, **Change Drop Cap**.

3 Click [Remove].

Notes:

- You cannot remove a drop cap by changing the font of the letter. You must return to the Drop Cap dialog box.

Align Paragraphs

Change the alignment of one or more paragraphs in a text or table frame. Text is aligned between the left and right margins of the frame.

Format → Indents and Lists...

Notes:

- You can align text with the right or left margin of the frame. You can also center it between the margins or justify it to evenly distribute the text between the margins. See the illustration on the next page for examples of these types of alignment.

- By default, text is left-aligned (lined up with the left margin of the frame).

- Don't justify large blocks of text. Justification adds space between words to stretch each line between the left and right margins. The extra spacing can make text difficult to read.

1 To change the alignment for a single paragraph, position the insertion point in the paragraph.

OR

Select multiple paragraphs to format.

2 Click **Format**, **Indents and Lists**. The Indents and Lists dialog box displays.

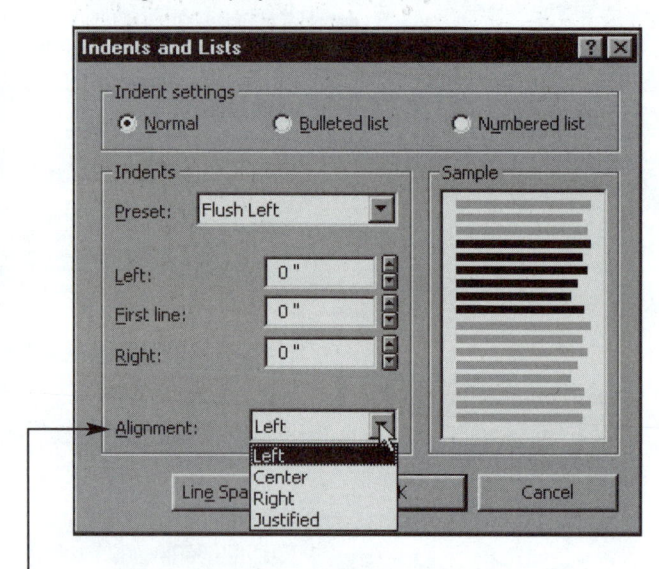

3 Click the alignment to apply:

- **Left**. Aligns text at the left margin of the frame. The right side of text will be ragged.
- **Center**. Centers text between the left and right margins of the frame.
- **Right**. Aligns text at the right margin of the frame. The left side of text will be ragged.
- **Justified**. Distributes text evenly between the left and right margins of the frame.

4 Click OK to align the text.

Notes:

- Alignment settings apply to entire paragraphs. Each paragraph in a story ends with a paragraph mark: ¶. Paragraph marks are visible when you show special characters (**View**, **Show Special Characters**). If the text is a single line, such as a title, there will not be a paragraph mark at the end.

The following figure illustrates the different alignment formats.

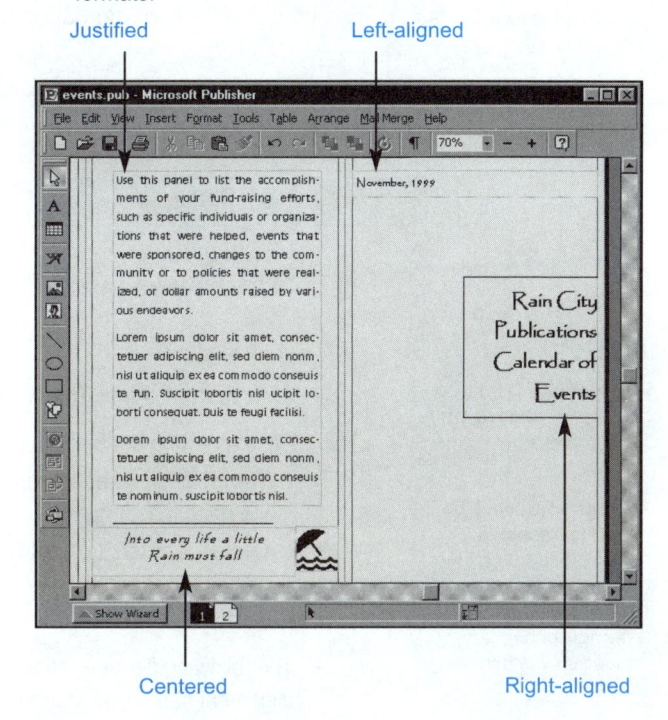

Justified Left-aligned

Centered Right-aligned

Align Using the Formatting Toolbar or Shortcut Keys

The tools on the Formatting toolbar vary depending on the kind of object that you are working with. You must be working in a text frame or table frame in order for alignment tools to appear on the toolbar.

1 Click **View**, **Toolbars**, **Formatting** to display the Formatting toolbar.

2 Select paragraphs to format.

3 Click a formatting tool or press a shortcut key:

- **Left-align**: Click **Align Left** or press **Ctrl+L**
- **Center**: Click **Center** or press **Ctrl+E**
- **Right-align**: Click **Align Right** or press **Ctrl+R**
- **Justify**: Click **Justify** or press **Ctrl+J**

115

Align Text Vertically

Vertical alignment positions text between the top and bottom margins of a frame.

Format ➡ Align Text Vertically

Notes:

- By default, text is vertically aligned with the top margin of the frame.

- These alignment settings apply to all of the text in a frame. You cannot vertically align separate paragraphs differently within a story.

- You cannot change the vertical alignment in a frame that contains overflow text (text that does not fit in the frame). The entire story must be placed before Publisher will be able to vertically align it.

1 Click the frame to select it.

2 Click **Format**, **Align Text Vertically**.

3 Click an alignment setting:
- **Top**. Aligns text at the top margin of the frame (this is the default setting).
- **Center**. Centers text between the top and bottom margins of the frame.
- **Bottom**. Aligns text at the bottom margin of the frame.

The following figure illustrates the available vertical alignment settings.

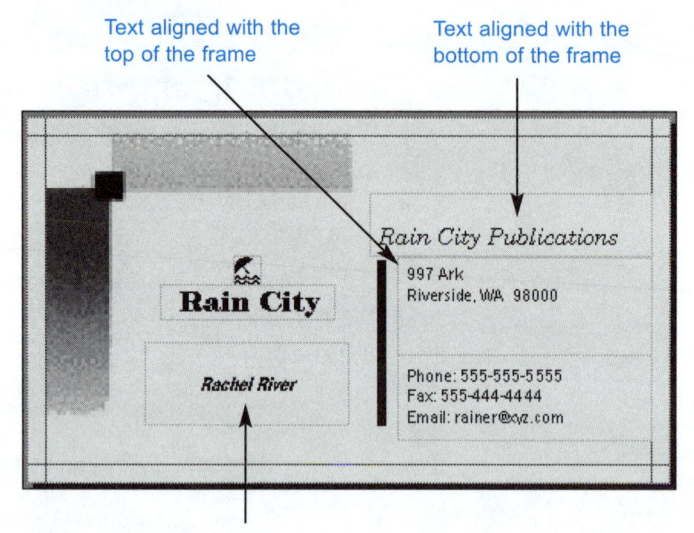

Text aligned with the top of the frame

Text aligned with the bottom of the frame

Rain City

Rachel River

Rain City Publications
997 Ark
Riverside, WA 98000

Phone: 555-555-5555
Fax: 555-444-4444
Email: rainer@xyz.com

Text vertically centered in the frame

116

Continue →

Format Characters

Change the font and the font size, and apply character formatting attributes such as bold, italic, and underlining to text.

Format ➡ A Font...

Notes:

- You can store formatting in a style and then apply the style to quickly format text. See *Edit a Style*.

- The Sample pane in the Font dialog box shows how characters will look with the currently selected formatting options.

- By default, Publisher applies Normal style to all new text. This style sets the default character formatting for new text, which is 10-point Times New Roman. To change the default character format, edit Normal style. See *Edit a Style*.

1 Select the text to format.

2 Click **Format**, **Font**. The Font dialog box displays.

3 Set character formatting options as desired.

4 To apply formatting to the selected text without closing the Font dialog box, click **Apply**.

   NOTE: *To move the dialog box to see the formatted text in your publication, drag the window title.*

   OR

   To apply the selected formatting and close the Font dialog box, click **OK**.

> **Notes:**
> - Shortcut keys and toolbar buttons are the quickest way to format text. However, some character attributes, such as character outlining and embossing, are available only using the Font dialog box.
> - The tools on the Formatting toolbar vary depending on the kind of object that you are working with. You must be working in a text frame or table frame in order for character formatting tools to appear on the toolbar.

Format Characters Using the Formatting Toolbar or Shortcut Keys

1. Click **View**, **Toolbars**, **Formatting** to display the Formatting toolbar.
2. Select the text to format.
3. Click a character formatting button or press the shortcut keys to apply formatting:

   - **Bold**: [B] or **Ctrl+B**
   - **Italics**: [I] or **Ctrl+I**
   - **Underline**: [U] or **Ctrl+U**

     NOTE: The Underline tool underlines with a single line under words and the spaces between the words. The Font dialog box has a variety of other underlining options, such as double lines, wavy lines, and words only underlining (not including the spaces between words).

   - **Font**: [Georgia]
   - **Any font size**: [12]
   - **Increase font size**: [A˄] or **Ctrl+>**
   - **Decrease font size**: [A˅] or **Ctrl+<**
   - **Font color**: [A]
   - **Subscript**: **Ctrl+=**
   - **Superscript**: **Ctrl+Shift+=**
   - **Small capitals**: **Ctrl+Shift+K**
   - **Remove character formatting**: **Ctrl+Spacebar**

> **Notes:**
> - A quick way to format text is to copy the formatting from one block of text to another. For example, if you have boldfaced and underlined some text, you can copy these formats to other text.

Copy Character Formatting

1. Select a formatted character.
2. Press **Ctrl+Shift+C**.
3. Select the text to format.
4. Press **Ctrl+Shift+V**.

119

Fit Text in a Frame

Use Publisher's automatic copyfitting feature to fit a certain amount of text into a frame of a specific size.

Format ➡ AutoFit Text

Notes:

- Normally, you resize a frame or create connected text frames in order to fit a story. Sometimes, however, you need to fit a story into a publication that has only a certain amount of space for it. Then, use automatic copyfitting.

- Publisher changes the font size of text in the frame in order to make it fit. If text is too small, try using one of the methods listed in *More Ways to Fit Copy* on the next page.

1 Select the text frame containing the story to fit.

In the following illustration, the text size of the selected text frame is 10 points.

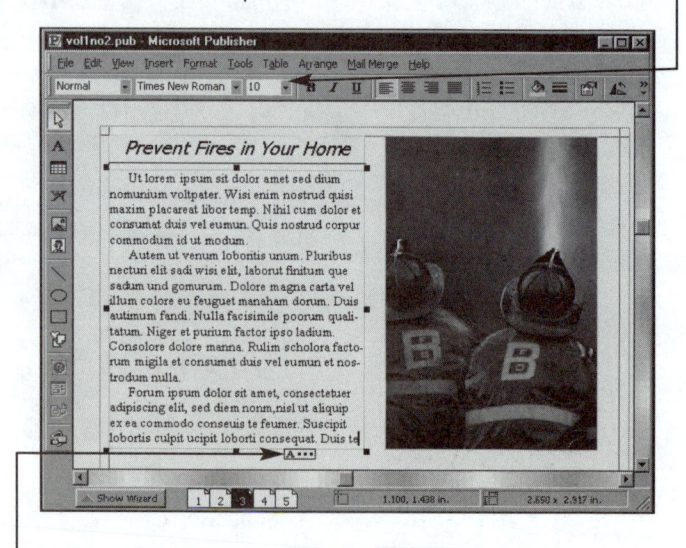

The **Text in Overflow** button indicates that the text does not fit in the frame.

2 Click **Format**, **AutoFit Text**.

3 Click an autofit option:

- **None**. Disables automatic copyfitting. This is the default setting.

- **Best fit**. Adjusts the size of the text so that it fits in the frame. When this option is selected, the size of the text changes when you add or delete text or resize the frame. The text always fits exactly in the frame.

- **Shrink Text on Overflow**. This option applies a smaller text size when there is text in the overflow area.

Notes:

- You cannot use automatic copyfitting in connected text frames.

When automatic copyfitting is applied, Publisher changes the text size in the frame to 9.5 points to fit the entire story in the frame.

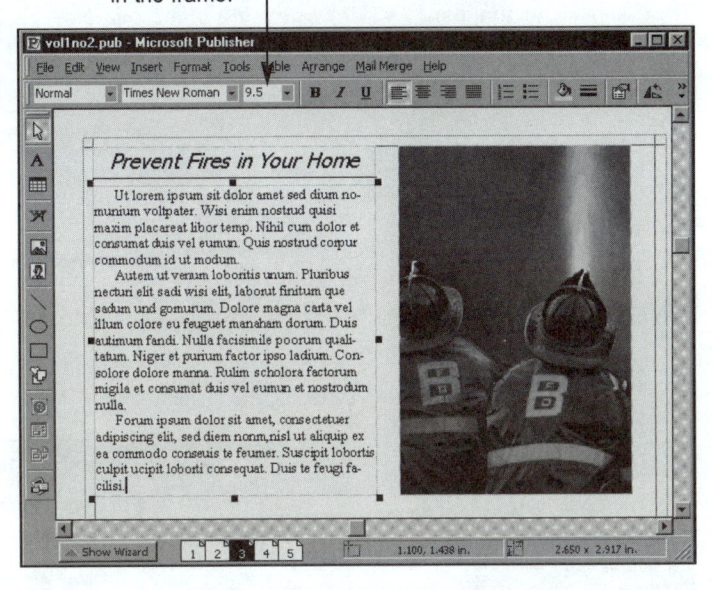

More Ways to Fit Copy

- Edit the story to add or remove text
- Adjust the space between lines and paragraphs
- Resize the frame
- Decrease or increase the frame margins
- Connect frames and continue the story on another page

Indent Paragraphs

Indent the first line of each paragraph in order to visually separate paragraphs in a story. Or, create hanging indents, where every line of the paragraph is indented except the first.

Format ➔ Indents and Lists...

Notes:

- Generally, you either add space between paragraphs or else indent the first line of each paragraph to visually separate paragraphs in long blocks of text. To add space between paragraphs, see *Set Line or Paragraph Spacing*.

1. Select the paragraphs to format.

2. Click **Format**, **Indents and Lists**. The Indents and Lists dialog box displays.

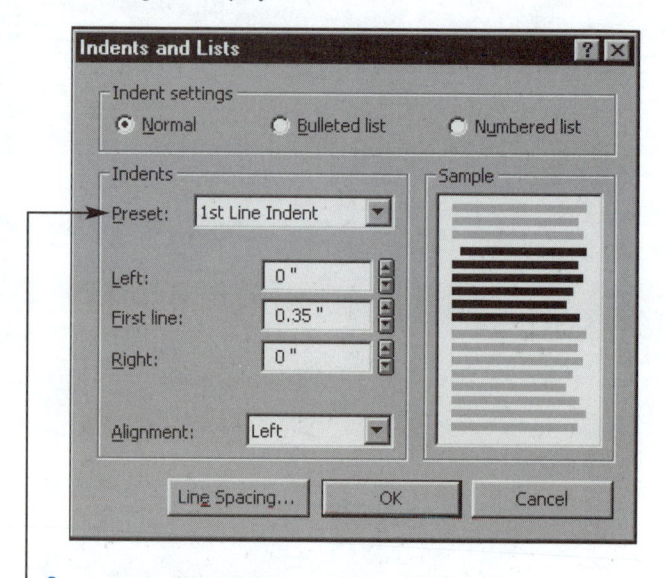

3. Select the type of indent from the **Preset** list:

   - **Original**. Removes indenting or, if a style is applied, returns to the indent specified by the style.
   - **Flush left**. No indent. All lines are flush left.
   - **1st Line Indent**. Indents the first line of each paragraph by the amount of space specified in the **First line** option.
   - **Hanging indent**. Indents all lines of the paragraph by the amount of space specified in the **Left** option with the exception of the first line, which is not indented.
   - **Quotation**. Indents all lines on both the left side and the right side by the amount of space specified in the **Left** and **Right** options.
   - **Custom**. Indents using the measurements that you specify in the **Left**, **First line**, and **Right** options.

> **Notes:**
>
> - Hanging indents are sometimes used to create bulleted or numbered lists. You can have Publisher create these for you. See *Create a Bulleted List* or *Create a Numbered List*.

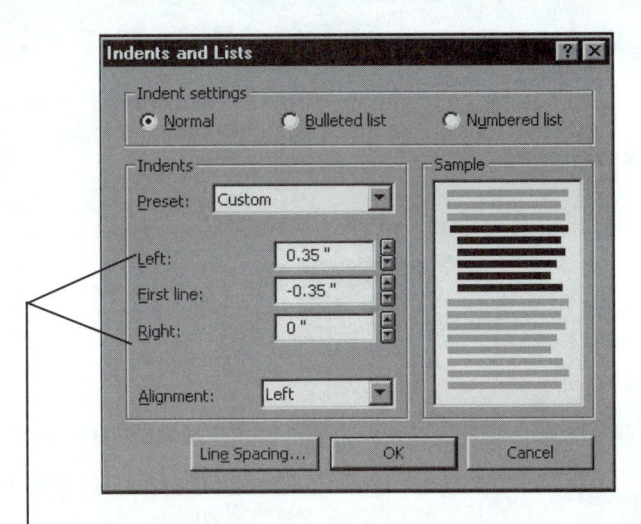

4 Type or select the amount of space to indent (you can type a negative number):

- **Left**. The amount of space to indent text from the left side.
- **First line**. The amount of space to indent the first line of the paragraph. To create a hanging indent, this should be a negative measurement, as shown in the dialog box illustration.
- **Right**. The amount of space to indent text from the right side. For example, long quotations in text are indented from both the left and the right sides.

5 Click **OK**. The following examples show different types of indents.

Hanging Indent

Mix·tec (mēs´tek´) *n.* a member of an Amerindian people who live in the Mexican states of Oaxaca, Guerrero, and Puebla
Mix·tecan (mēs tek´ ən) *n.* any of a family of three Amerindian languages spoken in Mexico

First Line Indent

Confucius said, A noble person takes as much trouble to discover what is right as lesser people take to discover what will pay.
Confucius said, A noble person covets the reputation of being slow in word but prompt in deed.

Quotation

Confucius believed that the only effective force for a ruler was that of his or her own moral force. Following is one of many examples of his teachings on the importance of leadership with integrity:

...they who rule by moral force are like the polestar, which remains in its place while the lesser stars do homage to it.

Confucius was primarily an educator who spoke on all facets of life.

123

Set Line or Paragraph Spacing

Add space between paragraphs to make the text easier to read and to add white space to a page. You can also set the space between lines in a paragraph. For example, you might want to double-space lines.

Format → Line Spacing...

Notes:

- You can set the amount of space between paragraphs by adding space either before or after paragraphs, or both.

- Generally, you either add space between paragraphs or else you indent the first line of each paragraph to visually separate paragraphs in a story. To create first-line indents, see *Indent Paragraphs*.

1. Select the paragraphs to format.

2. Click **Format**, **Line Spacing**. The Line Spacing dialog box displays.

3. Type or select the space **Between lines** to change line spacing.

    NOTE: *For example, to double-space lines of text, enter 2. To triple-space, enter 3. You can also make smaller adjustments to increase or decrease space between lines.*

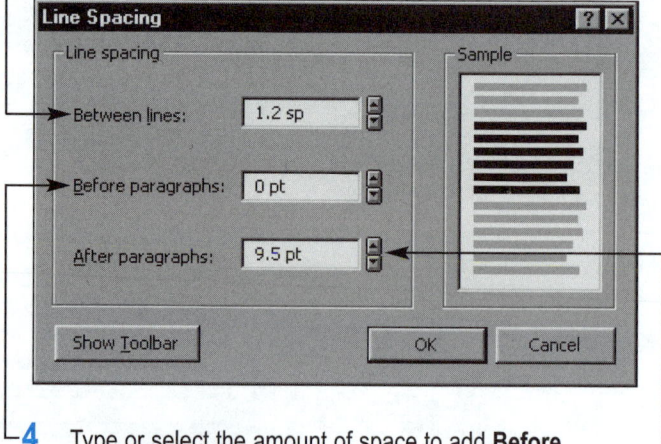

4. Type or select the amount of space to add **Before paragraphs**.

5. Type or select the amount of space to add **After paragraphs**.

Notes:

- Increase or decrease line spacing if the text within paragraphs appears too crowded or too spread out.

- These settings apply to entire paragraphs. You cannot apply them to individual lines within a paragraph.

6 Click [OK]. The following illustration shows text with space after paragraphs.

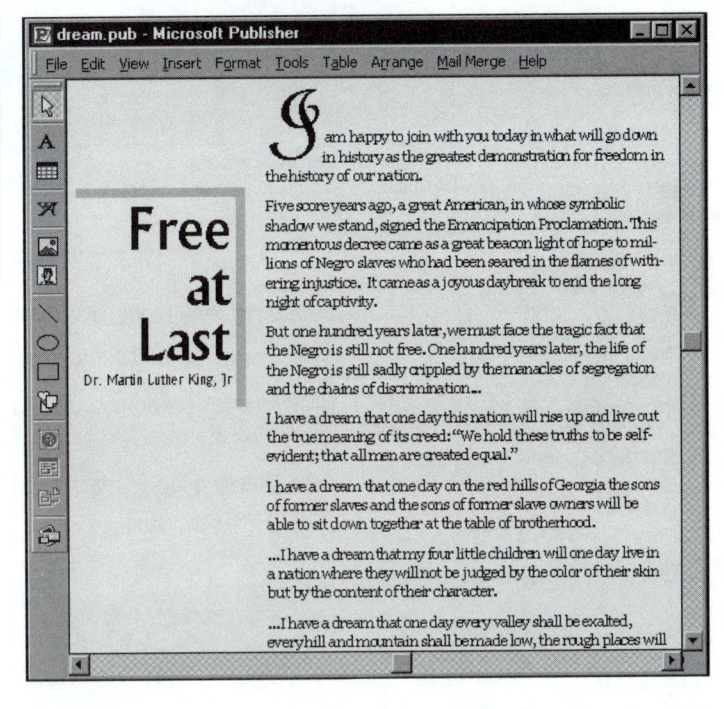

Create a Bulleted List

Add a graphic character, called a bullet, at the beginning of each paragraph.

Format ➡ Indents and Lists...

Notes:

- You can choose from a vast array of bullet characters. The standard bullet character used in most publications is a circle: ● Perk up a list with arrows, stars, smiley faces, or other symbols. You can use any character available in the fonts installed on your computer.

- In a bulleted list, the order of the items in the list is not important. To create sequential lists, see *Create a Numbered List*.

- When you select bullet options in the Indents and Lists dialog box, the Sample pane shows an example of what the list will look like.

1 Select the paragraphs to format.

NOTE: A bullet will be add to each selected paragraph.

2 Click **Format**, **Indents and Lists**. The Indents and Lists dialog box displays.

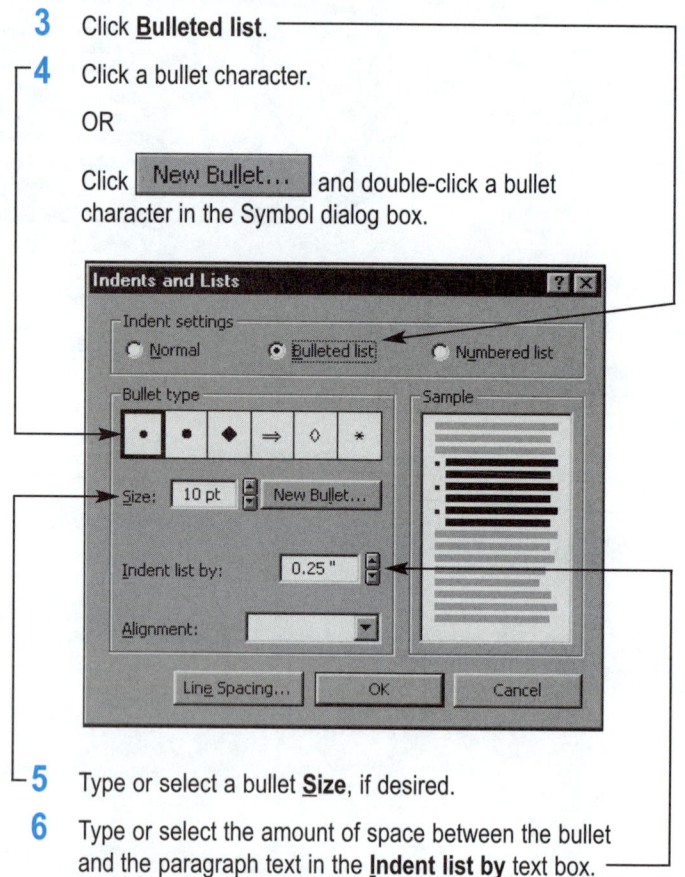

3 Click **Bulleted list**.

4 Click a bullet character.

OR

Click New Bullet... and double-click a bullet character in the Symbol dialog box.

5 Type or select a bullet **Size**, if desired.

6 Type or select the amount of space between the bullet and the paragraph text in the **Indent list by** text box.

7 Select a paragraph **Alignment**, if desired.

126

8   Click [OK]. The following example shows a bulleted list created using diamond bullets.

> **Learn Ballroom Dancing**
> ♦ Have fun
> ♦ Meet people
> ♦ Get an aerobic exercise workout
> ♦ Dazzle your partner
>
> Classes start next week. Call 555-5555

Notes:
- The Bullets tool creates a list using the bullet character selected in the Indents and Lists dialog box. By default, this is a circle. To use other bullet characters, use the Indents and Lists dialog box instead of the Formatting toolbar to create a list.
- To remove bullets, repeat the procedure.

Notes:
- Paragraphs return to the original indent style before you applied bullets.

Add Bullets Using the Formatting Toolbar

1   Select the paragraphs to format.

2   Click **Bullets** [icon] on the Formatting toolbar.

   NOTE: Click **View**, **Toolbars**, **Formatting** to show the Formatting toolbar if it is not displayed.

Remove Bullets

1   Select the bulleted paragraph.

2   Click **Format**, **Indents and Lists**. The Indents and Lists dialog box displays.

3   Click **Normal**.

4   Click [OK].

Create a Numbered List

Add numbers to paragraphs. Publisher will automatically renumber the list if items are moved or added.

Format → Indents and Lists...

Notes:

- Add numbers when the order of the items in a list is important. If the order is not important, use a bulleted list instead. See *Create a Bulleted List*.

- You can choose the character that separates the number and text. By default, the separator is a period: 1., 2., 3.

- You can use upper- or lowercase letters rather than numbers: a., b., c. or A., B., C.

1. Select the paragraphs to number.

2. Click **Format**, **Indents and Lists**. The Indents and Lists dialog box displays.

3. Click **Numbered list**.

4. Select a number **Format** (numbers or letters).

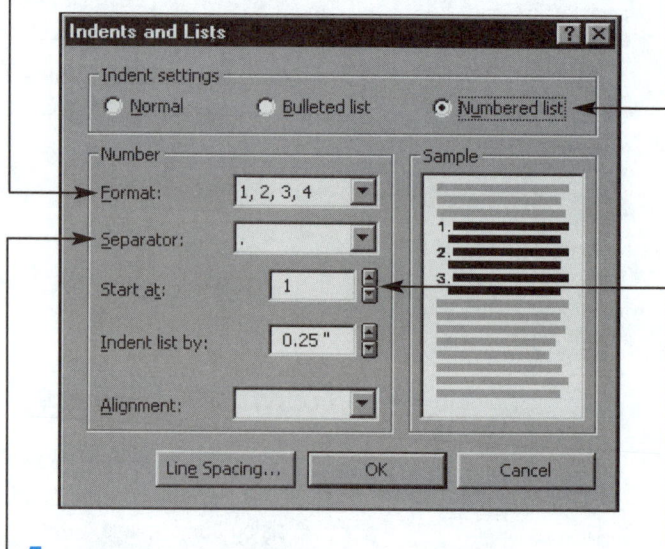

5. Select a number **Separator** (the character that appears after the number, before the text).

6. Select the starting number for the first paragraph in the list in the **Start at** option.

7. Type or select the amount of space between the number and the paragraph text at **Indent list by**.

8. Select a paragraph **Alignment** if you want to change the alignment of the paragraphs.

9. Click OK.

128

Notes:

- The Numbering tool creates a list using the number options as they are currently set in the Indents and Lists dialog box. By default, this is a number following by a period: 1., 2., 3., starting at the number 1.

- To remove numbers, repeat the procedure.

Number Paragraphs Using the Formatting Toolbar

1. Select the paragraphs to number.

2. Click **Numbering** on the Formatting toolbar.

   NOTE: Click View, Toolbars, Formatting to show the Formatting toolbar if it is not displayed.

Notes:

- Paragraphs return to the original indent style before you added numbers.

Remove Numbers

1. Select the numbered paragraph(s).

2. Click **Format**, **Indents and Lists**. The Indents and Lists dialog box displays.

3. Click **Normal**.

4. Click **OK**.

129

Set Tabs

Set tabs to indent and align lines of text.

Notes:

- The tab type sets the text alignment. Choose from four tab types: left-aligned, right-aligned, centered, and decimal. For example, a centered tab centers text around the tab stop. A decimal tab aligns a column of numbers with the decimal point. The illustrations show examples of tab types.

- By default, all paragraphs have preset left-aligned tab stops every half inch. Preset tabs are not visible on the ruler, but if you insert a tab in text it will indent text to the next half inch.

- Use tabs to indent part of the text within a line. For example, a header might have a left-aligned date, a centered title, and a right-aligned page number, as in the illustration on the next page.

1 Click **View**, **Rulers** if the rulers are not displayed.

2 Select the paragraphs to format.

3 At the intersection of the two rulers is a box with a symbol for the current tab type. To create a different type, click the box until the symbol for the type that you want to create is displayed:

- **Left-aligned**
- **Centered**
- **Right-aligned**
- **Aligned with decimal**

4 Click in the ruler to set the tab. The following illustration shows a decimal tab that lines up the decimals in a column of numbers.

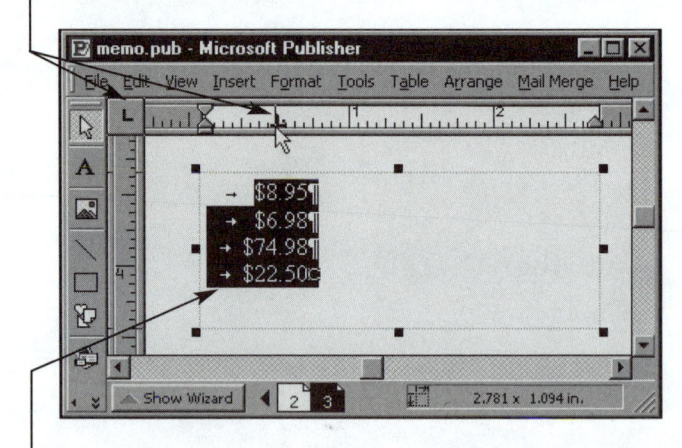

5 To insert a tab in text, press **Tab**. If special characters are shown (**View**, **Show Special Characters**), you can see the arrow symbols that represent tabs in text.

NOTE: To view tab settings for a paragraph, position the insertion point in the paragraph. Since tab settings may vary from paragraph to paragraph, the ruler shows only the tabs set in the current paragraph.

130

Notes:

- You can use tabs to set up columns of text. However, it might be easier to create a table to set up side-by-side paragraphs. See the **Tables** section.

- To indent the first line of all paragraphs in a story, it is easier to apply first-line paragraph indents than to use tabs. See *Indent Paragraphs*.

The following illustration shows a paragraph formatted with a center tab and a right-aligned tab.

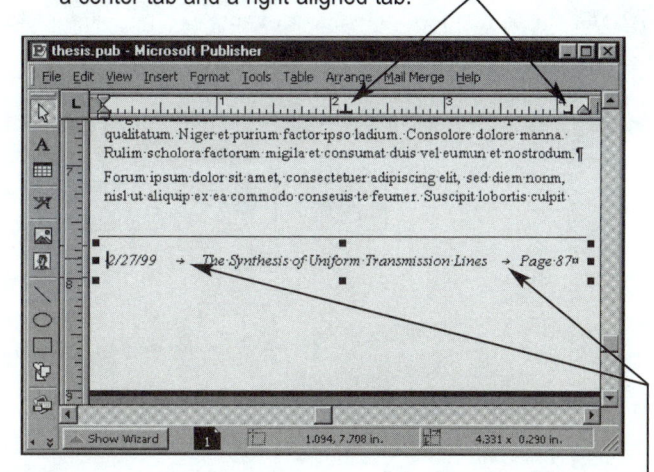

Symbols for tabs inserted in the paragraph appear when special characters are shown.

Notes:

- The ruler shows tab markers for the current paragraph (the paragraph containing the insertion point). Use this procedure to change tabs in the current paragraph.

Edit a Tab

- To move a tab, drag the tab marker in the ruler.

- To delete a tab, drag the tab marker off the ruler.

- To edit a tab (for example to add a leader character), double-click the tab marker in the ruler. Set options for the tab in the Tabs dialog box.

131

Create a Style

A style stores text formatting. For example, a headline style might boldface and center text. Applying a style to text applies formatting to the text.

Format ➡ Text Style...

1. Format the text as you want it to be in the style.
2. Select the formatted text.
3. Click in the **Style** box on the Formatting toolbar. This highlights the name of the current style.

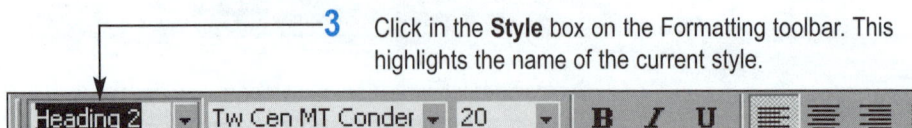

NOTE: *If the Formatting toolbar is not displayed, click* **View**, **Toolbars**, **Formatting**.

4. Type the name for the new style in the **Style** box.
5. Press **Enter**. The Create Style By Example dialog box displays.
6. Change the style name, if desired. 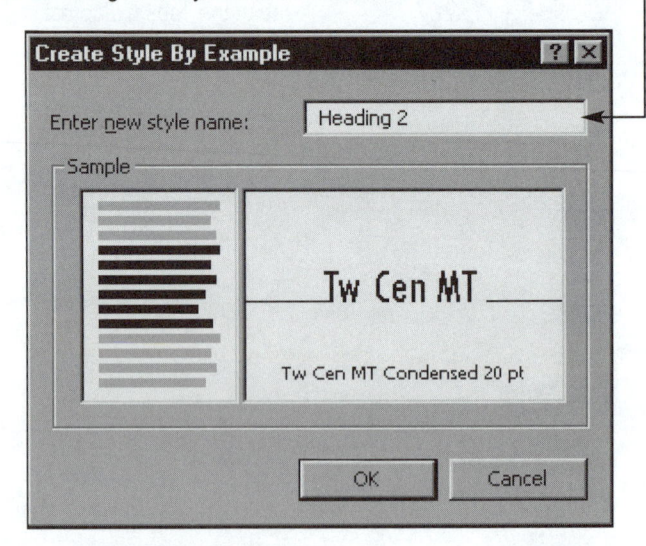
7. Click **OK** to save the style and apply it to the selected paragraph.
8. To apply the formatting of the style to other paragraphs, see *Apply a Style*.

Notes:

- Styles apply to entire paragraphs of text. They include both character formatting, such as typeface and font size, and paragraph formatting, such as alignment, tab settings, indents, and line and paragraph spacing.

- The quickest way to create a style is to use the Styles box in the Formatting toolbar as described in this procedure. You can also create, view, and otherwise work with styles using the Styles dialog box (**Format**, **Text Style**).

Edit a Style

Change the formatting of a style.

Format → Text Style...

Notes:

- Publisher comes with a preset Normal style that formats text in 10-point Times New Roman. This style appears by default in all publications and is the basis of all the other styles in the publication. Publisher applies Normal style to all new text that you type. To change the default formatting of new text, edit Normal style.

- Changes that you make to a style effect all paragraphs in the current publication to which the style has been applied.

- As you change the formatting of a style, the Sample pane in the Change Style dialog box shows you how the new formatting looks.

1 Click **Format**, **Text Style**. The Text Style dialog box displays.

2 Click **Change this style** >. The Change Style dialog box displays.

3 Select the style to edit in the **Choose style to change** list.

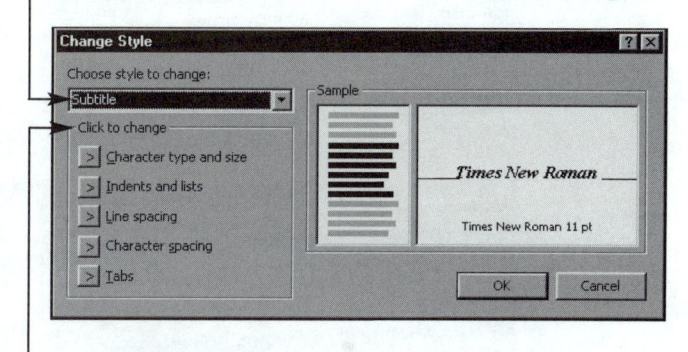

4 Use the **Click to change** buttons to change the style formatting.

5 Click OK twice to close both dialog boxes.

133

Apply a Style

Applying a style formats text using the formatting previously stored in the style.

Format → Text Style...

Notes:

- The quickest way to apply a style is to use the **Styles** box in the Formatting toolbar as described in this procedure. You can also apply styles by opening the Styles dialog box (**F**ormat, **Text** **S**tyle).

1 Position the cursor in the paragraph to format.

OR

Select multiple paragraphs to format.

NOTE: *If the Formatting toolbar is not displayed, click* **View**, **Toolbars**, **Formatting**.

2 Select the style to apply in the **Style** box on the Formatting toolbar. Publisher formats the text using the formatting stored in the style. The illustration shows the Subtitle style applied to the selected paragraph.

134

Notes:

- Use Format Painter to quickly apply the same style to different paragraphs in a publication. For example, use it to apply a subtitle style to several paragraphs on different pages of the publication.

Apply the Same Style Repeatedly

1 Click in a paragraph that has been formatted using the style that you wish to apply.

2 Double-click **Format Painter** in the Standard toolbar.

NOTE: You must double-click (instead of single click) so that the Format Painter remains active until you press **Esc**.

3 Click in the paragraph to format. Publisher applies the style to that paragraph.

4 Click in the next paragraph to format. Repeat as necessary.

5 Press **Esc** or click the **Format Painter** when finished formatting.

135

Import Styles from Another Publication

Share styles between similar publications. For example, if you have already created styles for a newsletter, you can import them into the different newsletter.

Format → Text Style...

Notes:

- This procedure imports all styles from another publication. You cannot import a subset of styles.

- If a style you are importing has the same name as a style in the current publication, you are given the choice of which style to keep.

1. Click **Format**, **Text Style**. The Text Style dialog box displays. The dialog box lists all styles available in the current publication.

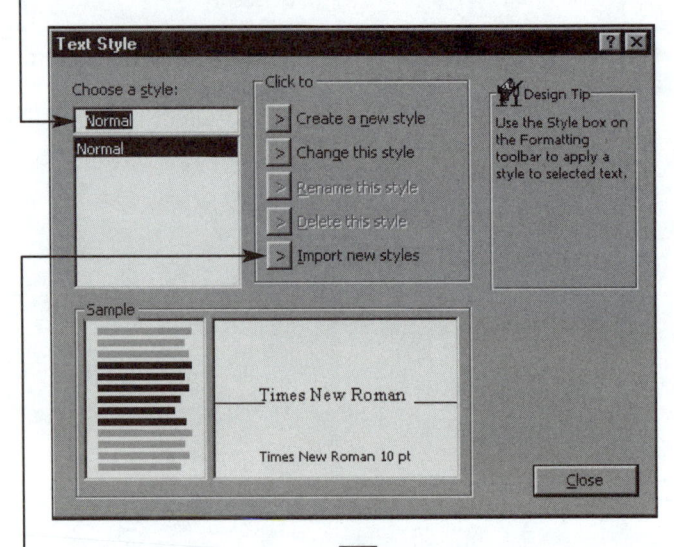

2. Click **Import new styles** [>]. The Import Styles dialog box displays.

3. Double-click the publication containing the styles to import.

4. If a style in the current publication has the same name as a style you are importing, the following prompt displays.

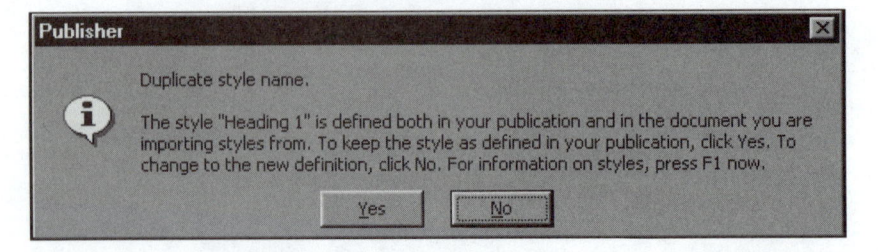

Notes:

- If you edit an imported style, the changes apply to the style in the current publication only. The style in the original publication is not affected.

5   Click **Yes** to choose not to import the style with the duplicate name.

OR

Click **No** to replace the style in the current publication with the incoming style.

When Publisher has finished importing styles, the Text Style dialog box displays. The imported styles have been added to the list of styles in the dialog box.

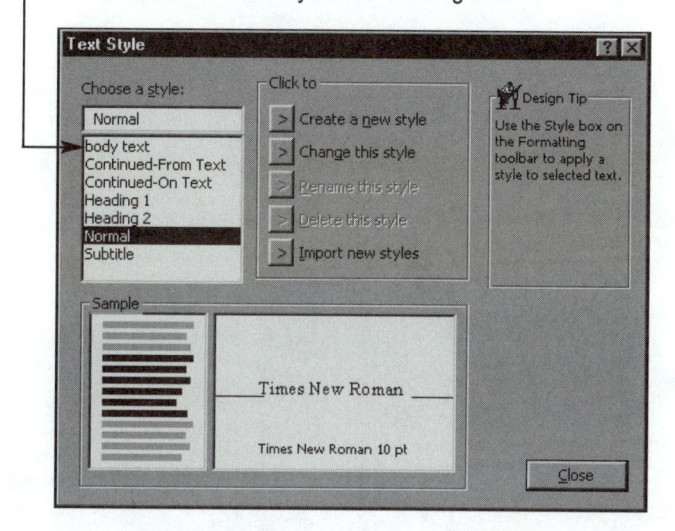

6   Repeat from step 2 to import styles from another publication, if desired.

7   Click **Close** or press **Esc** to close the Text Style dialog box when finished importing styles.

137

Drawing Objects

You don't have to be an artist to draw perfect squares, circles, and straight lines in Publisher. You can create simple graphics to enhance your publication. Publisher includes drawing object tools and AutoShape tools for creating shapes for graphics.

Use drawing object tools on the Objects toolbar to create graphics by drawing directly on the page. Because these shapes are not in frames, you can place them on top of frames. For example, use these tools to create callouts on a picture by drawing arrows from text frames to a picture frame. Or, draw lines between columns of text or under a headline.

AutoShape tools create shapes in a picture frame. You might decide to use AutoShape tools rather than the Objects toolbar for a particular drawing object because: 1) you can easily add text to AutoShape drawings, and 2) the AutoShapes toolbar provides more shapes than does the Objects toolbar. For example, you can create complex flowcharts using the AutoShapes Flowchart tools.

Draw Lines and Arrows

Draw a straight line. Transform the line into an arrow by adding an arrowhead.

Notes:
- Lines and arrows drawn using this procedure are not placed in frames; you draw them directly on the page.
- Lines can be used as a graphic element in many ways. For example, draw lines above or beneath titles or sidebars for emphasis or add lines between columns. This type of line is called a **rule**.
- Arrows are handy for creating figure callouts. Create text frames for callout text and draw arrows from the text to a picture.

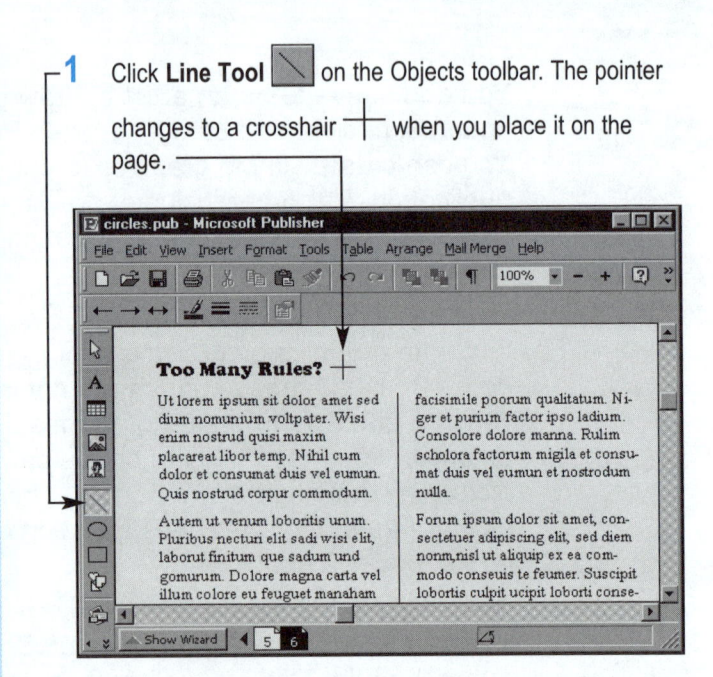

1. Click **Line Tool** on the Objects toolbar. The pointer changes to a crosshair when you place it on the page.

2. To draw a straight line, hold down the **Shift** key.

3. Drag to create the line.

4. When the line is the length you want it, release the mouse button and then the **Shift** key.
   - If the "snap to" feature is on, the line jumps to the nearest guide or object when you release the mouse button. See *Snap to Guides and Objects*.

140

Notes:

- See *Change the Line Style of a Drawing Object* to change the thickness or color of a line.

- You might want to group lines with the frames that they are placed on. Then if you move the frame, the lines will move with it. See *Group Frames and Objects*.

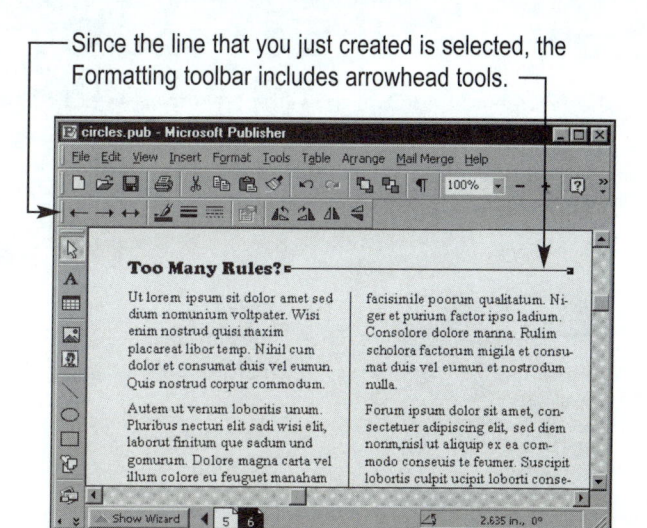

Since the line that you just created is selected, the Formatting toolbar includes arrowhead tools.

5 To add arrowheads to a line:

- To add an arrowhead to the left end of a horizontal line or to the top of a vertical line, click **Add/Remove Left Arrow**.

- To add an arrowhead to the right end of a horizontal line or to the bottom of a vertical line, click **Add/Remove Right Arrow**.

- To add an arrowhead to both ends of the line, click **Add/Remove Both Arrows**.

The following example shows how you can use arrows to create callouts from text frames to a picture.

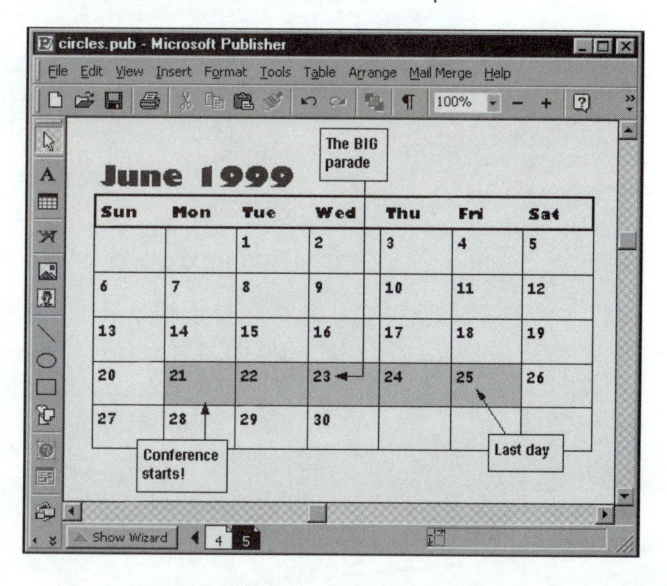

141

Draw Rectangles and Ovals

Use the Rectangle and Oval drawing object tools to draw shapes.

Notes:

- Publisher can constrain the shape of the object as you draw it in order to create perfect squares and circles.

- Shapes drawn using this procedure are not placed in a frame; you draw them directly on the page.

- After you create a rectangle or oval, see *Change the Line Style of a Drawing Object* to change the thickness or color of the lines.

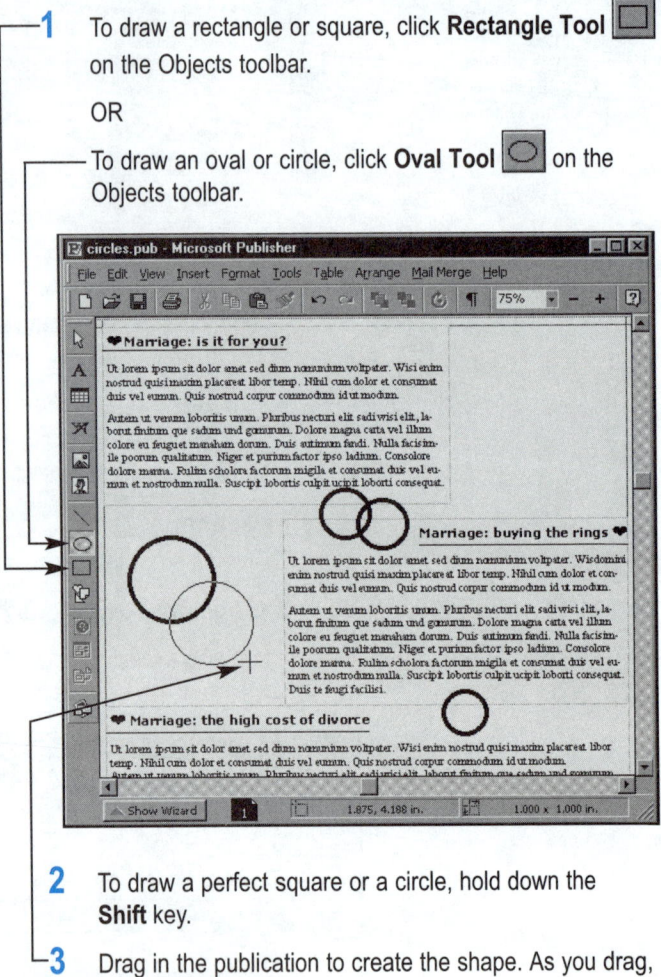

1. To draw a rectangle or square, click **Rectangle Tool** on the Objects toolbar.

   OR

   To draw an oval or circle, click **Oval Tool** on the Objects toolbar.

2. To draw a perfect square or a circle, hold down the **Shift** key.

3. Drag in the publication to create the shape. As you drag, the pointer changes to a crosshair:

   NOTE: It is difficult to control the placement of squares and circles created by holding down the **Shift** key. Don't worry if the object is not placed exactly where you want it. You can always move it later.

142

Notes:

- You can draw objects on top of other objects to layer them. For example, in the illustration on the previous page, a circle overlaps another circle.

- Do not use a rectangle as a border for a frame. Instead, apply a border to a frame (see *Apply Line Borders to a Frame*). That way, the border resizes and moves with the frame. To add an oval border, use the procedure on this page since an oval is not available as a frame border.

4 Release the mouse button and then the **Shift** key when the object is the size that you want it.

- If the "snap to" feature is on, the shape jumps to the nearest guide or object when you release the mouse button. See *Snap to Guides and Objects*.

The following illustration shows an oval used as a border around an imported picture.

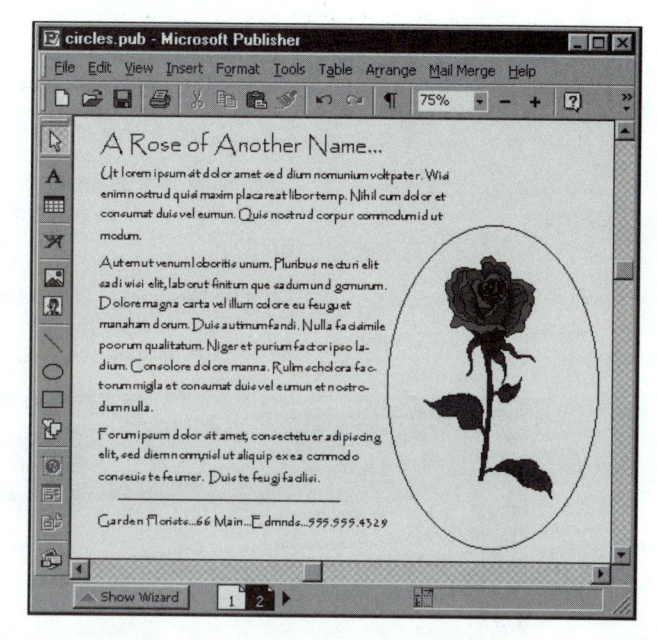

143

Draw Custom Shapes

A custom shape is a triangle, star, heart, or any other shape that the Custom Shapes tool can draw.

Notes:

- Shapes drawn using this procedure are not placed in a frame; you draw them directly on the page.

1 Click **Custom Shapes** on the Objects toolbar. The Custom Shapes toolbar opens.

2 Click the tool for the shape that you want to draw.

3 To constrain the shape to its original proportions (so the object won't be stretched out of shape), hold down the **Shift** key.

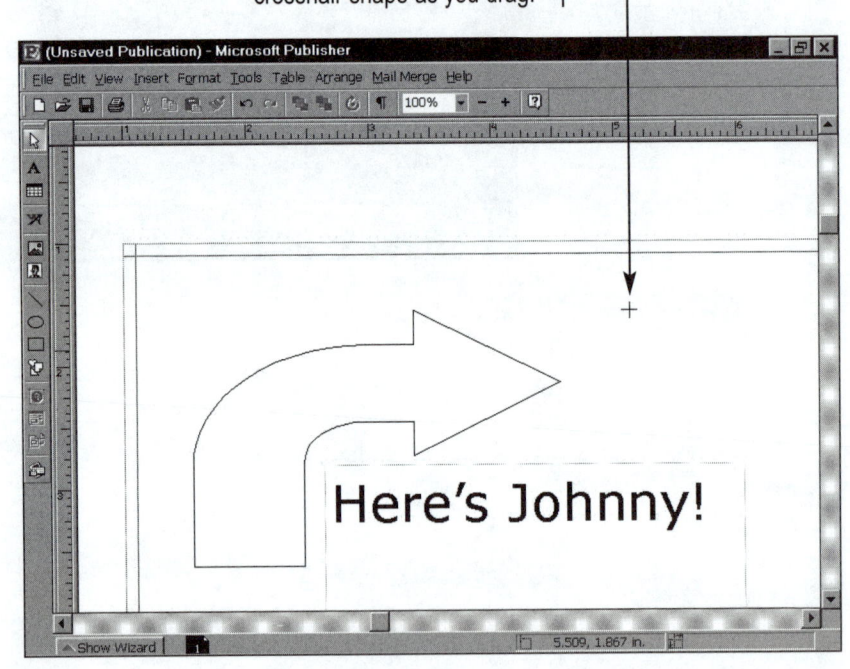

4 Drag on the page to create the shape. The pointer is a crosshair shape as you drag.

5. Release the mouse button and then the **Shift** key when the object is the size that you want it.

   Use custom shapes to quickly create simple graphics. In the following illustration, the first star was created using the Custom Shapes tool. The remaining stars were simply copied and pasted. When you paste each copy, Publisher staggers them evenly as shown in the illustration. The star on top of the stack is formatted with a drop shadow (select the drawing object and press **Ctrl+D**).

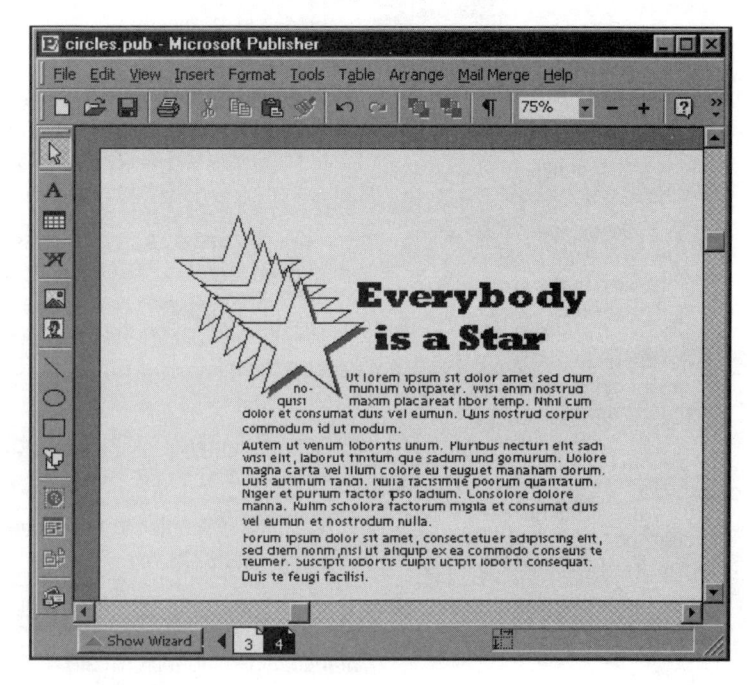

Draw a Balloon AutoShape

Use AutoShape tools to create balloons and bubbles of varying designs. This procedure shows you only how to create a balloon, but you can use it to draw any AutoShape.

Insert ➡ Picture

Notes:

- AutoShape objects are created in picture frames.
- The AutoShapes toolbar contains tools for drawing many shapes besides balloons. Experiment with the tools on the toolbar to create different shapes, such as hearts, stars, lines, and fancy arrows. Once you have learned to draw a balloon, you can draw any AutoShape.

1. Click **Insert**, **Picture**, **New Drawing**. A new frame for the drawing is placed in the window. The AutoShapes floating toolbar appears and the Drawing toolbar appears at the bottom of the window.

2. To resize the frame, drag a black selection handle on the frame boundary.

3. Click **Callouts** on the AutoShapes toolbar. The Callouts toolbar opens with tools for creating balloons of different shapes.

4. Click the callout tool for the shape that you would like to draw.

5. To retain the proportions of the shape as you create it, hold down the **Shift** key.

6. Drag in the frame to create the balloon. The pointer changes shape to a crosshair.

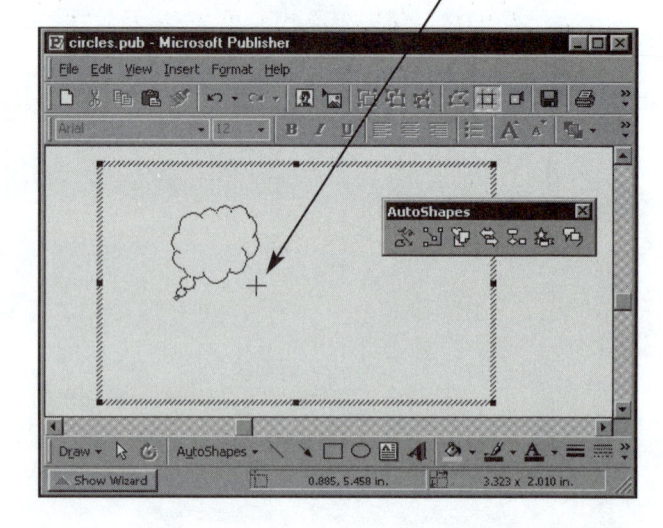

146

Notes:

- To edit an AutoShape drawing, double-click the frame. Use the Formatting, Drawing, and AutoShapes toolbars and the menu to edit the drawing.

7   When the shape is the size you would like it, release the mouse button and then the **Shift** key. The insertion point appears in the shape so that you can add text.

8   Type text, if desired.

  NOTE: *Even if text does not fit in the shape, continue typing all of the text. You can later change it to a smaller font size or make the shape larger (drag a selection handle on the shape).*

9   To format the text in a balloon:
   a. Drag across text to select it.
   b. Click **Format**, **Font**.
   c. Change settings in the Font dialog box and press **Enter**.

10 Repeat from step 3 to create more balloons or, experiment with other tools on the AutoShapes toolbar to draw different shapes.

11 To change the direction of the hook in a balloon:
   a. Click the object to select it. A triangle handle appears at the end of the hook.

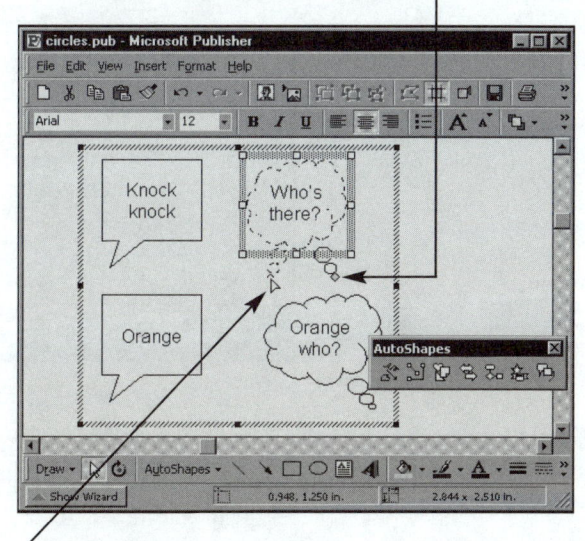

   b. Drag the triangle handle to a new direction. As you drag, a dotted line shows the hook's new position.
   c. Release the mouse button when the hook is correctly positioned.

12 Click anywhere outside of the drawing to exit AutoShapes.

147

Change the Line Style of an AutoShape

Change the thickness of the lines in an AutoShape. You can also apply colors.

Notes:

- Activate AutoShapes edit mode to work with an AutoShape. In edit mode, the AutoShapes and Drawing toolbars appear in the window.

- Use the Drawing toolbar at the bottom of the window to format line styles.

1. Double-click the AutoShape to activate edit mode. The AutoShapes and Drawing toolbars appear and the frame around the shape is visible.

2. Click the AutoShape to select it. White handles appear around the selected object.

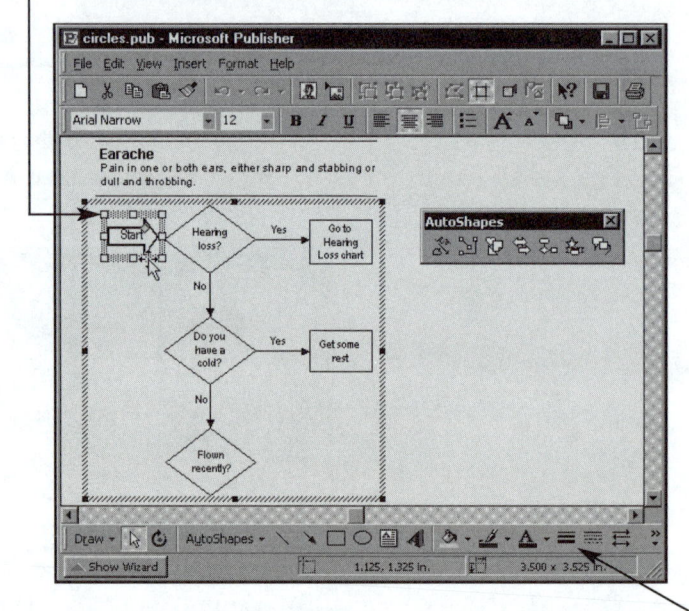

- To change the line thickness, click **Line Style** on the Drawing toolbar and select a style.

- To apply a dashed or dotted line, click **Dash Style** and select a style.

- To format or add an arrowhead, click **Arrow Style** and select a style.

- To change the color, click **Line Color** and select a color.

3. Click anywhere outside the AutoShape frame to exit edit mode.

148

Continue →

Change a Line Style of a Drawing Object

Change the thickness of the lines in a drawing object. You can also apply colors to lines.

Format → Line/Border Style

Notes:

- This procedure applies to drawing objects such as lines, arrows, rectangles, and ovals created using tools on the Objects toolbar. It does not apply to AutoShapes.

- The line style options available depend on the type of object you are formatting. For example, you can apply a dotted line style if formatting a line and you can apply border art if formatting a rectangle.

1 Click the object to select it.

OR

To select multiple objects, hold down the **Shift** key and click each object.

- When multiple items are selected, the **Group Objects** button appears. See *Group Frames and Objects* for information on this button.

- If the Formatting toolbar does not appear in the window, click **View**, **Toolbars**, **Formatting**.

2 If an arrow or line is selected, click **Dash Style** and select a dashed or dotted line, if desired.

NOTE: You cannot apply dashed or dotted line styles to other objects, such as rectangles or custom shapes.

3 To change the thickness of a line, click **Line/Border Style**. The Line/Border Style menu opens.

150

4 Select a line thickness from the menu.

OR

To select from more options and/or to apply a color, click **More Styles**. A dialog box opens with more line style options. The dialog box varies depending on the type of object selected. Select a line style and/or color to apply. Press **Enter** to close the dialog box.

- If the object that you are formatting is a line or arrowhead, the Line dialog box opens. You can select from different styles of arrowheads in this dialog box.
- If the object you are formatting is a rectangle, the Border Style dialog box opens. You can apply different weights to different sides of the rectangle and you can use border art. For more information on this dialog box, see *Apply Line Borders to a Frame*.

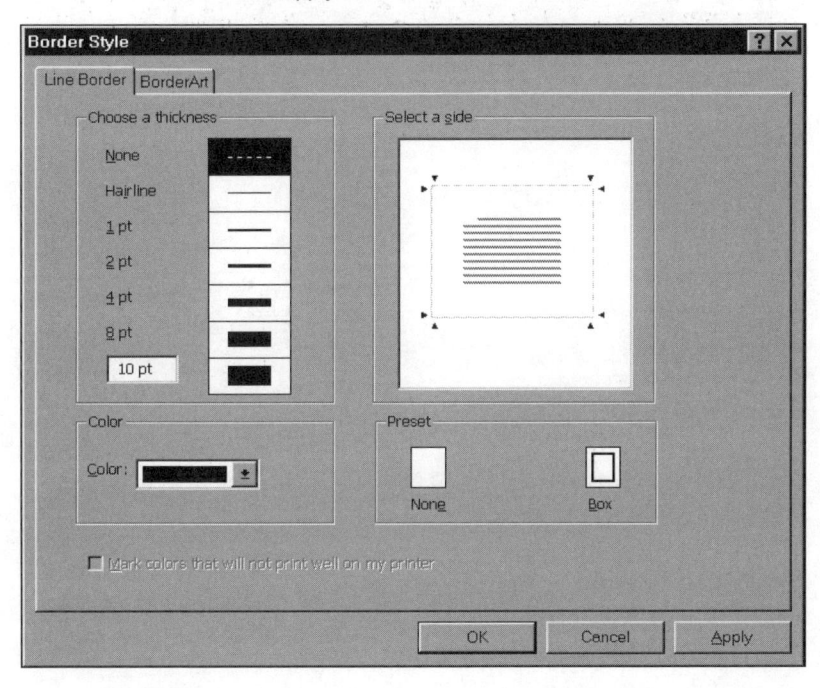

Pictures

You can have a lot of fun selecting pictures to add to your publication. Publisher comes with a Clip Gallery of hundreds of pictures, including some photographs, to use in your publications. You can also import your own pictures into a publication. The Publisher Design Gallery includes formatted design elements, such as calendars and sidebars, that are not pictures but that can add graphic elements to a page.

Pictures are placed in frames in your publication. See the **Frames** section for ways to format and work with frames after adding a picture.

You can also draw graphics with the Objects toolbar and the AutoShapes toolbar. See **Drawing Objects**.

You don't have to add a picture just because a page looks dull. You can use rules (lines), fonts, white space, a drop cap, and other elements to create inviting pages. If you decide to add a picture, choose it carefully. Find pictures that match the tone of your publication and are meaningful to the surrounding text.

Insert a Picture, Sound, or Video Clip

Add a clip art picture, a sound, or video clip from the Clip Gallery to your publication.

Insert ➡ Picture

Notes:

- The illustrations in this procedure demonstrate inserting clip art pictures from the Gallery. You can use the same procedure to insert a sound or motion (video) clip in a Web publication.

- The file size of your publication will be increased by the size of the clip that you insert. You can check the size of the clip when you insert it.

1 Click **Clip Gallery Tool** on the Objects toolbar.

2 Drag in the publication to create a frame.

NOTE: If you insert a sound or motion clip, the frame will be an object frame. If you insert clip art, it will be a picture frame.

3 Release the mouse button when the frame is the size you want. The Insert Clip Art dialog box displays.

4 Click the **Pictures**, **Sounds**, or **Motions** tab for the type of clip to insert.

5 Click a category to view clips by subject.

OR

Type one or more keywords and press **Enter** to find clips that might be useful to your story.

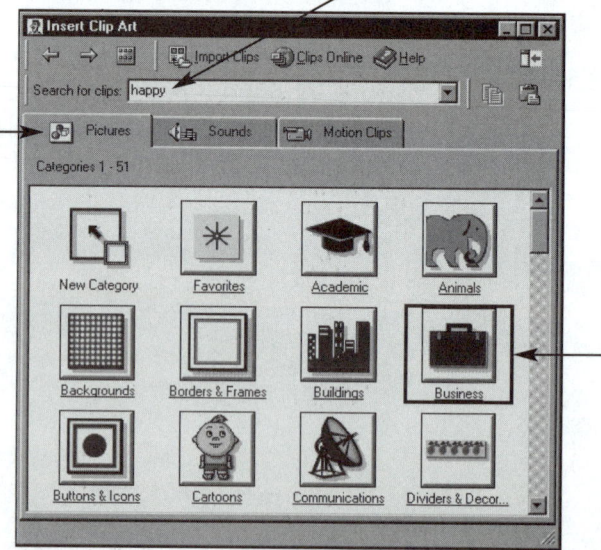

Clips matching the keyword(s) that you entered or the category that you selected are displayed in the Clip Gallery window.

154

Notes:

- The Clip Gallery installed with Publisher includes some photographs. Go to the Photographs category on the Pictures tab.

6 Place the mouse pointer over a picture to view the clip size and a brief description. Sound and motion clips include the clip length, such as 45 seconds.

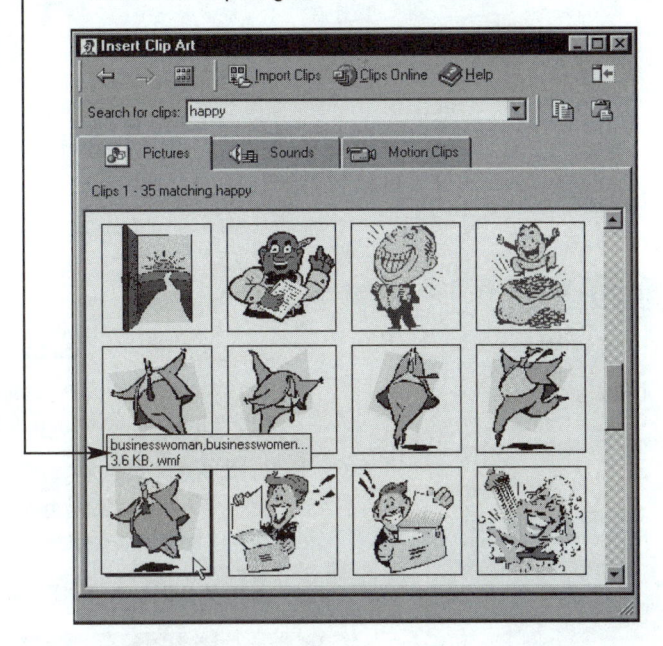

7 Use the buttons at the top of the dialog box to browse clips in the Gallery:

- Click a clip and then **Find similar clips** to find clips similar in subject matter. Specify the type of clip you are looking for.
- To return to the list of categories, click **All Categories**.
- To return to a previous screen, click **Back**.

8 To insert a clip in the publication, click it, then click **Insert clip**.

   NOTE: Publisher will resize the picture frame in order to retain the original proportions of a picture (if the picture would have to stretch to fit in the frame).

9 Click to close the Clip Gallery.

155

Clips: Organize Clips in the Gallery

If you have many clips in the Clip Gallery, keep them organized so that you can locate them easily.

Insert → Picture

Notes:

- Create categories for clips in the Clip Gallery. Go to the All Categories page in the Gallery to browse clips by category.

- Add and edit keywords to search for a particular clip. Enter keywords in the search box located under the Clip Gallery toolbar.

- To enter keywords or to add a clip to a category, the clip must be in the Clip Gallery.

- Clips downloaded from the Web (see *Clips: Download Clips from the Web*) are located in the Downloaded Clips category. These clips already have keywords and categories assigned to them. You can place them in different categories and edit keywords.

1. Open Clip Gallery:

   a. Click **Clip Gallery Tool** on the Objects toolbar.

   b. Drag in the publication to create a frame. When you release the mouse button, the Gallery opens.

2. To create a new category:

   a. Click the tab for the type of media (pictures, sounds, or motion clips) to organize.

   b. Click **All Categories** to list current categories.

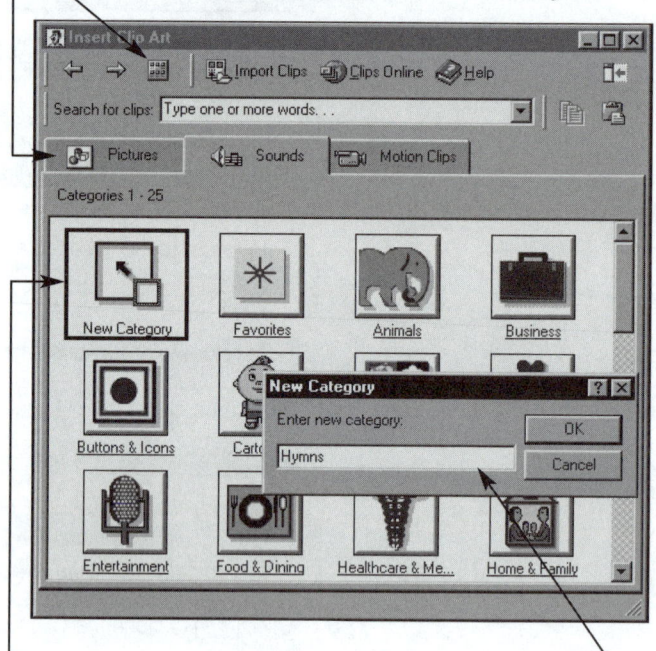

   c. Click New Category.

   d. Type a name for the new category and press **Enter**. The category is added to the All Categories page.

3. To add a clip to a category:

   a. Display the icon for the clip.

   b. Click the icon to open a pop-up menu.

Notes:

- You can add a single clip to multiple categories. Deleting a category (right-click the category icon and select **Delete Category**) removes only the category. Clips in the category are not deleted.

c. Click **Add clip to Favorites or other category**. The menu expands.

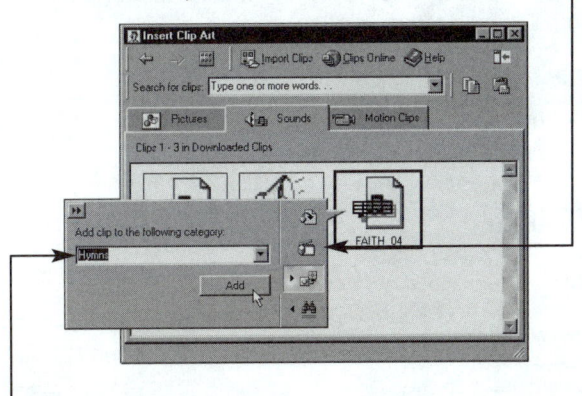

d. Type or select a category.

NOTE: *Typing the name of a category that does not exist creates a new category.*

e. Click **Add** to add the clip to the category.

4 To add or edit the keywords for a clip:

a. Right-click the icon for the clip and select **Clip Properties**.

b. Click the Keywords tab.

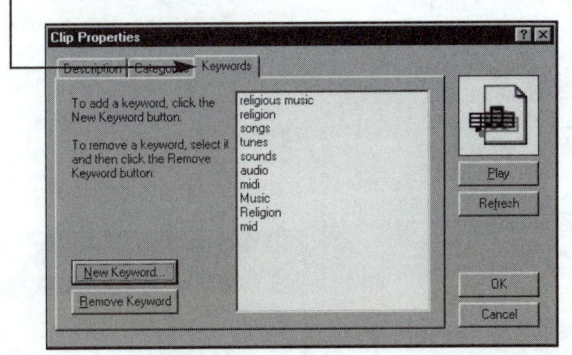

c. To add a keyword, click **New Keyword...** and type the keyword. Click **OK** to add the keyword to the list.

d. To remove a keyword, click the keyword in the list and click **Remove Keyword**.

e. Click **OK** to close the Clip Properties dialog box.

5 Click ✗ to close the Clip Gallery when finished organizing clips.

6 Delete the frame that you created in step 1.

157

Clips: Download Clips from the Web

Visit the Microsoft Clips Online Web site and download clip files including clip art pictures, sound files, and video (motion) clips.

Notes:

- You must have an Internet connection and a Web browser that supports frames and JavaScript (such as Internet Explorer version 4.0 or later).

- Clips downloaded from the Web are added to Clip Gallery categories as appropriate. In addition, they are added to the Downloaded Clips category, which is created the first time you download from the Web site.

- Microsoft periodically updates the Clip Gallery Live Web site. When you visit the site, it might not match the illustrations in this procedure.

1. Click **Clip Gallery Tool** on the Objects toolbar.

2. Drag in the publication to create a frame.

3. Release the mouse button when the frame is the size you want. The Insert Clip Art dialog box displays.

4. Click **Clips Online** on the Clip Gallery toolbar. The Connect to Web prompt displays.

5. Click **OK**. Publisher starts your Web browser and connects to the Clip Gallery Live Web site home page.
   - If unable to connect, start your Web browser and establish a connection to the Internet. Then, start this procedure from step 1.
   - You might be presented with a license agreement before you can access the Clip Gallery Live site.

6. Browse the site to find clips to download.

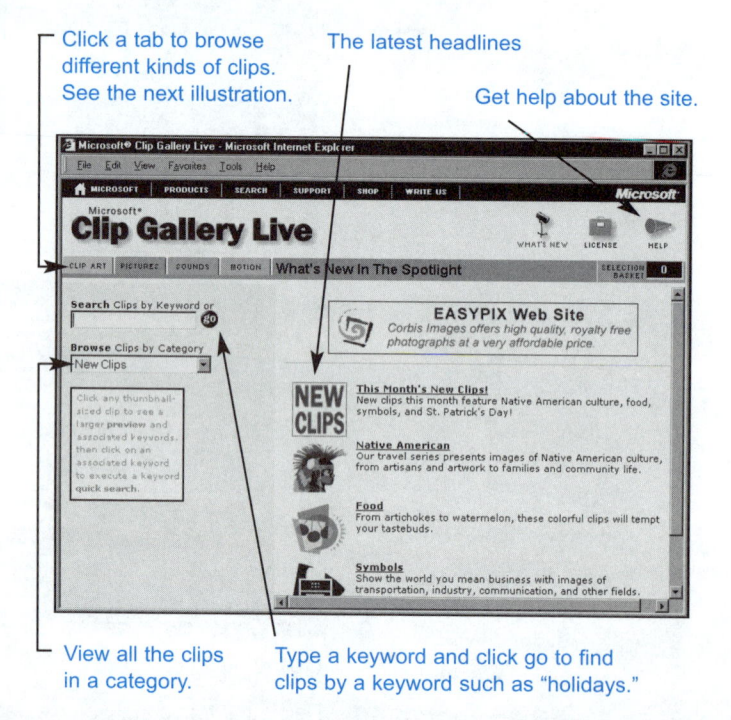

Click a tab to browse different kinds of clips. See the next illustration.

The latest headlines

Get help about the site.

View all the clips in a category.

Type a keyword and click go to find clips by a keyword such as "holidays."

158

7 Browse and download clips matching the selected category or keyword.

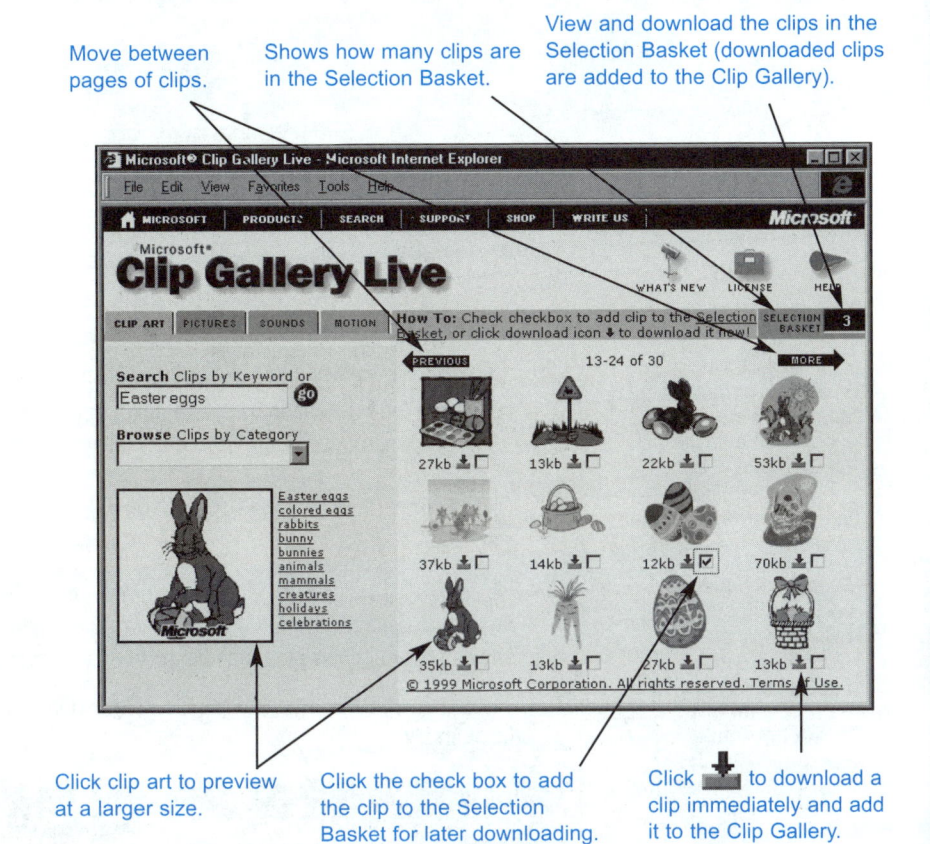

Move between pages of clips.

Shows how many clips are in the Selection Basket.

View and download the clips in the Selection Basket (downloaded clips are added to the Clip Gallery).

Click clip art to preview at a larger size.

Click the check box to add the clip to the Selection Basket for later downloading.

Click to download a clip immediately and add it to the Clip Gallery.

8 Use your Web browser to exit and close the connection to the Internet.

9 To view clip(s) you downloaded, click the Downloaded Clips category in the Clip Gallery.

159

Clips: Add Clips to the Gallery

Add sound, video, or pictures located in files on your computer to the Clip Gallery.

Insert → Picture

Notes:

- The illustrations in this procedure demonstrate adding pictures to the Clip Gallery. Dialog boxes for adding sound and video clips are similar.
- Files must be located on your computer or an attached drive (such as a shared network drive) in order for you to import them into the Gallery.

1. To open the Clip Gallery:
   a. Click **Clip Gallery Tool** on the Objects toolbar.
   b. Drag in the publication to create a clip frame. When you release the mouse button, the Clip Gallery opens.

2. Click **Import Clips** to open the Add clip to Clip Gallery dialog box.

3. Select the type of clip to import—pictures, sounds, or motion clips—from the **Files of type** list. The illustration shows how to import pictures (clip art).

4. Display the folder containing the file to import in the **Look in** list.

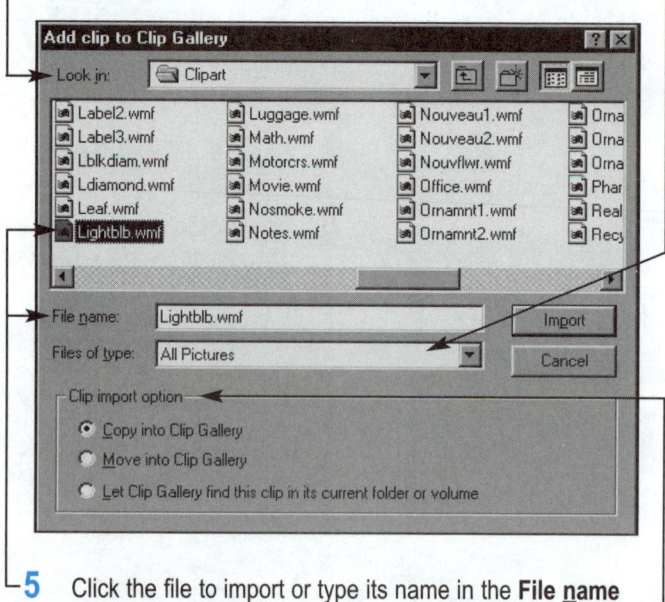

5. Click the file to import or type its name in the **File name** text box.

6. Click an import option:
   - **Copy into Clip Gallery**. Places a copy of the clip into the Clip Gallery.

Notes:

- When you import, you enter a list of keywords that you can later use to find the clip again. You also specify which categories to place the clip in. For example, you could add a clip to both the Favorites and the Symbols categories.

- **Move into Clip Gallery**. Copies the clip into the Gallery and then deletes the original file.

- **Let Clip Gallery find this clip in its current folder or volume.** The file is not placed in the Clip Gallery. Instead, a pointer to the current location of the file is added to the Clip Gallery. The clip file might be located on a zip disk, CD-ROM, or shared network drive. When you insert the clip into a publication, Publisher uses the pointer to locate the file and copy it into the publication.

7 Click [Import] to display the Clip Properties dialog box.

8 Type a short description of the clip. This description displays in a pop-up tip when you place the mouse pointer over the clip in the Clip Gallery.

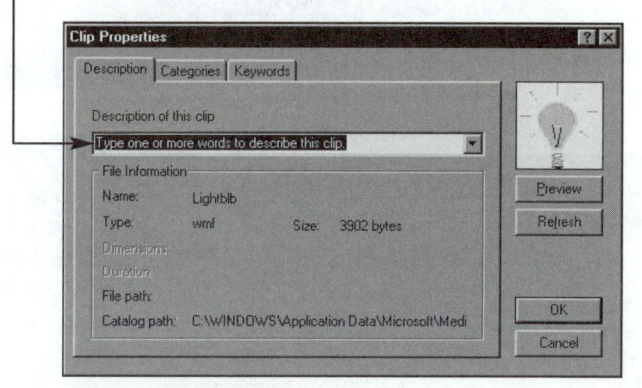

9 Click the **Categories** tab and select the check box next to each category you'd like to add the clip to.

   NOTE: These are the categories in the Clip Gallery. You can add a clip to multiple categories.

10 To enter a list of keywords you can use to find the clip in the Clip Gallery:

    a. Click the **Keywords** tab.

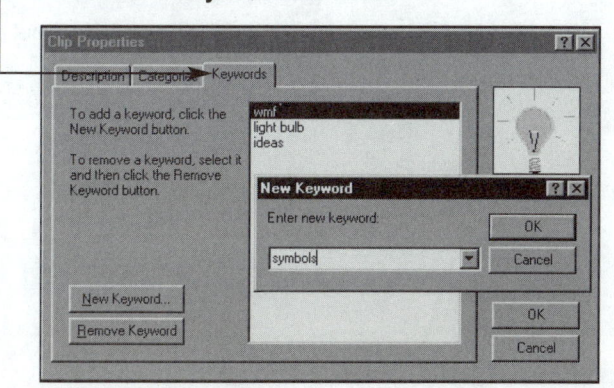

Clips: Add Clips to the Gallery

(continued)

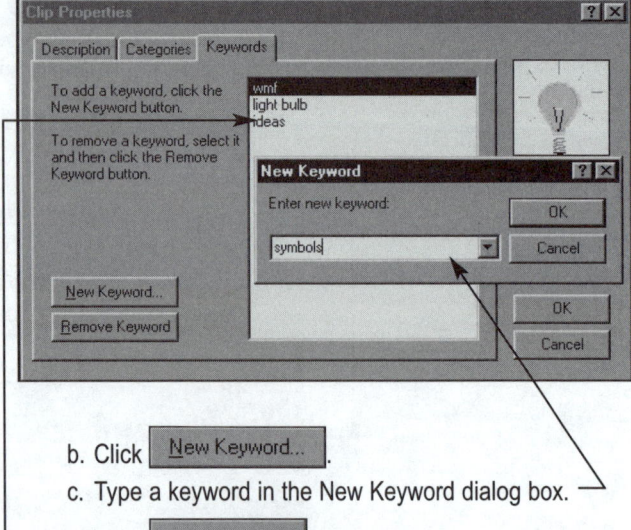

b. Click **New Keyword...**.

c. Type a keyword in the New Keyword dialog box.

d. Click **OK** to add the keyword to the list in the Clip Properties dialog box.

e. To remove a keyword, click the keyword in the list and click **Remove Keyword**.

f. Repeat from step 10a until the list of keywords is complete.

11 Click **OK** when finished setting clip properties.

12 To insert the clip into the frame that you created in step 1:

a. Click the clip.

b. Click **Insert clip**.

13 Click **X** to close the Clip Gallery.

14 Delete the frame that you created in step 1, if desired.

Continue →

Import a Picture

Insert a picture from a file on your computer.

Insert → Picture

Notes:

- You can insert a copy of the picture in a publication so that the picture is saved as part of the publication. The original file remains on disk and the two pictures are not connected in any way. Or, you can insert a link to the picture file. Then when you change the picture in the original file, the changes also appear in the publication. The picture itself is not stored in the publication.

- You can import files in a number of graphic file formats. The formats that you can insert are listed in the Insert Picture dialog box.

1 Click **Picture Frame Tool** on the Objects toolbar.

2 Drag on the page to create the picture frame. The frame is selected (handles appear around it).

3 Click **Insert**, **Picture**, **From File**. The Insert Picture dialog box displays.

4 Click the picture to insert. The right pane shows a preview of the picture (not available for all file types).

NOTE: To view a list of file types that you can import, scroll through the **Files of type** list.

164

Notes:

- If you have a graphic of a format that you cannot import, try opening it in a graphics program and saving it in a file type that Publisher can use.

- Pictures are imported into picture frames. After you import a picture, you can resize, crop, scale, rotate, format the picture frame, and otherwise work with the picture in your publication.

5 To link to the picture file, click the [Insert ▼] arrow to open the drop-down menu and click **Link to File**.

OR

Click [Insert ▼] to place a copy of the picture in the file.

The following illustration shows the picture inserted in a picture frame.

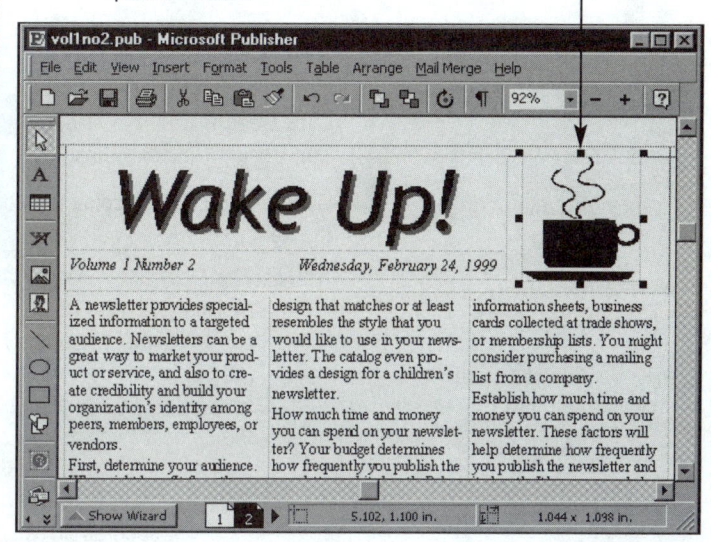

165

Insert a Design Gallery Object

The Publisher Design Gallery contains hundreds of predesigned objects that you can insert and customize to create pull quotes, sidebars, advertisements, calendars, titles, and other objects in your publication.

Insert → Design Gallery Object...

Notes:

- Most Design Gallery objects include sample text and graphics that you can replace with your own choices.
- Use the **Wizard** button to change the design of an object inserted from the Design Gallery. The **Wizard** button appears below the object when it is selected.

1. Click **Design Gallery Object** on the Objects toolbar. The Design Gallery opens.

2. Click a category to display the objects in that category in the right pane.

   NOTE: The Objects by Design tab and the Objects by Category tab list the same Design Gallery objects, but arranged differently. The Objects by Design tab groups all objects that you can create using a single design. For example, you can browse all of the objects that you can create using the Arcs design or the Waves design. The Objects by Category tab lists the same type of object together, such as all sidebars and all pull quotes.

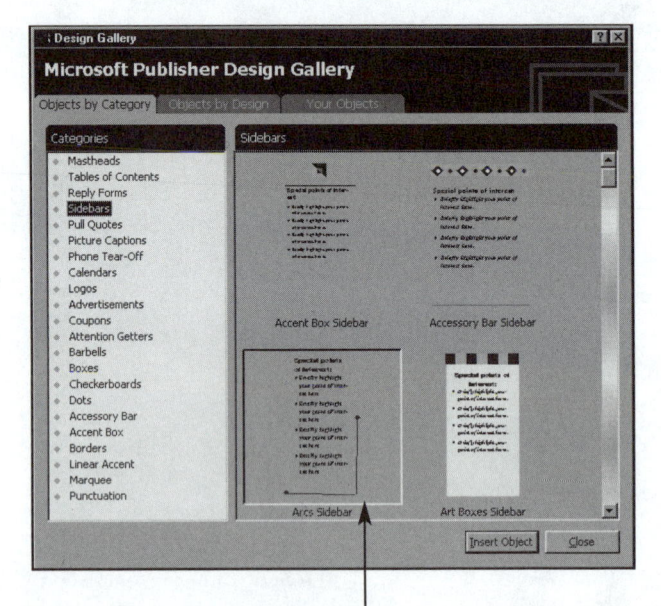

3. Click the object to insert.

4. Click **Insert Object** to insert the selected object on the publication page.

Notes:
- You can move, copy, rotate, resize, edit and format sample text, and otherwise work with Design Gallery objects the same way you work with other frames and their contents.

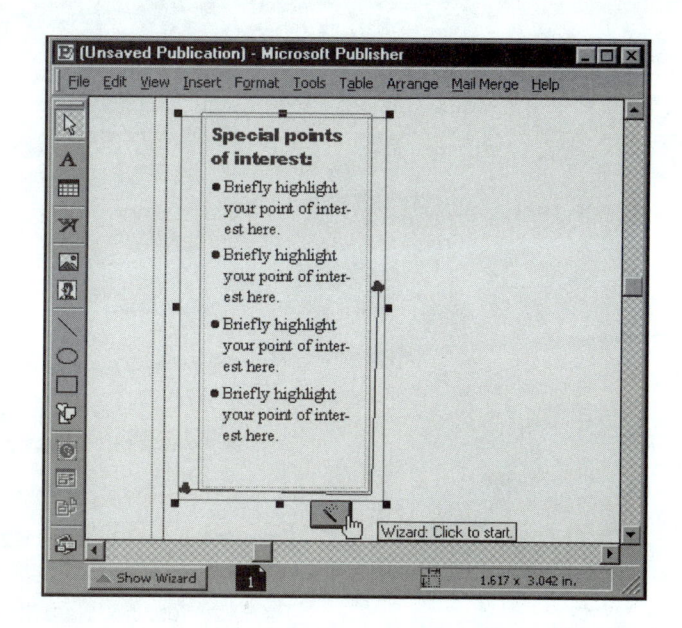

   NOTE: When a Design Gallery object is selected, the Wizard button appears at the bottom of the object.

5 Click **Wizard** to apply a different design to the object, if desired.

6 To change the text in an object, click the sample text and type your own text. See *Type and Edit Text*.

7 To move the object, see *Copy or Move a Frame*.

8 To see the different edits that you can make to an object (such as apply a border or change the frame margins), right-click the object to open a shortcut menu.

   NOTE: What you can do with the object depends on the type of frame that it is in. For example, calendars are set up in table frames, sidebars and pull quotes are in text frames.

167

WordArt: Create a WordArt Picture

Publisher comes with WordArt, a feature that transforms text into graphics.

Insert ➡ Object...

Notes:

- WordArt is a set of tools that you can use to distort, mold, stretch, and otherwise work with text to create a graphic. It is installed with Microsoft Publisher 2000.

1 Click **WordArt Frame Tool** on the Objects toolbar.

2 Drag on the page to create a frame.

3 Release the mouse button when the frame is the size you want.

The Enter Your Text Here dialog box displays. The WordArt toolbar and menu appear in the Publisher window. The WordArt frame is surrounded by a gray border, as shown in the following illustration.

NOTE: Clicking the page outside of the WordArt frame exits WordArt. To re-enter WordArt, double-click the frame.

168

Notes:

- It is easy to accidentally exit WordArt. If you click outside of the WordArt frame, WordArt closes. Double-click the frame to start it again.

4 Type the text that you will work with in WordArt in the Enter Your Text Here dialog box. Press **Enter** to begin text on a new line, if necessary.

5 Click **Insert Symbol...** and select a symbol to insert, if desired.

> NOTE: You can only select from symbols in the current font at this point in the process of creating the picture. To insert symbols from another font, see WordArt: Change Font and Attributes.

6 Click **Update Display**. The text that you typed appears in the WordArt frame in the publication.

7 See *WordArt: Change Font and Attributes* and *WordArt: Mold Text into a Shape* to add special effects.

8 To type different text, repeat steps 4 to 6.

> NOTE: If the Enter Your Text Here dialog box is closed, click **Edit**, **Edit WordArt Text**.

9 When finished creating the picture, click anywhere outside of the WordArt frame.

> NOTE: To open WordArt and edit the picture, double-click the WordArt frame.

169

WordArt: Change Font and Attributes

Change the typeface or the font size, and apply font attributes such as boldfacing and italics to the text in a WordArt picture.

Notes:

- The WordArt toolbar contains tools for changing the font, rotating and aligning text, and setting the amount of space between characters.

- Font and attribute formatting applies to all of the WordArt text. You cannot format individual characters in a WordArt picture.

1. Select a font from the font list.

    NOTE: See WordArt: Create a WordArt Picture *if you have not yet opened WordArt and entered text.*

2. Select a specific font size or else Best Fit from the font size list.

    NOTE: The Best Fit setting sizes text to fit in the frame. This is the default setting.

3. Use the WordArt toolbar to format text:

    - **B** Boldface text

    - *I* Italicize text

    - Ee Make uppercase and lowercase letters the same height, as in the following sign:

    Free Lunch

170

- ◧ Stack letters so that text reads from top to bottom:

Widgets

- ◧ Stretch text left-to-right to fill the frame horizontally
- ◧ Center, left-align, right-align, or justify text
- ◧ Set space between characters
- ◧ Rotate or slant text
- ◧ Apply a pattern such as the following bricks:

FOR SALE

- ◧ Apply a shadow:

Welcome

- ◧ Outline each letter; the following text has a brick pattern with a thin outline around each letter:

FOR SALE

WordArt: Mold Text into a Shape

Form text into different shapes.

Notes:

- Some of these shapes rotate the text. Try out different shapes and see how they look.
- How text wraps into a shape depends on how many lines of text you are working with.

1. Open the shapes list in the WordArt toolbar and select a shape.

   NOTE: See WordArt: Create a WordArt Picture *if you have not yet entered the text to work with.*

2. Click **Format**, **Stretch To Frame** to expand the text to fill the entire WordArt frame, if desired.

   NOTE: Repeat to remove the stretch. When a check mark appears next to the option, the text is stretched.

3 Repeat from step 1 to experiment with different shapes. The following illustration shows some different WordArt shapes.

Crop a Picture

Cropping a picture hides part of it.

Format → Crop Picture

Notes:

- Cropping trims a picture.

- The cropped section remains part of the picture; it is simply hidden. You can uncrop to restore the picture. Repeat the procedure on this page to uncrop. Or, to completely restore the picture to its original condition (uncrops the picture and undoes any resizing), see *Restore a Picture* in the *Scale a Picture* procedure.

1. Click the picture to select it.

2. Click **Crop Picture** on the Formatting toolbar.

   NOTE: *Click **View**, **Toolbars**, **Formatting** to display the Formatting toolbar.*

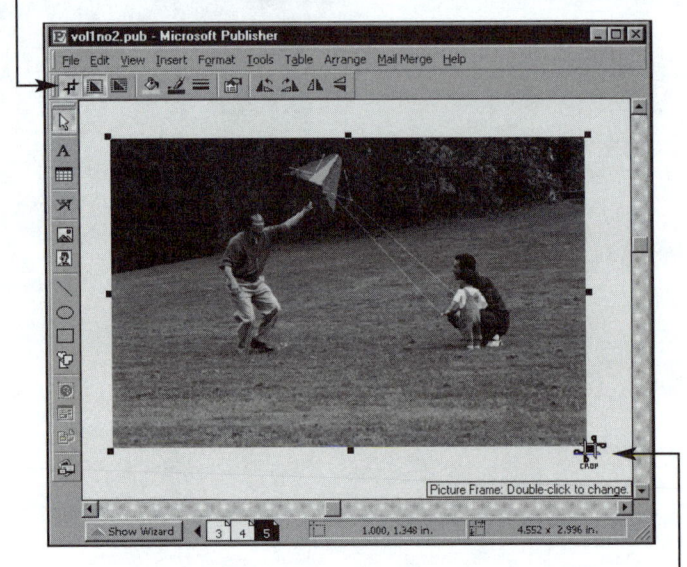

3. Place the pointer over a selection handle. The pointer changes to:

4. To crop multiple sides of the picture at once, hold down the **Ctrl** key.
   - If you crop multiple sides of the picture using a handle on a side of the picture, the picture is cropped from that side and the side opposite it. (For example, if you crop using a handle on the top of the picture, both the top and bottom are cropped.)
   - If you crop multiple sides of the picture using a corner handle, all four corners of the picture are cropped.

174

5 Drag the handle. As you drag, the picture is cropped.

6 If you crop too much, drag in the reverse direction to reveal the trimmed part of the picture.

7 Release the mouse button when finished. In this illustration, the picture has been cropped on three sides to eliminate excess background.

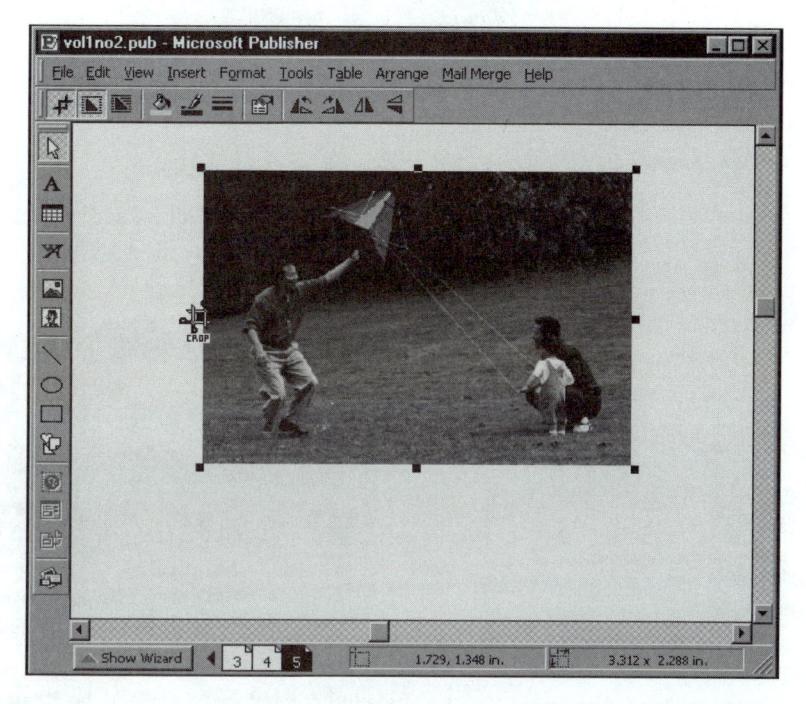

NOTE: To change the picture size, see Scale a Picture *or* Resize a Frame.

Scale a Picture

Resize a picture by entering a percentage of its original size.

Format → Scale Picture...

Notes:

- Use the Scale Picture dialog box to resize a picture by typing a percentage of the original size. The original height and width is 100%. Scaling a picture to 200% doubles its size. Scale to 50% to make it one half its original size.

- To retain the proportions of the original picture, type the same percentage for the picture height and the width.

- You can also resize a picture by resizing the picture frame. See *Resize a Frame*.

1 Select the picture to scale.

2 Click **Format**, **Scale Picture** or **Scale Object** (depending on the frame type). The Scale Picture or Scale Object dialog box displays.

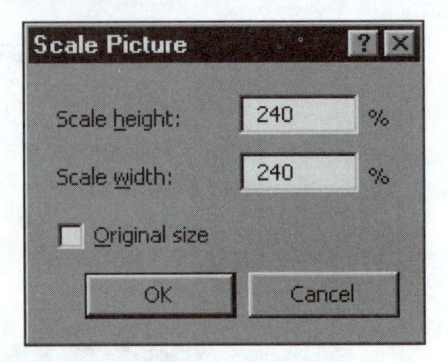

Scale Picture
Scale height: 240 %
Scale width: 240 %
☐ Original size
OK   Cancel

3 Type the percentage to scale in the **Scale height** and **Scale width** text boxes.

4 Click OK.

Restore a Picture

Restore the original size and proportions to a picture that you have resized.

If you have cropped the picture, this procedure unhides the cropped part.

1 Select the picture to restore.

2 Click **Format**, **Scale Picture** or **Scale Object** (depending on the frame type).

3 Click the **Original Size** check box to mark it.

4 Click OK.

176

Frames

Work with frames of all types—text frames, picture frames, WordArt frames, and also table frames. Move, copy, resize, and jazz up frames by adding borders and rotating them.

Apply Line Borders to a Frame

Add line borders of varying width around a text frame or picture frame.

Format ➡ Line/Border Style

Notes:

- See *Apply Table Borders* to apply borders to table cells.

- You specify which sides of the frame to border. For example, you could add borders only at the top and bottom of the frame.

- Publisher has a number of preset line weights (**weight** refers to the thickness of the line) that you can apply. Or, specify the weight by entering the number of points.

- To add other types of lines, such as lines between columns, see *Draw Lines and Arrows*.

1 Click the frame to select it.

2 Click **Format**, **Line/Border Style**, **More Styles**. The Border Style dialog box displays.

   NOTE: To apply standard borders around the entire frame, click one of the line styles on the **Line/Border Style** drop-down menu. You will have more selections in the Border Style dialog box.

3 Click the **Line Border** tab, if necessary.

4 To specify which sides of the frame should have a border, click a side to add or remove borders in the **Select a side** preview pane.

   NOTE: When a side is selected, triangles appear on each end of the line. In the dialog box illustration, only the bottom of the frame will have a border.

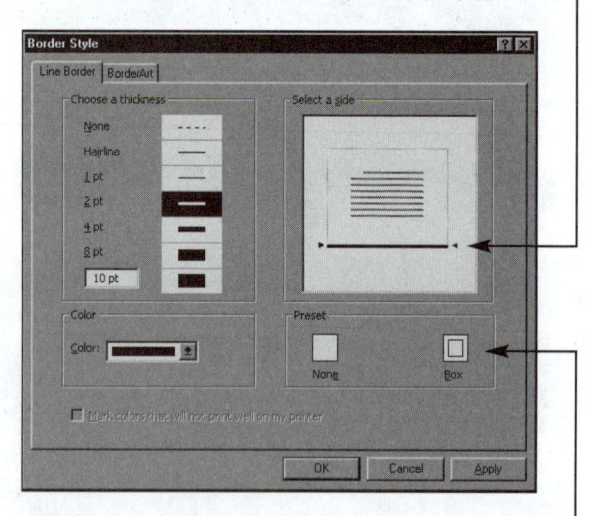

- To select all sides of the frame, select **Box** in the Preset options.

- To remove borders from all sides of the frame, select **None** in the Preset options.

178

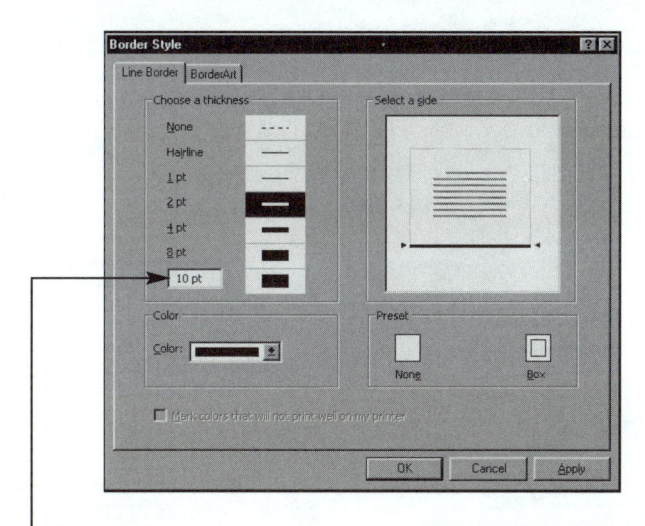

5 Select a preset thickness.

OR

Type the number of points to set the thickness of the line.

6 To apply a different color, select the color from the **Color** drop-down list.

7 Click **OK**.

8 To apply a drop shadow, click the frame to select it and press **Ctrl+D**. The following illustration shows a text frame with a border and drop shadow.

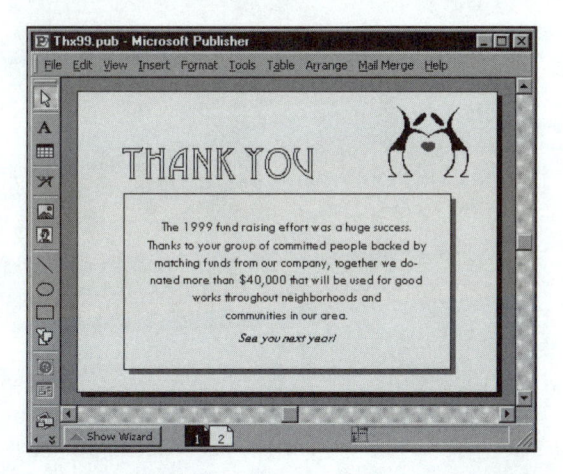

Remove Borders

1 Right-click the frame to open the shortcut menu.

2 Click **Change F_rame**, **Line/_Border Style**, **_None**.

NOTE: To remove a drop shadow, select the frame and press Ctrl+D.

Notes:

- This procedure removes the borders from all sides of a frame.

179

Apply BorderArt Borders

BorderArt borders are made up of pictures. For example, you can add a border consisting of lots of little umbrellas or cats or balloons.

Format ➡ Line/Border Style

Notes:

- You can create some wild effects using BorderArt borders. But be careful that your design does not become too cluttered, unless you are specifically trying to achieve a chaotic, attention-grabbing look.

- BorderArt borders usually work best with titles or other bold text.

1. Click the frame to select it.
2. Click **Format**, **Line/Border Style**, **More Styles**. The Border Style dialog box displays.
3. Click the **BorderArt** tab.
4. Scroll through the list of **Available Borders**.
5. Click the style to apply. The selected style appears in the Preview pane on the right side of the window.
6. Type or select a different **Border size,** if desired. The new size is displayed in the preview pane. See step 7 to retain the proportions of the pictures as you resize.
   - The border size refers to the size of the pictures that comprise the frame, not the size of the frame itself. For example, if the selected border consists of cats, the cats will become smaller or larger when you change the size.
   - To return to the original size, click **Use Default Size**.

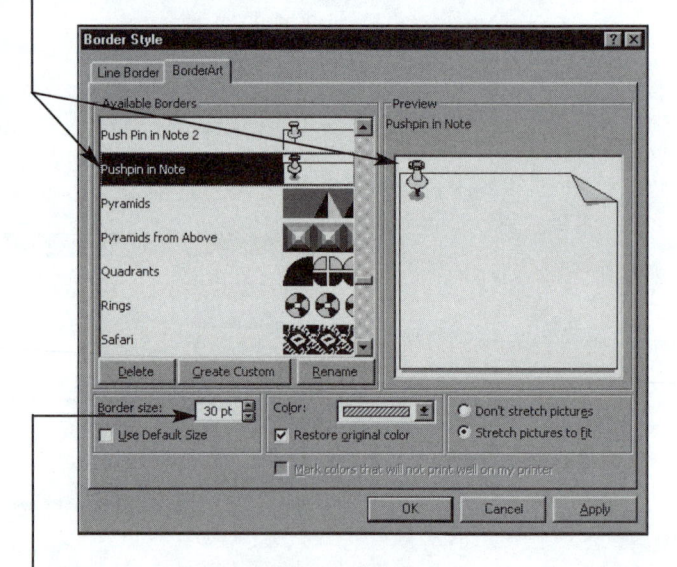

7 If you resize the border (step 6), the shape of the pictures will be distorted if **Stretch pictures to fit** is selected. To prevent this, select **Don't stretch pictures**.

*NOTE: For example, if you enlarge the border, the pictures will become thinner so that they do not touch each other if **Stretch pictures to fit** is selected. If **Don't stretch pictures** is selected, fewer pictures will be used in the border when you make the border size larger. The best way to see how this feature works is to experiment with these two options using various border sizes.*

8 To change the border colors, select from the **Color** list.

*NOTE: To return to the original colors, click **Restore original color**.*

9 To apply the border to the frame without closing the dialog box, click **Apply**.

NOTE: Use this option to experiment with different borders to see how they look in the publication. If the dialog box is in the way, you can move it by dragging the title bar.

10 To apply the border to the frame and close the dialog box, click **OK**.

Rotate a Frame

Rotate a picture, text, drawing object, or table frame.

Arrange → Rotate or Flip

Notes:

- You can rotate objects using tools on the Formatting toolbar or using the Custom Rotate dialog box. If you use the Custom Rotate dialog box, you can see the object rotating on the page. Move the dialog box to see the rotation by dragging its title bar.

- Do not rotate important text in a Web publication. Rotated text frames convert to pictures when you publish the site. Users who disable the display of pictures in order to speed up Internet browsing will not see the text.

Rotate 90 Degrees

1. To display the Formatting toolbar, click **View**, **Toolbars**, **Formatting**.

2. Click the frame to select it.

3. Click **Rotate Right** on the Formatting toolbar

   OR

   Click **Rotate Left** on the Formatting toolbar.

   Publisher rotates the frame 90 degrees to the right or left. The following illustration shows a text frame rotated 90 degrees to the left.

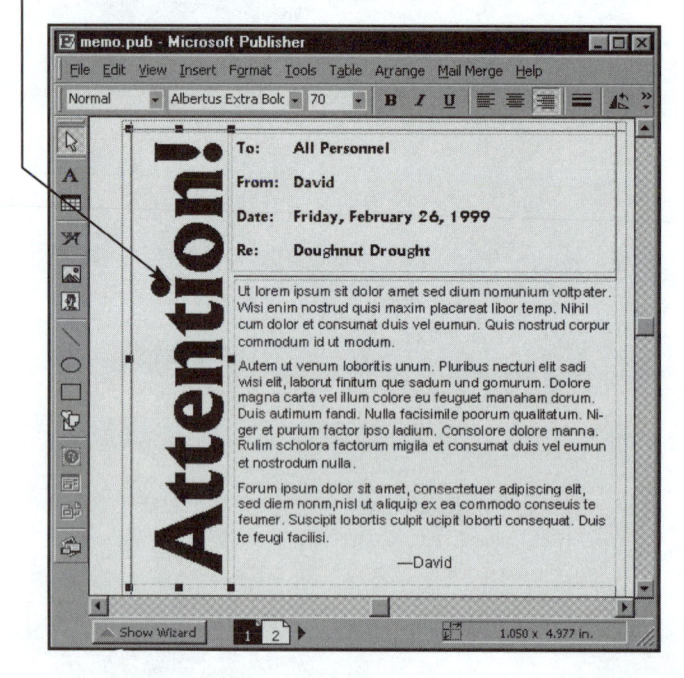

Rotate by Dragging

1 Click the frame to select it.

2 Hold down **Alt**.

3 Place the pointer over a selection handle until it changes to: 🔄

4 Drag to rotate the frame.

Rotate Using the Custom Rotate Dialog Box

1 Click the frame to select it.

2 Click **Custom Rotate** 🔄 in the Standard toolbar. The Custom Rotate dialog box displays.

3 To rotate the frame in increments of 5 degrees in either direction, click a rotate button.

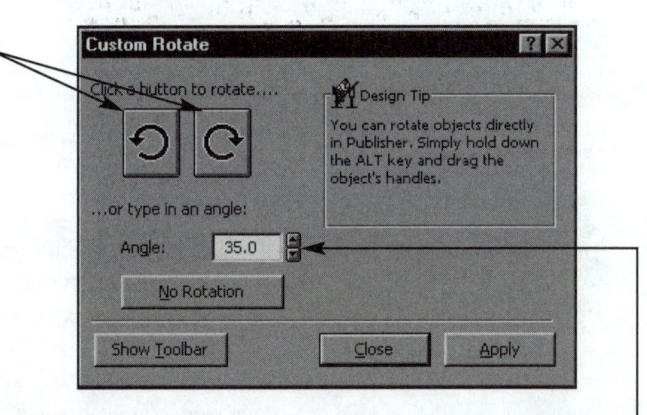

OR

To rotate the frame in increments of one degree, click an **Angle** option arrow button.

OR

Type the number of degrees to rotate the frame in the **Angle** option and click Apply.

OR

To remove rotation and return the object to its original position, click No Rotation.

4 Click Close when finished.

183

Set the Default Formatting for a Frame

Set frames to format automatically with the formatting that you use most often. For example, if you usually apply borders to picture frames, have Publisher automatically apply them to all new picture frames that you create.

[Format]

Notes:

- This procedure sets the default formats of all frames of a particular type, such as picture frames, text frames, or table frames.

- For example, the default margin for text frames is .04". If you usually change the top and bottom margins to 0" whenever you create a new text frame, change the default margin for all text frames to 0". You save time by not having to change the margins each time you create a text frame.

- By default, Publisher formats text in 10-point Times New Roman. To change the default font in text frames, change the font in Normal style. See *Edit a Style*.

- Click the tool on the Objects toolbar for the type of frame that you would like to format:

    - For text frames, click **Text Frame Tool** [A].
    - For tables, click **Table Frame Tool** [⊞].
    - For WordArt objects, click **WordArt Frame Tool** [𝒜].
    - For imported picture frames, click **Picture Frame Tool** [🖼].
    - For clip art, click **Clip Gallery Tool** [🖼].

    NOTE: *Do not create a frame. The pointer changes to ┼ as if you were going to create a frame using the selected tool.*

- Use any command on the **Format** menu that is active (not dimmed) to set default formatting.

    - For example, use the **Frame Properties** command to set margins and other options specific to the type of frame that you are working with, or use the **Line/Border Style** command to apply borders.
    - If a command on the **Format** menu is dimmed, the format cannot be applied to the frame.

- Click **Pointer Tool** [▶] on the Objects toolbar to deactivate the selected frame tool.

    NOTE: *The next time you create a frame of the selected type, your formatting will automatically be applied.*

Select Frames

Before you can format, move, copy, or otherwise work with a frame, you need to select it.

Notes:

- Selecting all objects on the entire page selects all text frames, table frames, picture frames, and drawing objects.

- When a frame or object is selected, square boxes (called selection handles) appear around the edges of the object. A single selected object has black selection handles. When multiple objects are selected, selection handles are gray and the Group Objects button displays.

- The Ungroup Objects button appears when you select a grouped object. See *Group Frames and Objects*.

To select:	Do this:
A single object	Click the object
Multiple objects	Hold down **Shift** and click each object
All objects on the page	Click **Edit**, **Select All**

NOTE: *In Two-Page view, all objects on both pages are selected.*

Objects next to each other	Drag around the objects

Selection handles

Multiple objects are selected so the Group Objects button displays.

NOTE: *If you cannot select an object because it is placed behind another object, you need to move objects in the stack. Select the top object and click **Arrange**, **Send Backward**. Repeat until you can access the object.*

185

Copy or Move a Frame

Copy and move frames and other objects within a publication.

Edit → Copy / Cut

Notes:

- Use this procedure to move the frame or object to a page that is visible in the window.
- To move in small increments, nudge the object.
- If a Snap To feature is enabled, the frame or object will be pulled to the nearest ruler mark, guide, or object. See *Snap to Guides and Objects*.

1 Click the frame or object to select it.
2 Place the mouse pointer over a boundary until it changes to:
3 To move in a straight line, hold down **Shift**.
4 Drag to the new position.
5 Release the **Shift** key.
6 Release the mouse button.

Copy/Move a Frame

The copy is placed on top of the original.

1 Click the frame or object to select it.
2 Press **Ctrl+C** to copy the frame.

   OR

   Press **Ctrl+X** to move the frame.
3 Press **Ctrl+V**.

Notes:

- Place the frame or object in the scratch area, then switch to the page that you want to move it to.

Move a Frame to Another Page

1 Click the frame or object to select it.
2 Place the mouse pointer over a boundary until it changes to:

3   Drag the picture off the page to the scratch area, as shown in the following illustration.

4   Click the icon in the status bar to go to a different page.

    OR

    Press **Ctrl+G** and type the page number to go to.
    Press **Enter**.

5   Drag the picture from the scratch area to the page.

Notes:

- It is difficult to move a frame small distances using the mouse. Nudging moves a frame or object in small increments.

- By default, each time you nudge, the frame or object is moved .13". You can adjust this amount.

Nudge a Frame

1   Select the frame.

2   Hold down the **Alt** key.

3   Press an arrow directional key.

    NOTE: To adjust the amount that objects are moved when you nudge them or to use a dialog box to nudge the selected object, click **A̱rrange**, **N̰udge**.

187

Resize a Frame

Change the size of a frame. Resizing a picture frame changes the size of the picture.

Format ➔ Size and Position...

Notes:

- Drag to resize an object when you want to line it up with boundaries on the page.

- If a Snap To feature is enabled, the frame jumps to the nearest guide or object when you resize it. See *Snap to Guides and Objects*.

- If you resize a frame containing a graphic, including WordArt and clip art graphics, the graphic is resized along with the frame.

- If you resize a text frame, the font size of the text changes if automatic copyfitting is enabled for the text frame. See *Fit Text in a Frame*.

- If you resize a grouped object, all objects in the group are resized. See *Group Frames and Objects*.

Resize by Dragging

1 Click the frame or object to select it.

2 Place the mouse pointer over a selection handle until it changes to the resize pointer.

NOTE: To proportionally resize the height and width at the same time, place the mouse pointer over a handle on one of the corners of the frame or object. Place the pointer on a handle on the side to change only the width. Top or bottom handles will change only the height.

3 To resize proportionally, hold down the **Shift** key.

NOTE: If you selected a corner handle, you do not need to hold down **Shift**. The object will be sized proportionately as you drag.

4 Drag to resize.

5 Release the mouse button and the **Shift** key when the object is the size you want.

Notes:

- When you know exactly what size the picture should be, enter the measurements in the Size and Position dialog box.

- To see the size of an object in the Publisher window, select the object. The object measurements are displayed in the lower-right corner of the status bar.

Resize by Typing Measurements

1 Select the picture to resize.

2 Click **Format**, **Size and Position**. The Size and Position dialog box opens.

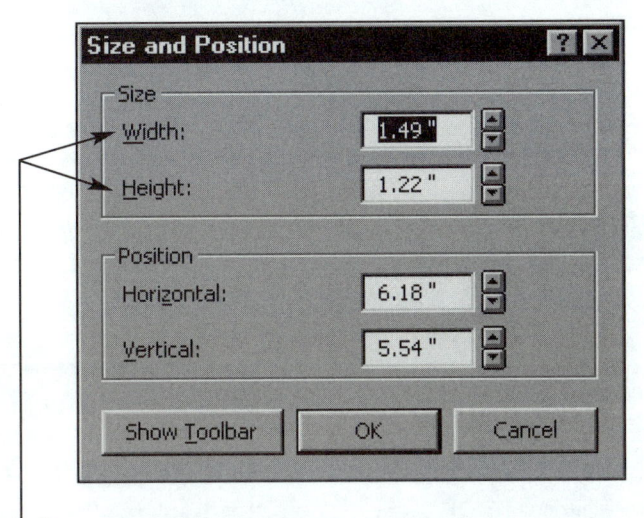

3 Type or select the **Width** and/or **Height** measurements.

4 Click OK.

189

Line Up Frames

Use this procedure to line up a group of frames at the top, bottom, left, or right boundaries of the page. You can also line them up with a margin or center a frame in the middle of the page.

Arrange → Align Objects...

Notes:

- Use this procedure to line up frames in a row or column.
- You can use this procedure to place a single frame in the center of the page.
- You can also add a ruler guide and then drag each frame to the guide. See *Add Ruler Guides.*

1. Select the frame(s) to line up. The following illustration shows a number of text and picture frames. To clean up this page, start by selecting the picture frames at the top of the page.

2. Click **Arrange**, **Align Objects**. The Align Objects dialog box displays.
   - Click a **Left to right** option to line up objects horizontally across the page.

     NOTE: *The **Centers** option places the selected frame(s) in the center of the page. You can use this option to center a frame between the left and right margins.*

190

- Click a **Top to bottom** option to line up objects vertically.

    NOTE: The **Centers** option places the selected frame(s) in the center of the page. You can use this option to center a frame between the top and bottom margins.

- Click **Align along margins** to line up frames with a margin. This lines up the frames along the margin guide.

    NOTE: In the illustration below, the row of picture frames is lined up with the top margin. The text frames are not all placed against a margin so you would not use the margins to line them up.

3. Click [Apply] to see how the selected options line up the frames in the publication.

    - If the dialog box is in the way, drag it by the title bar to move it.
    - If you do not like the way frames are lined up, click the **No change** option and repeat step 6.

4. Click [OK].

    The following illustration shows pictures and text frames lined up. First the row of picture frames were lined up top to bottom at their top edges along the margin. Then, the text frames were lined up top to bottom at their top edges.

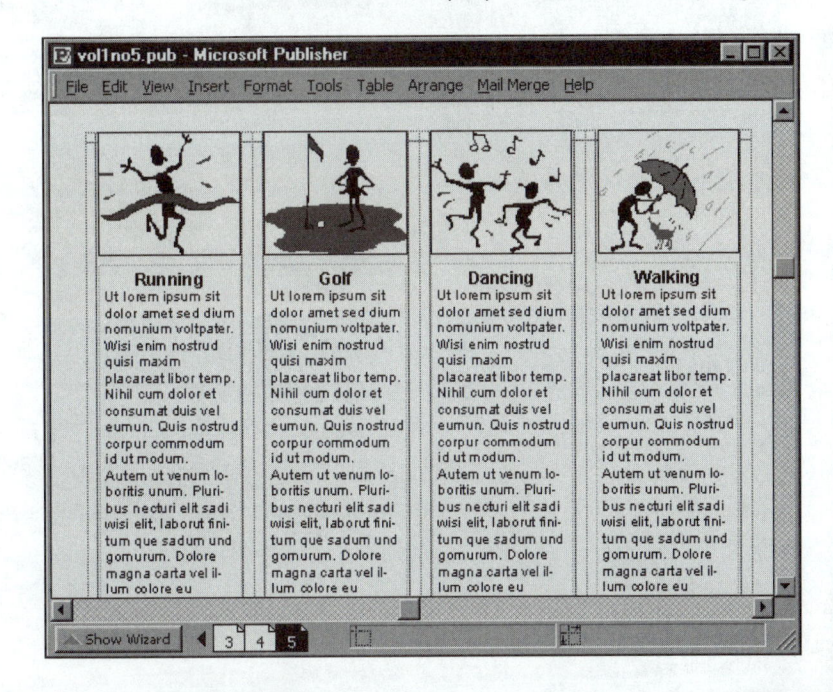

191

Group Frames and Objects

Combine multiple frames and/or drawing objects into a group to work with all of the items at the same time.

Notes:

- A grouped object is treated as a single item. When you move, resize, or otherwise edit a grouped object, all of the objects within the group are changed.

- Group frames and objects when you want them to stay together. For example, if you group a picture frame and the text frame containing its caption, the caption stays with the picture when you move the picture frame.

- You can work with the individual items in a grouped object to some extent. For example, you can edit text in a text frame that is grouped. However, you cannot apply formatting, such as changing the border of a frame, in the group. You must first ungroup the object to edit it. See *Ungroup Objects* on the next page.

- You can group different types of objects. For example, you can group a picture frame, text frames containing callout text, and callout lines.

Arrange → Group Objects

1 To select each object that will be included in the group, hold down the **Shift** key and click each object.

When multiple objects are selected, the handles around each object are gray instead of black and the **Group Objects** button appears.

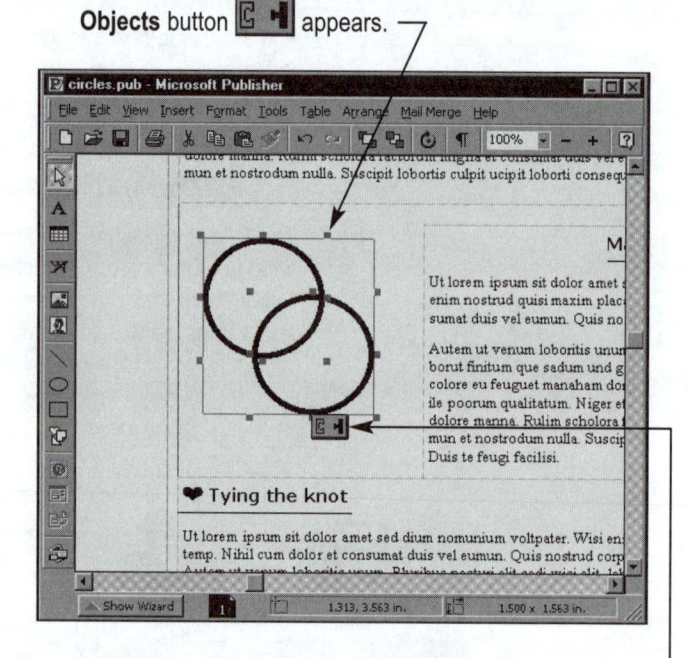

2 Click the **Group Objects** button. The objects are now grouped into a single object.

When a grouped object is selected, the handles around the object are black (instead of gray). In addition, the **Ungroup Objects** button appears, as in the illustration on the next page.

Notes:

- Publisher remembers the original grouped items. You can divide the group back into its individual, separate frames and objects.

- When you ungroup a grouped object, each frame and object in the group becomes a single, separate object.

Ungroup Objects

1 Click the grouped object to select it.

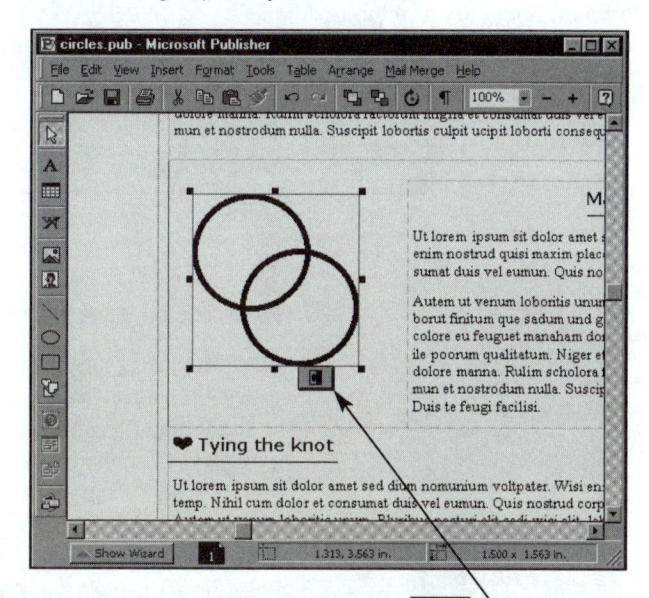

2 Click the **Ungroup Objects** button.

193

Change Frame Margins

Every frame has margins that you can set to adjust the amount of white space between the frame boundary and the text.

Format → Text Frame Properties...

Notes:

- By default, the margins for picture frames are 0" so that there is no white space between a picture and its frame.

- By default, the margins for text frames are .04" on each side of the frame.

- To change the default margins for all new frames of a particular type, see *Set the Default Formatting for a Frame*.

1. Right-click the frame to format.

2. Click **Change Frame**, **Picture Frame Properties**. The Frame Properties dialog box displays.
   - The **Frame Properties** command name varies depending on the frame type. For example, it might be **Text Frame Properties** or **Picture Frame Properties**.
   - Options on the Frame Properties dialog box differ depending on the type of frame you are formatting. The following illustration shows the Picture Frame Properties dialog box.

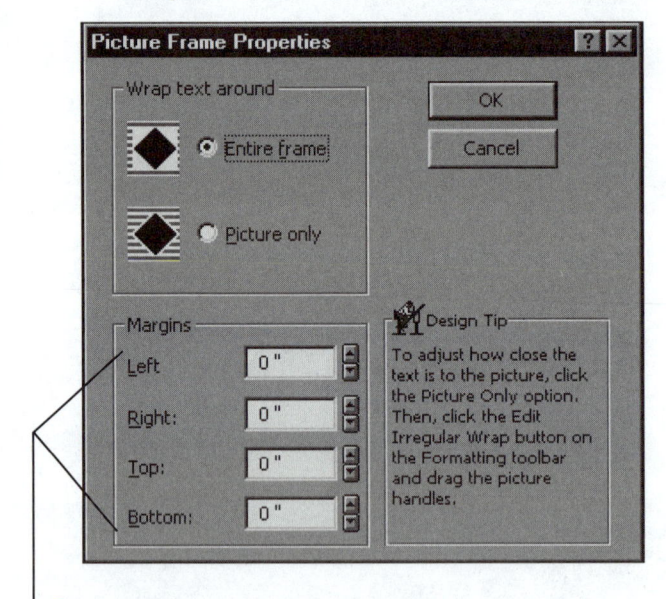

3. Type or select new margin measurements, as desired.

4. Click OK.

194

Tables

Use tables to set up side-by-side paragraphs where information is organized in columns and rows. Tables are placed in table frames, which you can work with like any other frame.

Create a Table

Specify the size and the number of rows and columns to include, and select a preset format for a new table.

Notes:

- When you create a table you can select a preset format which might apply borders, fills, and other formatting to the new table.
- Tables are placed in a table frame.
- When you first create a table, it has columns of equal width. See *Change Column Width or Row Height* to create columns of unequal width.
- See *Enter Text in a Table* for tips on adding and editing table text.

1. Click **Table Frame Tool** on the Objects toolbar. When you place the pointer on the page, it changes shape to: ┼

2. Drag on the page to create a frame the size you will want the table to be. When you release the mouse button, the Create Table dialog box displays.

3. Type or select the **Number of rows** for the table.

   NOTE: When you calculate how many rows you need, add an extra row for column headings if necessary. If you are not sure how many rows you need, you can add more later.

4. Type or select the **Number of columns** for the table.

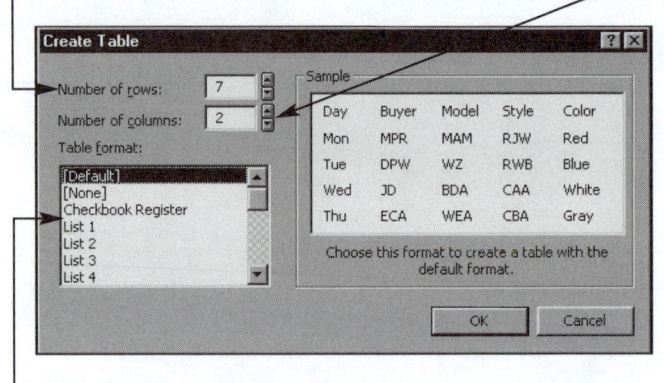

5. Click a preset **Table format** or click **[None]** to create a plain table without formatting. A sample of the selected format appears in the Sample pane.

   NOTE: To set up the formatting for the [Default] option, see Set the Default Formatting for a Frame.

6. Click **OK** to close the dialog box.

If you specified more rows or columns than will fit in the table frame, Publisher displays the following prompt.

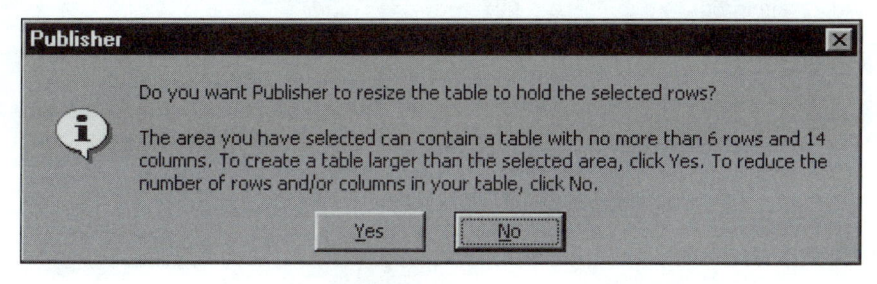

Publisher

Do you want Publisher to resize the table to hold the selected rows?

The area you have selected can contain a table with no more than 6 rows and 14 columns. To create a table larger than the selected area, click Yes. To reduce the number of rows and/or columns in your table, click No.

[Yes]   [No]

Click [Yes] to have Publisher resize the table to fit the number of rows or columns you specified.

OR

Click [No] to return to the Create Table dialog box, where you can enter fewer rows or columns.

Publisher creates the table, as in the following illustration. Gridlines (dotted lines) define each cell. The insertion point is located in the top left cell. When a table is active, it shows buttons at the top of each column and left of each row. Clicking these buttons selects columns and rows.

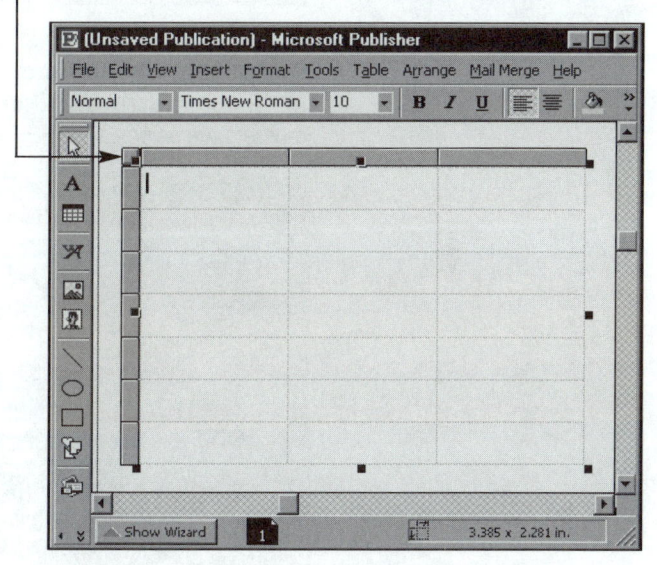

> **Notes:**
> - Monthly calendars are created using tables. The Design Gallery has some calendars that you can insert in your publication. See *Insert a Design Gallery Object*.

*NOTE: If you do not see table gridlines, click **View**, **Show Boundaries and Guides**.*

Apply Table Borders

Add printing borders to make a table easier to read.

Format → Line/Border Style

Notes:

- A table frame has gridlines (dotted lines) that define each cell. However, cell gridlines do not print. Use this procedure to add borders to print.

- The thickness of a line is also called the **weight**. For example, a thicker line has a heavier weight.

1. Select the cell(s) to format.

2. Click **Format**, **Line/Border Style**.

   NOTE: To apply a border of equal thickness around all sides of the selected cell(s), click the border to apply in the menu and skip the remainder of this procedure.

3. Click **More Styles**.

4. To apply, remove, or change the weight of one side of selected cells, click the gridline to format. To select additional sides, hold down **Shift** and click the next gridline.

   Triangular handles appear on both ends of a selected gridline. In the following illustration, the top and bottom borders are selected.

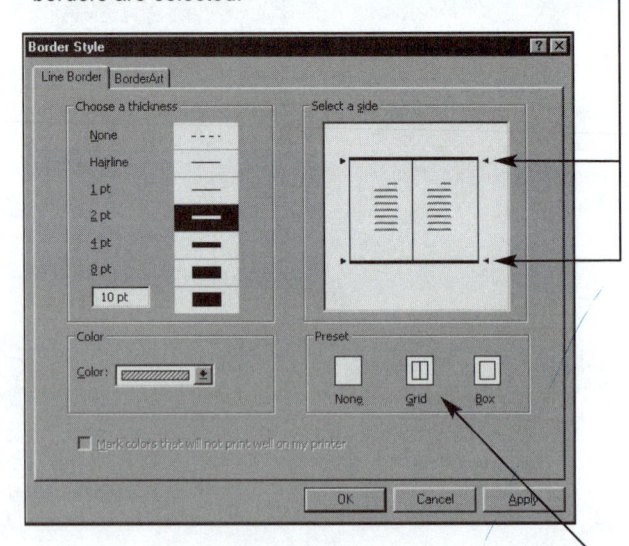

   - To apply borders around all selected cells, click **Grid**.

     NOTE: The following table is formatted with a grid border. Heavier lines were applied separately to the top and bottom gridlines of the top row.

198

Notes:

- Before you apply borders, you select the cells to format. See *Select in a Table* for help.

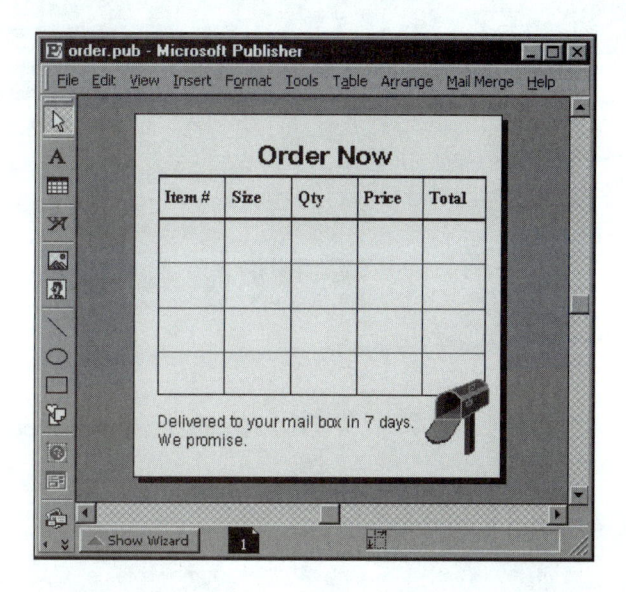

- To apply borders around the outside of the selected cells, click **Box**.

5 Click the thickness of the border to apply.

OR

Type the number of points to specify the line thickness.

6 Select a color to apply, if desired.

7 To apply different borders to different sides of the selected cells, repeat from step 4 as necessary.

8 Click **OK** to close the dialog box.

Remove Borders

Remove all borders or individual borders from selected cells.

1 Select cells to format.

2 Click **Line/Border Style** on the Formatting toolbar.

3 Click **More Styles**.

4 Click the gridline for the border to remove and click **None** under the line thickness options.

OR

To remove all borders, click **None** from the Preset options at the bottom of the dialog box.

5 Click **OK** to close the dialog box.

199

Shade Cell Backgrounds

Shade or color the background of cells to emphasize cell content.

Format → Fill Color

Notes:

- If you are printing in black and white, choose a pale grey background. Pick a light shade so that it is easy to read text in the cell.

- Background shading is often used for table titles. For example, you could apply a black background and set the color of the text to white. To change text color, see *Format Characters*.

1. Select the cell(s) to shade.
2. Click **Format**, **Fill Color**, **More Colors**.
3. Click a color to apply.
4. To see how the selected color will look in the table, click Apply.

   NOTE: *If the Colors dialog box is in the way of the table, drag the title bar to move it.*

5. Click OK to apply the color and close the dialog box.

   The following illustration shows a table that uses background shading to emphasize the highest numbers in a table.

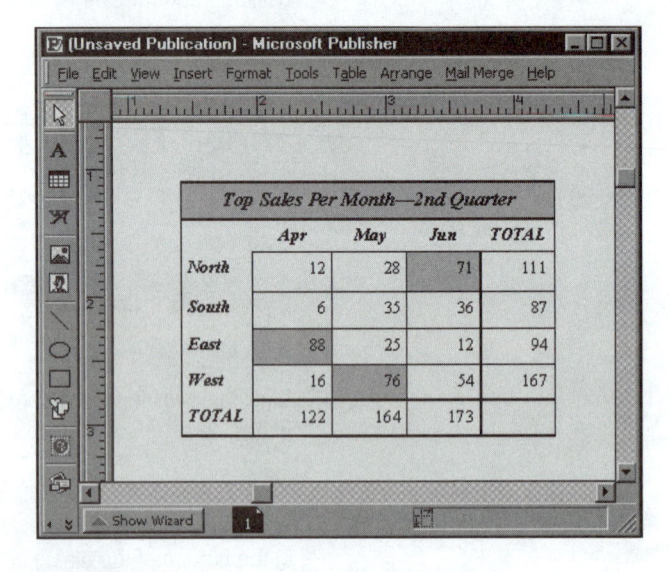

   Top Sales Per Month—2nd Quarter

	Apr	May	Jun	TOTAL
North	12	28	71	111
South	6	35	36	87
East	88	25	12	94
West	16	76	54	167
TOTAL	122	164	173	

Apply a Fill Using the Formatting Toolbar

The Fill Color tool includes a few standard colors that you can quickly apply to selected cells.

1 Select the cell(s) to fill.

2 Click **Fill Color** on the Formatting toolbar.

   NOTE: *If the Formatting toolbar is not displayed, click* **View**, **Toolbars**, **Formatting**.

3 Select a color from the drop-down menu.

   In the following table, the cells in the top row have been merged to create a row of one cell for the title (see *Merge Cells*). The top row is formatted with a black background fill.

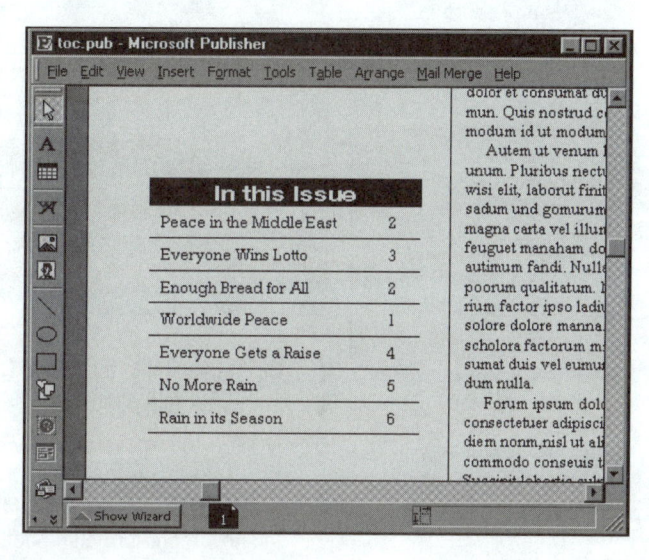

Notes:

- If you want selected cells to be transparent, press **Ctrl+T** after removing the fill. When cells are transparent you can see layout guides and other objects placed under the table.

Remove a Fill

Delete the fill from selected cells. Cell background will be white.

1 Select the cell(s) to format.

2 Click **Fill Color** on the Formatting toolbar.

3 Click **No Fill**.

Apply a Preset Table Format

Preset table formats, called AutoFormats, include fills and borders. Apply a preset format to quickly format a table.

T<u>a</u>ble ➡ Table Auto<u>F</u>ormat...

Notes:

- When you create a table you can select from a number of preset table formats. Use this procedure to apply a format to an existing table.

- You can specify which of the formats included in the AutoFormat to apply. For example, you might apply all formats in a particular AutoFormat except for cell shading.

- After you apply an AutoFormat, you can customize the formatting in the table. For example, you might change the shade of a fill or change the thickness of a border.

1 Click the table to select it.

2 Click T<u>a</u>ble, Table Auto<u>F</u>ormat. The Auto Format dialog box displays.

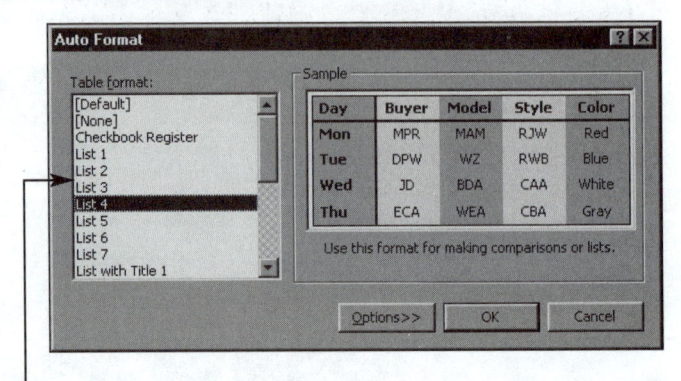

3 Click a format in the **Table format** list to view an example in the Sample pane.

NOTE: To remove an AutoFormat, click [None].

4 Click <u>O</u>ptions>> to expand the Auto Format dialog box to show more formatting options.

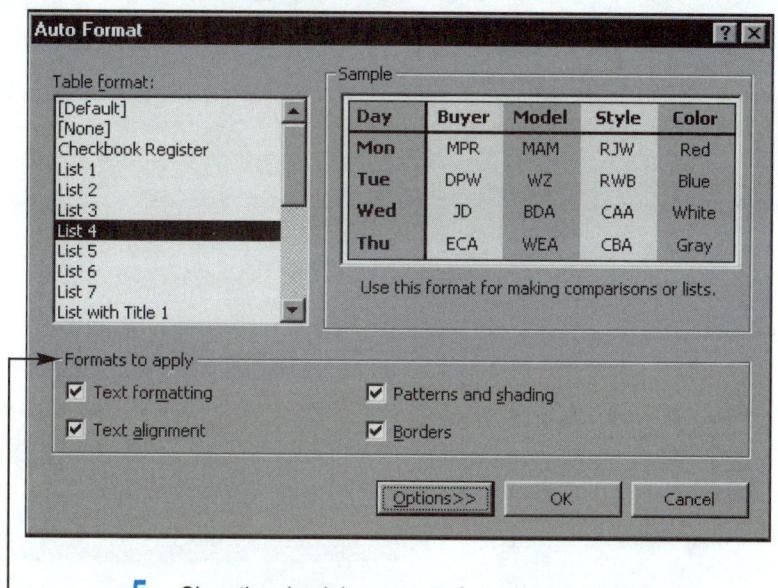

5 Clear the check box next to formats that you do not want applied.

6 Click **OK** to apply formatting.

Copy Cell Formatting

1 Select the cell with formatting you wish to copy.

2 Click **Format**, **Pick Up Formatting**.

3 Select cell(s) to format.

4 Click **Format**, **Apply Formatting**.

Notes:

- This procedure copies all of the formatting for a cell, including borders, shading, and cell margins.

203

Change Column Width or Row Height

When you create a table, all columns are the same width and all rows are the same height. Use this procedure to resize rows and/or columns.

Notes:

- You resize a column or row in one of two ways. You can resize the table so that it adjusts to the new column width or row height. For example, if you expand a column or row, the table will be larger. Or, you can have the size of surrounding columns and rows adjust so that the table stays the same size.

- The row height expands automatically to fit text that you enter in a cell. The height of the rows will be as large as that of the cell in the row with the most amount of text. To prevent the row from expanding to accommodate text, see *Lock the Row Height* on the next page.

1. To resize multiple columns or rows, select them.

2. To change the column width, place the mouse pointer on the border of the column. If multiple columns are selected, place the pointer on the border of any of the selected columns. The pointer changes to: ⇔ADJUST

OR

To change the row height, place the mouse pointer on the border of the row to resize. If multiple rows are selected, place the pointer on the border of any of the selected rows. The pointer changes to: ⇕ADJUST

3. To resize without changing the size of the entire table, press **Shift**.

4. Drag to resize.

Following is a table with varying column widths created for a table of contents. The columns with titles are wider than the columns with page numbers.

Notes:

- When you type text in a cell, the row height automatically expands to fit all text that you enter. To prevent this, lock the row height.

- If the row height is locked, you can fit text by using a smaller font size. Also try reducing the size of cell margins.

- When you type more text than will fit in a cell in a locked table, the text is in the table cell but is not visible.

Notes:

- By default, cells have a .04" margin all the way around the cell.

Lock the Row Height

1. Click the table to select it.
2. Click **T**a**ble**, **G**r**ow to Fit Text** to deselect the option.

Change Cell Margins

Changing cell margins adjusts the amount of white space between the text in a cell and the cell boundaries.

1. Select the cell(s) to format.
2. Click **F**o**rmat**, **Table Cell Prop**e**rties**.

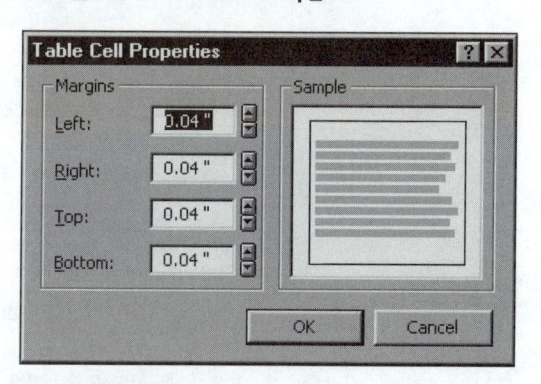

3. Type or select new margin measurements, as desired.
4. Click **OK** to close the dialog box.

205

Insert or Delete Columns or Rows

Add or remove columns and/or rows in a table.

Table ➡ Insert Rows or Columns... / Delete Rows or Columns...

Notes:

- Adding rows or columns changes the size of the table. The table expands to accommodate the new cells.

- Use this procedure to add multiple columns and rows before or after the current cell.

Insert Columns and Rows

1. Click a cell in a column or row adjacent to where you will insert the new columns or rows.

2. Click **Table**, **Insert Rows or Columns**. The Insert dialog box displays.

3. Specify whether to add **Rows** or **Columns**.

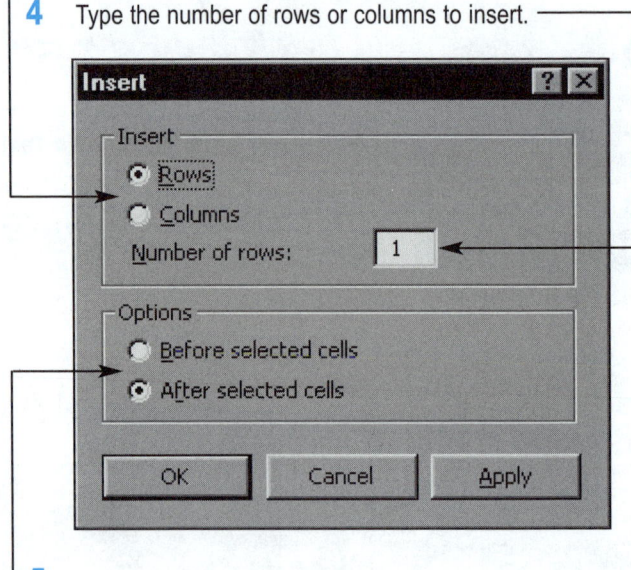

4. Type the number of rows or columns to insert.

5. Select to insert new cells before or after the current cell.

6. Click **Apply** to view the change in the table in the publication, if desired.

    NOTE: Drag the dialog box by the title bar if it is in the way.

7. Click **OK**.

206

Notes:

- To add a new row when you are editing text, press **Tab** from the last cell in the table.

Quickly Insert One or a Few Columns or Rows

Adding rows or columns changes the size of the table. The table expands to accommodate the new cells. The width of a new column will be the same as the width of the column to the right of the selected column. The height of a new row will be the same as the height of the row beneath the selected rows.

1. Select one or more columns that will appear to the left of new column(s).

   OR

   Select one or more rows that will appear above the new row(s).

   NOTE: *Select as many columns or rows as you would like to insert. For example, to insert two rows, select two rows.*

2. Click T**a**ble.

3. Click **I**nsert Columns or **I**nsert Rows.

   - Publisher inserts new columns to the right of the selected columns or new rows beneath the selected rows.
   - To add many columns or rows, use the Insert dialog box. Click T**a**ble, **I**nsert Rows or Columns.

Notes:

- Deleting columns or rows changes the size of the table. The table will be smaller.

Delete Columns or Rows

1. Select column(s) or row(s) to delete.

2. Click T**a**ble.

3. Click **D**elete Columns or **D**elete Rows.

   NOTE: *To undo the deletion, press* **Ctrl+Z** *before you do anything else in the publication.*

207

Merge Cells

Combine multiple cells into a single cell.

Table → Merge Cells

Notes:

- The merge feature is often used to merge all cells in a row in order to center a title over a table.
- You cannot merge the cells in a column. Cells must be in the same row in order to merge them.

1. Select the cells to combine.
2. Click **Table**, **Merge Cells**. Two of the rows in the following illustration are merged into single cells.

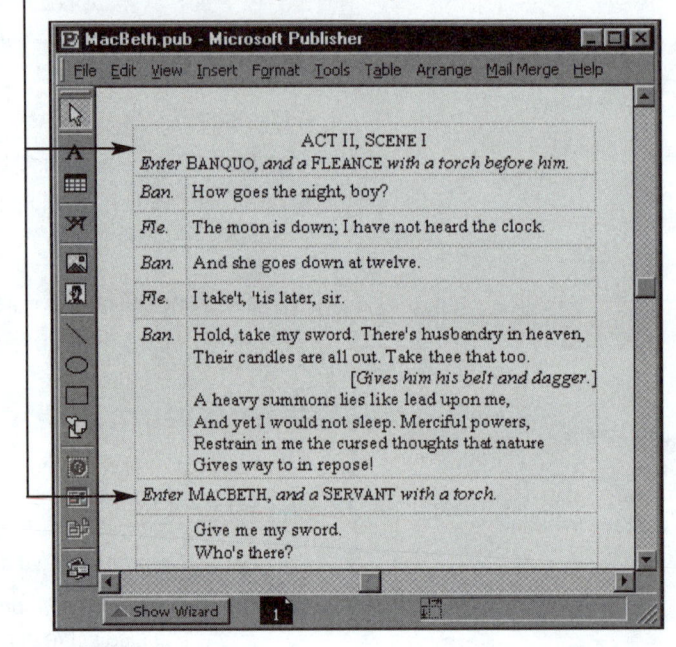

Notes:

- You can only split cells that have previously been merged. Publisher remembers which cells were merged and splits them into the original number of cells.

Split Merged Cells

1. Select the merged cell.
2. Click **Table**, **Split Cells**.

208

Enter Text in a Table

Type and edit text in table cells.

Notes:

- To select the contents of a cell, see *Select in a Table*.

- You can add a picture to a table cell by creating a picture frame the size of the cell and placing it over the cell. The picture is not actually in the cell; it is on top of it. To store the picture with the table, group the table and the picture frame. See *Group Frames and Objects*.

- Format text as you would in a text frame. Use the procedures in the **Format Table** section.

- Use the Fill feature to copy the contents of a cell into cells to the right of it (across the row) or into cells beneath it (down a column).

- Existing text in the cells you are copying to will be replaced.

1. Type text in the first cell of the table.
   - To delete the selected text or the current character, press **Delete**.
   - To delete the previous character, press **Backspace**.

2. Press **Tab** to move to the next cell.
   - Pressing **Tab** at the end of a row moves the insertion point to the next row.
   - Pressing **Tab** at the last cell in the table inserts a new row.
   - Press **Shift+Tab** to return to the previous cell.
   - Click in any cell to go to that cell. The insertion point will be active.

3. Repeat steps 1 and 2 to add text to the table.

Copy Text Across a Row or Down a Column

1. Select the cells containing the text to copy and the cells where you will copy to.

2. Click T**a**ble.

3. Click **Fill Down** to copy the data from the top selected cell to the remaining selected cells in a column.

   OR

   Click **Fill Right** to copy the data from the leftmost selected cell to the remaining selected cells in a row.

209

Select in a Table

To work with specific columns, rows, or cells in a table, you first need to select them.

Notes:

- Selected cells are darkened.
- When you select, the cell pointer changes to:

- To select a column, click the button at the top of the column.

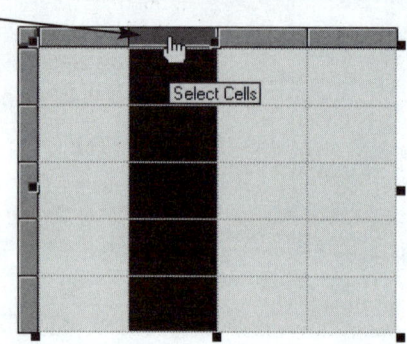

- To select multiple columns, drag across column buttons.
- To select a row, click the button to the left of the row.

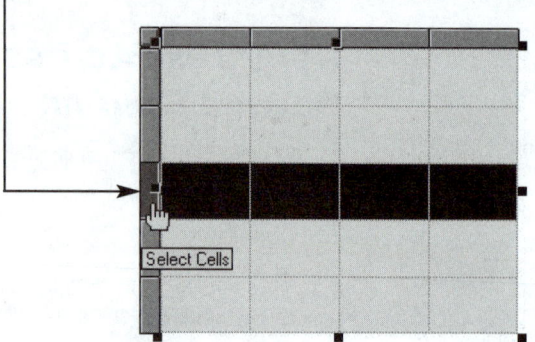

- To select multiple rows, drag across row buttons.
- To select the current cell, press **Ctrl+A**.

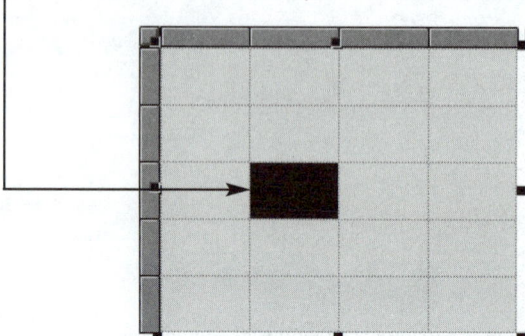

210

- To select individual cells, drag across cells to select.
- To select all cells in the table, click the button at the intersection of the columns and rows.

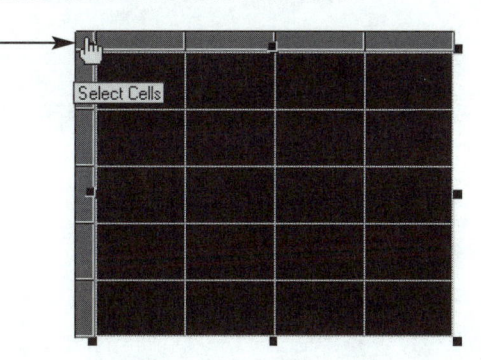

Select Text in a Cell

To select:	Do this:
A word	Double-click the word
Any text	Drag across text OR Click first character, **Shift**+click last character
From the insertion point to the end of the text in the cell	**Shift+End**
From the insertion point to the beginning of the text in the cell	**Shift+End**
All text in the cell	**Ctrl+A**
Character-by-character or line-by-line	**Shift**+arrow keys

Mail Merge

Merge a file of names and addresses with a publication to create documents for mass mailings. For example, you might print a letter and envelope for each of your clients notifying them of a change of address. Publisher will create an envelope and a letter for every client in your address list. Each envelope and letter will include the client name and address.

Create an Address List

If you do not have an existing list of names and addresses to merge, you can create one in Publisher. If you already have an address list, this section includes a list of file formats that you can use with Publisher.

Mail Merge → Create Publisher Address List...

1 Click **Mail Merge**, **Create Publisher Address List**.

2 Fill in the fields with information for one name and address.

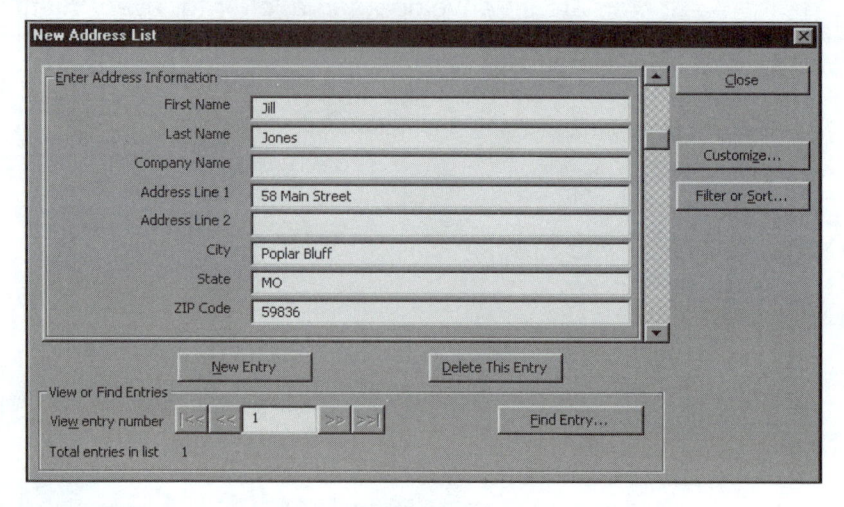

NOTE: Click the scroll bar to display more fields.

Notes:

- Publisher stores the address list in Microsoft Access (database) file format. If you have Access installed, you can use it to work in the file.

- The address list is called the **data source** in Publisher mail merge operations. It contains the names and addresses that will be merged with the publication.

3 Click **New Entry**.

4 Add the next name and address.

5 Repeat steps 3 and 4 to create your address list.

6 Click **Close** to display the Save As dialog box.

NOTE: The Save As dialog box only displays the first time you save the address list.

214

7 Display the folder in which to save the address list file in the **Save in** list.

```
Save As
Save in: [Project X]              clients.mdb
File name: clients.mdb                    Save
Save as type: Microsoft Publisher address lists   Cancel
```

8 Type a name for the address list. Publisher includes the .mdb Microsoft Access extension.

9 Click [**Save**].

*NOTE: To open the address list to edit names and addresses, click **Mail Merge**, **Edit Publisher Address List**.*

Data Source File Formats Publisher Can Use

You can use address lists created in any of the programs listed here.

- Microsoft Access (all versions)
- Microsoft Excel versions 3.0, 4.0, 5.0, 7.0, and 8.0
- Microsoft FoxPro 2.0, 2.5, and 2.6
- Microsoft Outlook (all versions)
- Microsoft Word tables or data documents
- Microsoft Works (database cannot contain formulas)
- dBase III, IV, and V
- Delimited ASCII text files (not files with fixed-width fields)

Sort an Address List

Sorting an address list alphabetizes it in a particular order, such as by last name or by state.

Mail Merge → Edit Publisher Address List...

Notes:

- Publisher merges publications in the order in which names appear in the address list. If you want to merge names and addresses in a particular order, sort the address list in that order. For example, to print labels in ZIP Code order, sort the list by ZIP Code.

- You can sort in either ascending (a to z) or descending (z to a) order.

- If you are using an address list created in a separate program, use that program to sort the data source file.

1. Click **Mail Merge**, **Edit Publisher Address List**. The Open Address List dialog box displays.

2. Double-click the address list file to open it.

3. Click **Filter or Sort...** to display the Filtering and Sorting dialog box.

4. Click the **Sort** tab.

5. Select the field to sort by.

6. Select **Ascending** or **Descending** order.

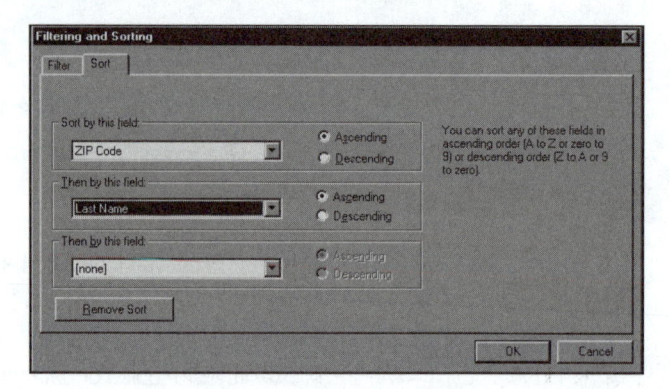

7. If desired, select more fields to sort by.

   NOTE: In the above dialog box, addresses are sorted by ZIP Code. Within each ZIP Code, addresses are grouped by last name.

8. Click **OK** to close the Filtering and Sorting dialog box.

9. Click **Close** to close the address list.

Continue →

Merge an Address List with a Publication

Combine information from the address list with a publication. For example, print addresses on publications that you will mail, such as postcards, flyers, form letters, mailing labels, and envelopes.

Mail Merge ➡ Merge

Notes:
- First, create the publication with which you will merge the address list. See *Create a Publication Using a Wizard* or *Create a Blank Publication*.
- You must have a file with names and addresses to merge with the publication. This file is called an **address list** or **data source**. See *Create an Address List*.

1. Open the publication.
2. To attach a data source (address list) to the publication:
   a. Create a text frame in the publication where you will place names and addresses. See *Create a Text Frame*.
   b. Click the text frame to select it.
   c. Click **Mail Merge**, **Open Data Source**. The Open Data Source dialog box displays.
   d. Click **Merge information from an Outlook contact list**. Publisher locates your Outlook contact list. If Outlook is not currently running or if you have multiple contact lists, Publisher will prompt you for information.
   OR
   Click **Merge information from another type of file** to use a Publisher address list or a file created in another program. Double-click the data source file to use.
   NOTE: You only have to attach a data source to the publication once. After that, whenever you open the file and merge, Publisher will know which data source to use.
3. Use the Insert Fields dialog box to add fields from the data source to the publication:
   a. Click a field to add.
      NOTE: Add fields in the order in which they will appear in the publication.

Notes:

- Publisher merges records in the order in which they appear in the data source. Sort the address list so that names and addresses appear in the order in which you want to merge them. For example, sort by ZIP Code or by last name to merge in that order. See *Sort an Address List* to sort a data source created in Publisher.

- If the merge feature is not installed, Publisher prompts you to install it the first time you merge.

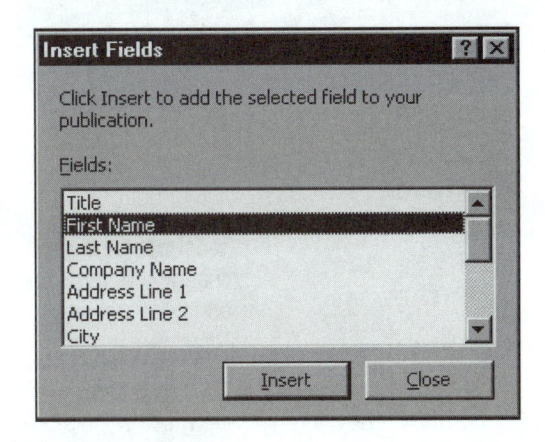

b. Click **Insert** to place a code for the selected field in the text box.

c. In the text frame, add text, spaces, commas, or start a new paragraph, as necessary.

- For example, you will want to add a space after the First Name field before you insert the Last Name field. Press **Enter** to start a new paragraph after you add the name fields so that the Address field(s) will be placed on the next line.

- To move the Insert Fields dialog box if the text frame is hidden, drag the dialog box title bar.

d. Repeat from step a. to add fields until the address is complete.

e. Click **Close** when finished adding fields.

The following illustration shows an envelope with data source field names in a text frame.

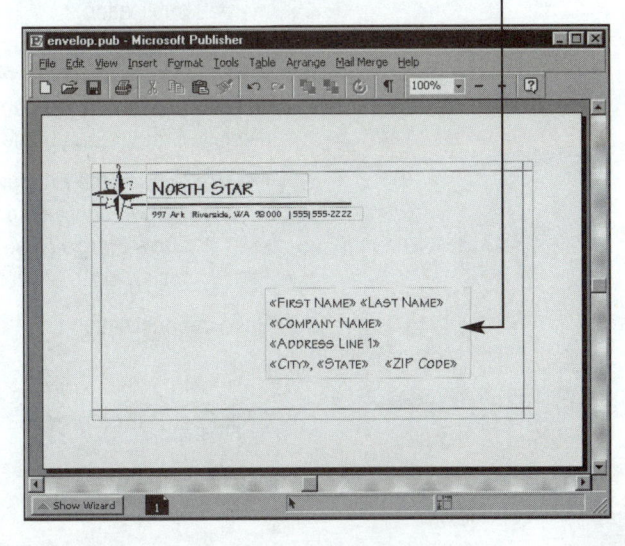

219

Merge an Address List with a Publication *(continued)*

4 To format the address, select all the field code(s) and then change the font, font size, and character formatting attributes just as you would any other text. See *Format Characters.*

5 Click **Mail Merge**, **Merge**. Publisher merges and displays the Preview Data box.

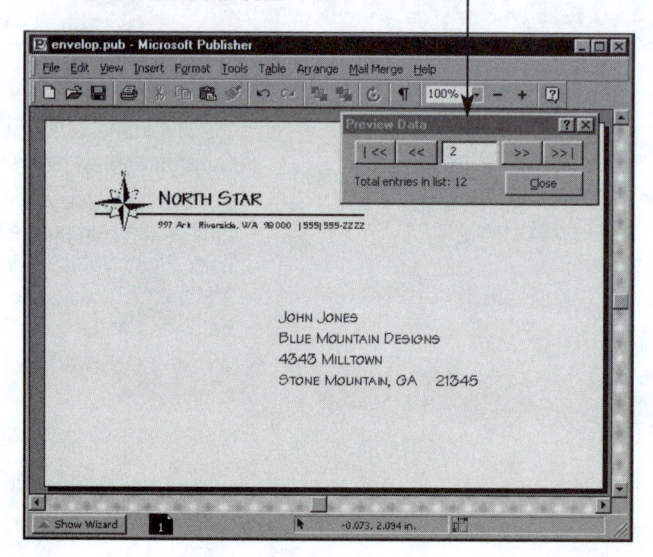

6 Use the buttons in the Preview Data box to preview the merged publication.

7 Click **Close** to close the Preview data box when finished previewing the publication. Field codes are displayed rather than names and addresses.

*NOTE: To open the Preview Data box to preview the merged publication at any time, click **Mail Merge**, **Show Merge Results**. Once you have merged, this option is always available.*

8 Save the publication for later printing.

OR

Click **File**, **Print Merge** to print the merged documents.

220

Print

These procedures tell you how to set print options and print on your local printer. If you are printing the final output at a commercial printing service, work with the service to prepare the publication for printing on their equipment.

Choose a Printer

The printer you currently have selected determines how your publication will appear in the Publisher window.

File → Print Setup...

Notes:

- Publisher displays publications as they will look when printed on the printer specified in the Print Setup dialog box.

- Choose the printer *before* you design your pages. Each printer prints pages a little differently. If the currently selected printer does not print exactly like the one on which you will print the final output, you might have to do a lot of adjusting to compensate.

- If you will be sending the final publication to a commercial printing service, set the printer to a driver that is closest to the one they will be using. Ask the service which printer driver to use. They might provide you with a custom driver that you can install in Windows.

- Use the **Tools**, **Commercial Printing Tools** command to set up a publication for a commercial printing service. Work with your printing service to set these options.

1. Click **File**, **Print Setup**. The Print Setup dialog box displays.

2. Click the drop-down arrow to open the list of printers.

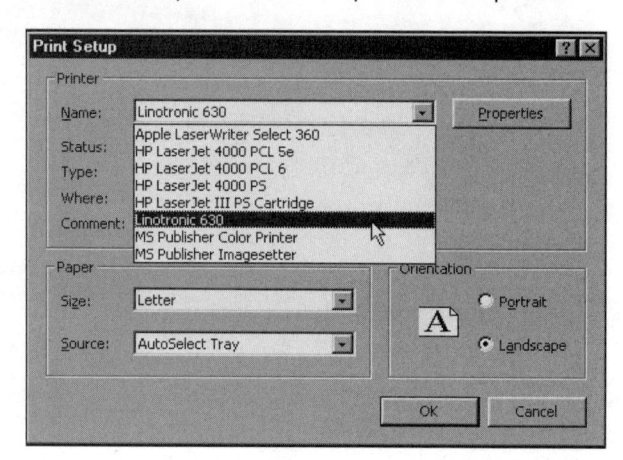

3. Click the printer to use.

   NOTE: If the printer is not listed, install it from your Windows CD or install the driver supplied by your printing service. To install a driver, click the **Start** button [Start] on the Windows taskbar. Click **Settings**, **Printers**, and then double-click the **Add Printer** icon. Follow the wizard prompts.

4. Click OK.

- The QMS Colorscript 100 printer driver is often used for publications that will be printed by a service. Publisher comes with several generic drivers that will work with most commercial services.

- The MS Publisher Color Printer driver is for digital color and the MS Publisher Imagesetter driver for offset printing. It does not matter whether or not you have the printer. Publisher uses the printer driver specifications to display pages.

Change the Paper Size

Set the size of the paper that you will print the publication on.

File → Print Setup...

Notes:

- If you will be sending the publication to a printing service, ask the service which paper size to use.

- This procedure changes the size of the paper on which you will need to print the publication. This is not necessarily the size of the publication. To set the size of the publication, see *Change the Page Size*.

1. Click **File**, **Print Setup**. The Print Setup dialog box displays.

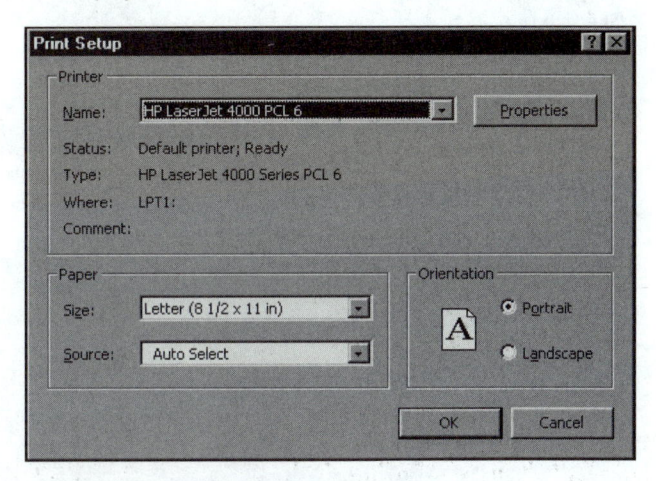

2. Select a paper size from the **Size** list.

3. Click OK.

223

Print Crop Marks

Print crop marks when printing a publication smaller than the paper on which it is printed.

[File] ➡ [Print...]

Notes:

- Crop marks show the size of a small publication printed on large paper. For example, if you print a single 5"x3" publication on an 8.5"x11" page, the crop marks will show where the publication should be cut to make it the correct size.

- If you send the publication to a commercial printing service, the service will use the crop marks to trim the publication to the correct size. Or, you can use a paper cutter to trim it.

1 Click **File**, **Print**. The Print dialog box displays.

2 Click [Advanced Print Settings...]. The Print Settings dialog box displays.

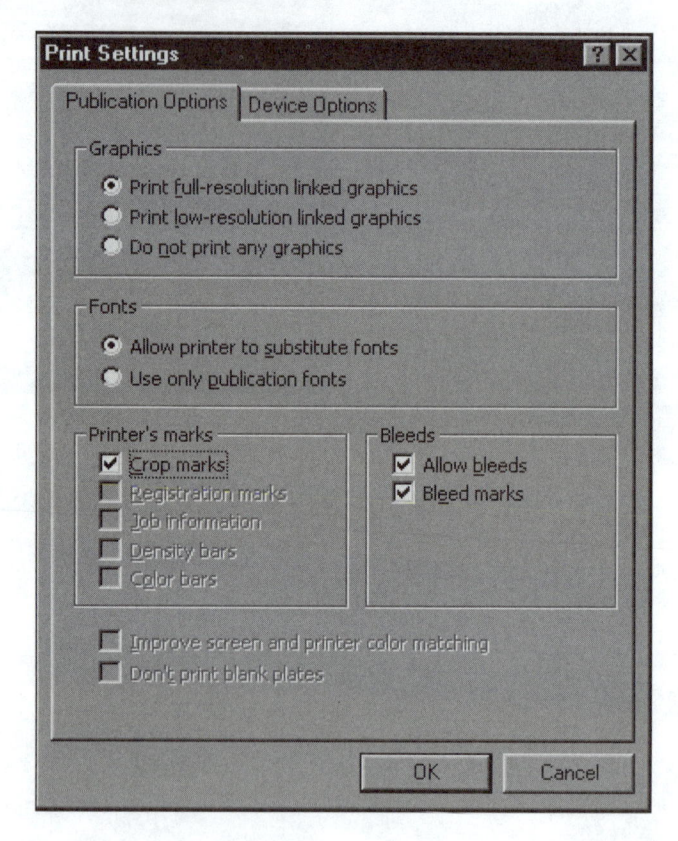

3 Select the **Crop marks** check box.

4 Click [OK].

224

Notes:

- Often when you print a small publication, such as a label or postcard, multiple copies of the publication print on a single page. For example, when you print labels, you usually print an entire sheet. Use this procedure to print a single copy of a small publication.

- The small publication will print in the center of the page.

- Print crop marks when you print a small publication on a larger sheet of paper. That way you will know where the boundaries of the publication are.

Print a Single Copy of a Small Publication on a Page

1 Click **File**, **Print**. The Print dialog box displays.

2 Click [Page Options...] to display the Page Options dialog box.

> *NOTE: If the **Page Options** button does not appear on the Print dialog box, this option is not available for the current publication.*

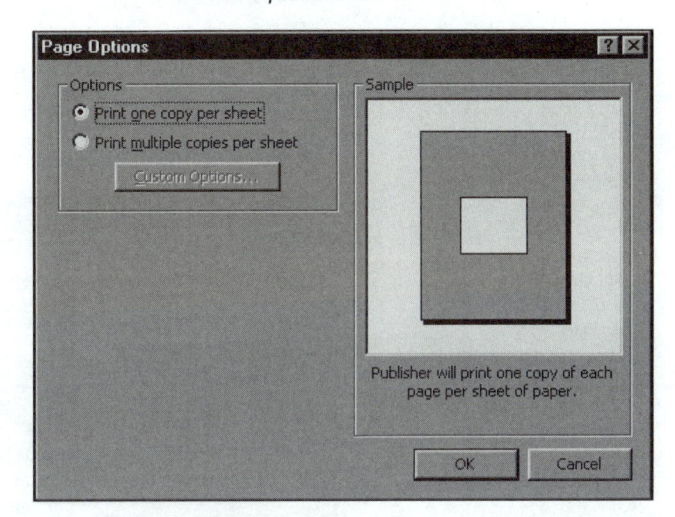

3 Select **Print one copy per sheet**.

4 Click [OK] twice.

225

Print on a Desktop Printer

Use this procedure to print on your local or network printer. If you are using a commercial printing service, use this procedure to print a draft of your publication on your printer.

File ➡ Print...

Notes:

- This procedure prints the publication on your local printer. See *Choose a Printer*.

- If the publication will be printed at a commercial printing service, use the **Tools**, **Commercial Printing Tools** command to set up the publication for printing. Work with your printing service to set these options.

1. Click **File**, **Print**. The Print dialog box displays.
2. Type or select the pages to print.

   NOTE: By default, all pages in the publication will print.

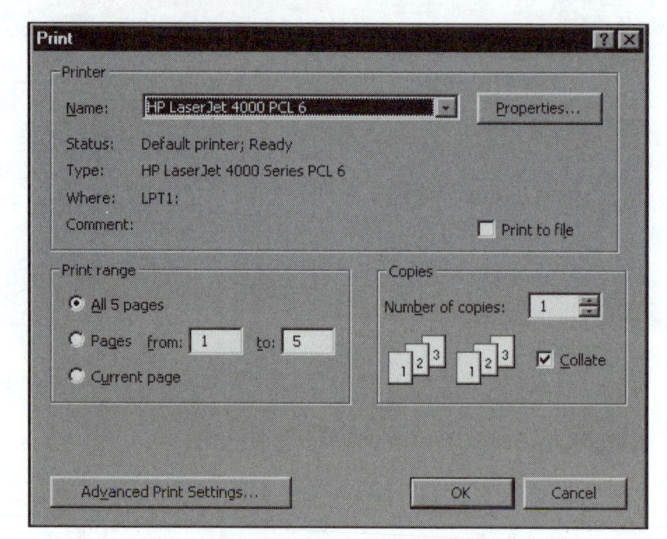

3. Type or select the number of copies to print.
4. Click OK.

Index

A

Add a Drop Cap 112
Add Continuation Notices 80
Add Grid Guides 44
Add Headers and Footers.............52
Add Ruler Guides 42
Align Paragraphs........................114
Align Text Vertically 116
Apply a Preset Table Format 202
Apply a Style 134
Apply BorderArt Borders 180
Apply Line Borders to a Frame ..178
Apply Table Borders 198
Arrange Toolbars............................8

C

Change a Line Style of a
  DrawingObject......................150
Change Column Width or
  Row Height 204
Change Frame Margins 194
Change Page Margins 46
Change the Line Style of an
  AutoShape............................148
Change the Page Orientation 51
Change the Page Size 48
Change the Paper Size..............223
Check Spelling 102
Choose a Printer 222
Clips: Add Clips to the Gallery ..160
Clips: Download Clips from
  the Web................................158
Clips: Insert a Picture, Sound,
  or Video Clip 154
Clips: Organize Clips in the
  Gallery..................................156
Copy or Move a Frame 186
Create a Blank Publication 22

Create a Bulleted List 126
Create a Numbered List 128
Create a Publication Using
  a Wizard 18
Create a Style 132
Create a Table............................196
Create a Text Frame 70
Create an Address List 214
Create Connected Text Frames ..72
Crop a Picture 174
Customize Toolbars........................6

D

Delete Text 84
Disable Publication Wizard
  Steps 34
Draw a Balloon AutoShape........146
Draw Custom Shapes 144
Draw Lines and Arrows..............140
Draw Rectangles and Ovals 142

E

Edit a Story in Microsoft Word 92
Enter Text in a Table 209

F

Find Text 98
Fit Text in a Frame 120
Flow a Long Story 78
Format Characters 118

G

Get Help Using the Answer
  Wizard 12
Get Help Using the Office
  Assistant 10
Group Frames and Objects........192

227

H

Hide the Catalog at Startup 4
Hyphenate.................................106

I

Import a Picture..........................164
Import Styles from Another
    Publication............................136
Import Text 76
Indent Paragraphs......................122
Insert a Design Gallery Object ..166
Insert a Page..............................56
Insert a Symbol 94
Insert or Delete Columns
    or Rows................................206
Insert the Current Date/Time........96

L

Line Up Frames 190

M

Maintain a Personal Information
    Set..28
Merge an Address List with
    a Publication 218
Merge Cells...............................208
Move Rulers 36

O

Open a Publication 26

P

Place Text or Graphics on
    All Pages...............................54
Preview Web Pages 66
Print Crop Marks........................224
Print on a Desktop Printer..........226
Publisher Window 3

R

Replace Text 100
Resize a Frame..........................188
Rotate a Frame..........................182
Run Design Checker...................64

S

Save a Publication 24
Scale a Picture 176
Select Frames...........................185
Select in a Table 210
Select Text.................................90
Set AutoSave Options.................30
Set Line or Paragraph Spacing..124
Set Tabs 130
Set the Default Formatting for
    a Frame................................184
Set the Default Publication
    Folder 32
Set the Unit of Measure 40
Set the Zero Point.......................38
Set Up Columns in a
    Text Frame 82
Set Up Facing Pages 50
Set Web Page Properties 62
Shade Cell Backgrounds 200
Snap to Guides and Objects........49
Sort an Address List 216
Start Publisher.............................2

T

Type and Edit Text 86

V

View Two Pages 58
Visit the Office Update Web Site..14

W

WordArt: Change Font and
    Attributes 170
WordArt: Create a WordArt
    Picture.................................168
WordArt: Mold Text into
    a Shape................................172
Wrap Text Around Pictures 110

Z

Zoom In or Out 60

Notes

Notes

Notes

Notes

Notes

Notes

Notes

2/99 HR

Less Surfing, More Answers—FAST

These books bring the specific Internet information you need into focus so that you won't have to spend a lifetime surfing for it. Each book provides you with practical Web sites plus these skills:

- **common e-mail system** (like AOL, Outlook, Messenger)
- **search engines and browsing** (keywords, Yahoo, Lycos, etc.)
- **refining searches** (Boolean searching, etc.), for minimizing search time

FOR BEGINNERS
Cat. No. HR3 • ISBN 1-56243-603-1

FOR MANAGERS
Cat. No. HR2 • ISBN 1-56243-602-3

FOR SALES PEOPLE
Cat. No. HR4 • ISBN 1-56243-604-X

FOR STUDENTS
Cat. No. HR1 • ISBN 1-56243-601-5

BUSINESS COMMUNICATION & E-MAIL
Cat. No. HR6 • ISBN 1-56243-676-7

101 THINGS YOU NEED TO KNOW
Cat. No. HR5 • ISBN 1-56243-675-9

FOR SENIORS
Cat. No. HR7 • ISBN 1-56243-695-3

ENTERTAINMENT & LEISURE
Cat. No. HR8 • ISBN 1-56243-696-1

FOR SHOPPERS & BARGAIN HUNTERS
Cat. No. HR9 • ISBN 1-56243-697-X

HEALTH & MEDICAL RESOURCES
Cat. No. HR10 • ISBN 1-56243-713-5

INVESTING & PERSONAL FINANCE
Cat. No. HR11 • ISBN 1-56243-758-5

ROMANCE & RELATIONSHIPS
Cat. No. HR12 • ISBN 1-56243-772-0

Preview any of our books at:
http://www.ddcpub.com

$10 ea.

DDC Publishing
275 Madison Ave.
New York, NY 10016

To order call 800-528-3897 fax 800-528-3862

Quick Reference Guides find software answers faster because you read less

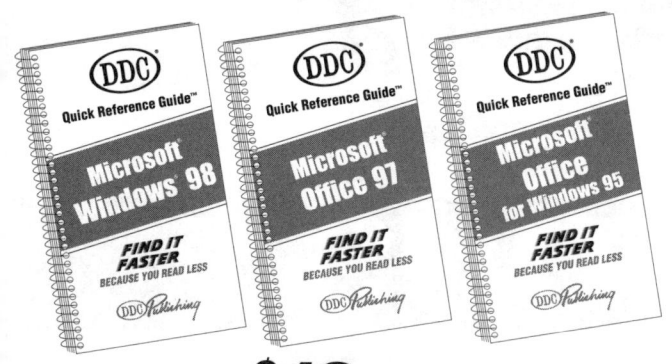

$12 ea.
Did We Make One for You?

Find it quickly and get back to the keyboard—fast

The index becomes your quick locator. Just follow the step-by-step illustrated instructions. We tell you what to do in five or six words.

Sometimes only two.

No narration or exposition. Just "press this—type that" illustrated commands.

The spiral binding keeps pages open so you can type what you read. You save countless hours of lost time by locating the illustrated answer in seconds.

The time you save when this guide goes to work for you will pay for it the very first day

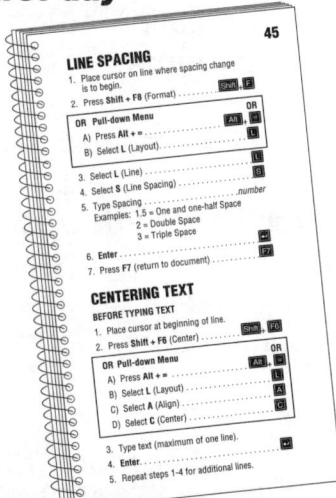

TITLE	CAT.No
Access 2 for Windows	OAX2
Access 7 for Windows 95	AX95
Access 97	G28
Access 2000	G55
Business Communication & Style	G41
Claris Works 5 for Macintosh	G39
Computer & Internet Dictionary	G42
Computer Terms	D18
Corel WordPerfect Suite 8	G32
Corel WordPerfect 7 Win 95	G12
Corel WordPerfect Suite7 Win 95	G11
DOS 5	J17
DOS 6.0 - 6.22	ODS62
Excel 5 for Windows	F18
Excel 7 for Windows 95	XL7
Excel 97	G27
Excel 2000	G49
Internet, 2nd Edition	I217
Lotus 1-2-3 Rel. 3.1 DOS	J18
Lotus 1-2-3 Rel. 3.4 DOS	L317
Lotus 1-2-3 Rel. 4 DOS	G4
Lotus 1-2-3 Rel. 4 Win	03013
Lotus 1-2-3 Rel. 5 Win	L19
Lotus 1-2-3 Rel. 6 Win 95	G13
Lotus Notes 4.5	G15
Lotus Smart Suite 97	G34
Office for Win. 3.1	M017

TITLE	CAT.No
Office for Win 95	MO95
Office 97	G25
Office 2000	G47
PageMaker 5 for Win & Mac	PM18
PowerPoint 4 for Win	OPPW4
PowerPoint 7 for Win 95	PPW7
PowerPoint 97	G31
PowerPoint 2000	G51
Quattro Pro 6 for Win	QPW6
Quicken 4 for Windows	G7
Quicken 7.0 (DOS)	OQK7
Quicken 8.0 (DOS)	QKD8
Windows NT 4	G16
Windows 3.1 & 3.11	N317
Windows 95	G6
Windows 98	G35
Word 6 for Windows	OWDW6
Word 7 for Windows 95	WDW7
Word 97	G26
Word 2000	G48
WordPerfect 5.1+ for DOS	W-5.1
WordPerfect 6 for DOS	W18
WordPerfect 6 for Win	OWPW6
WordPerfect 6.1 for Win	W19
Works 3 for Win	OWKW3
Works 4 for Win 95	WKW4

Preview any of our books at our Web site:
http://www.ddcpub.com

To order call 800-528-3897
fax 800-528-3862

DDC Publishing
275 Madison Ave., New York, NY 10016

2/99 Q

MOUS

Microsoft® initiated the **MOUS (Microsoft® Office User Specialist) program** to provide Office users a means of demonstrating their level of proficiency in each application in the Office suite. After the successful completion of the certification test in an application, users receive a certificate that reflects their level of proficiency.

The **MOUS program** establishes the criteria for both proficient and expert levels in Word, Excel, PowerPoint, FrontPage, and Access, and proficient skill levels in Outlook.

Tests are given at Authorized Testing Centers around the country. Each test takes about 45 minutes to complete.

For more information on how you can become MOUS certified, visit our Web site!
www.ddcpub.com

2/99 L

Fast-teach Learning Books

How we designed each book

Each self-paced hands-on text gives you the software concept and each exercise's objective in simple language. Next to the exercise we provide the keystrokes and the illustrated layout; step by simple step—graded and cumulative learning.

Did we make one for you?

Titles $27 each   Cat. No.
- Creating a Web Page w/ Office 97 .... Z23
- Corel Office 7 .... Z12
- Corel WordPerfect 7 .... Z16
- Corel WordPerfect 8 .... Z31
- DOS + Windows Z7
- English Skills through Word Processing Z34
- Excel 97 .... Z21
- Excel 5 for Windows E9
- Excel 7 for Windows 95 .... Z11
- Internet Z30
- Internet for Business Z27
- Internet for Kids Z25
- Keyboarding/Word Processing with Word 97 .... Z24
- Keyboarding/Word Processing for Kids Z33
- Lotus 1-2-3 Rel. 2.2–4.0 for DOS L9
- Lotus 1-2-3 Rel. 4 & 5 for Windows ... B9
- Microsoft Office 97 .... Z19
- Microsoft Office for Windows 95 ..... Z6
- PowerPoint 97 .... Z22
- Windows 3.1 – A Quick Study WQS1
- Windows 95 .... Z3
- Windows 98 .... Z26
- Word 97 .... Z20
- Word 6 for Windows 1WDW6
- Word 7 for Windows 95 .... Z10
- WordPerfect 6 for Windows Z9
- WordPerfect 6.1 for Windows H9
- Works 4 for Windows 95 .... Z8

Microsoft® OFFICE 2000

Titles $29 each   Cat. No.
- Accounting Applications with Excel 2000 .... Z41
- Access 2000 .... Z38
- Create a Web Page with Office 2000 .... Z43
- Desktop Publishing with Publisher 2000 .... Z47
- Excel 2000 .... Z39
- Office 2000 .... Z35
- **Office 2000 Deluxe Edition $34** ... Z35D
  - Includes advanced exercises an illustrated solutions for each exercise
- Office 2000: Advanced Course Z45
- PowerPoint 2000 .... Z40
- Web Page Design with FrontPage 2000 .... Z49
- Windows 2000 .... Z44
- Word 2000 .... Z37

each with CD-ROM

Preview any any of our books at:
http://www.ddcpub.com

DDC Publishing

to order call:
800-528-3897
fax 800-528-3862

2/99 OD

Our One-Day Course has you using your software the next day

$18 ea.
Includes diskette

Here's how we do it
We struck out all the unnecessary words that don't teach anything. No introductory nonsense. We get right to the point—in "See spot run" language. No polysyllabic verbiage. We give you the keystrokes and the illustrated layout; step by simple step.

You learn faster because you read less
No fairy tales, novels, or literature. Small words, fewer words, short sentences, and fewer of them. We pen every word as if an idiot had to read it. You understand it faster because it reads easier.

Illustrated exercises show you how
We tell you, show you, and explain what you see. The layout shows you what we just explained. The answers fly off the page and into your brain as if written on invisible glass. No narration or exposition. No time wasted. **Each book comes with a practice disk to eliminate typing the exercises.**

DID WE MAKE ONE FOR YOU?

Cat. No.	Title
DC2	Access 97, Day 1
DC29	Access 97, Day 2
DC30	Access 97, Day 3
DC1	Access 7 for Windows 95
DC50	Basic Computer Skills
DC4	Excel 97, Day 1
DC27	Excel 97, Day 2
DC28	Excel 97, Day 3
DC39	Excel 2000
DC22	FrontPage
DC5	Internet E-mail & FTP w/Sim. CD
DC48	Internet for Sales People w/Sim. CD
DC49	Internet for Managers w/Sim. CD
DC6	Intro to Computers and Windows 95
DC51	Intro to Office 2000
DC21	Local Area Network
DC35	Lotus Notes 4.5
DC8	MS Explorer w/ Sim. CD

Cat. No.	Title
DC10	Netscape Navigator w/ Sim. CD
DC11	Outlook 97
DC52	Outlook 98
DC12	PageMaker 5
DC14	PowerPoint 97, Day 1
DC31	PowerPoint 97, Day 2
DC13	PowerPoint 7 for Windows 95
DC34	Upgrading to Office 97
DC47	Upgrading to Windows 98
DC56	Upgrading to Windows 2000
DC20	Visual Basics 3.0
DC16	Windows 95
DC24	Windows NT 4.0
DC18	Word 97, Day 1
DC25	Word 97, Day 2
DC26	Word 97, Day 3
DC36	Word 2000
DC17	Word 7 for Windows 95
DC19	WordPerfect 6.1

Preview any of our books at: http://www.ddcpub.com

DDC Publishing To order call **800-528-3897** fax **800-528-3862**
275 Madison Avenue • New York, NY 10016